Emotions and Beliefs

How Feelings Influence Thoughts

Edited by

Nico H. Frijda
University of Amsterdam

Antony S. R. Manstead
University of Amsterdam

and

Sacha Bem
Leiden University

Editions de la Maison des Sciences de l'Homme
Paris

CAMBRIDGE
UNIVERSITY PRESS

PUBLISHED BY THE PRESS SYNDICATE OF THE UNIVERSITY OF CAMBRIDGE
The Pitt Building, Trumpington Street, Cambridge, United Kingdom and
EDITIONS DE LA MAISON DES SCIENCES DE L'HOMME
54 Boulevard Raspail, 75270 Paris Cedex 06, France

CAMBRIDGE UNIVERSITY PRESS
The Edinburgh Building, Cambridge CB2 2RU, UK
  http://www.cup.cam.ac.uk
40 West 20th Street, New York NY 1011–4211, USA
  http://www.cup.org
10 Stamford Road, Oakleigh, Melbourne 3166, Australia

First published 2000

Printed in the United Kingdom at the University Press, Cambridge

Typeset in Palatino 10/12pt   [CE]

A catalogue record for this book is available from the British Library

Library of Congress cataloguing in publication data
Emotions and beliefs: how feelings influence thoughts / edited by
Nico H. Frijda, Antony S. R. Manstead, and Sacha Bem.
    p.   cm. – (Studies in emotion and social interaction)
Includes bibliographical references.
ISBN 0 521 77138 2 (hardback) – ISBN 0 521 78734 3 (paperback)
1. Emotions and cognition.   2. Belief and doubt.
I. Frijda, Nico H.   II. Manstead, A. S. R.   III. Bem, Sacha.   IV. Series.
BF531.E513   2000
152.4–dc21   99–059880

ISBN 0 521 77138 2 hardback
ISBN 0 521 78734 3 paperback
ISBN 2 7351 0879 1 hardback (France only)

Contents

Contributors

Sacha Bem, Leiden University, The Netherlands
Herbert Bless, University of Trier, Germany
Ian Brissette, Carnegie Mellon University, USA
Margaret S. Clark, Carnegie Mellon University, USA
Gerald L. Clore, University of Illinois at Urbana-Champaign, USA
Michael W. Eysenck, Royal Holloway College, University of London, UK
Klaus Fiedler, University of Heidelberg, Germany
Joseph P. Forgas, University of New South Wales, Sydney, Australia
Nico H. Frijda, University of Amsterdam, The Netherlands
Karen Gasper, University of Illinois at Urbana-Champaign, USA
Eddie Harmon-Jones, University of Wisconsin-Madison, USA
Antony S. R. Manstead, University of Amsterdam, The Netherlands
Batja Mesquita, Wake Forest University, USA
Keith Oatley, Ontario Institute for Studies in Education, University of Toronto, Canada

The influence of emotions on beliefs

Nico H. Frijda, Antony S. R. Manstead, and Sacha Bem

Emotion theory has changed quite dramatically during the last three decades. To a large extent this change has been due to a keen interest in the role of cognition in emotion. We have seen the emergence of "cognitive emotion theory" (e.g., Lazarus, 1991), which has in turn stimulated a considerable body of research. Within this theory, beliefs are viewed as major antecedents of emotions, a point that is particularly emphasized by what is known as "appraisal theory" (e.g., Scherer, 1999). According to appraisal theory, emotions result from how the individual believes the world to be, how events are believed to have come about, and what implications events are believed to have.

Beliefs thus are regarded as one of the major determinants of emotion, and therefore an important part of the study of emotion can properly be seen as falling under the umbrella of cognitive psychology. Oddly enough, however, the reverse direction of influence in the relation between emotion and cognition has received scant attention. This is in itself rather odd, because one might easily regard emotions as being among the determinants of an individual's beliefs. They can be seen as influencing the content and the strength of an individual's beliefs, and their resistance to modification. Indeed, such an influence has traditionally been considered to be one of the most important things to be said about emotions. Spinoza (1677/1989) defined emotions as "states that make the mind inclined to think one thing rather than another." The influence of emotions upon beliefs can be viewed as the port through which emotions exert their influence upon human life. Beliefs fueled by emotions stimulate people to action, or allow them to approve of the actions of others in political contexts. That is why Aristotle provided a detailed discussion of emotions in his *Rhetorica*. Emotion arousal was viewed as essential in persuasive formation of judgment. "The orator persuades by means of his hearers, when they are roused to emotion by his speech; for the judgments we deliver are not the same when we are influenced by joy or sorrow, love or hate" (*Rhetorica* I, II.5).

The notion that emotions determine beliefs was a common assumption during much of human history, and probably still is. It was the starting point of the views of human well-being in Epicurean and Stoic philosophy. Facing up to one's fear of death allows one to correct the beliefs that such fear has generated, argued Lucretius, as well as the beliefs, the *phantaseia*, from which the fear had sprung (Nussbaum, 1994). This is why Seneca condemned emotions such as anger. "Reason herself, to whom the reins of power have been entrusted, remains mistress only so long as she is kept apart from the passions: if once she mingles with them and is contaminated, she becomes unable to hold back those whom she might have cleared from her path. For when once the mind has been aroused and shaken, it becomes the slave of the disturbing agent" (Seneca, *De Ira*, I, viii.1).

In most discussions of the relations between emotion and cognition, the emphasis has been on the assumption that the former distorts the latter. For Kant, emotion was an illness of the mind. Unreason as a consequence of emotions makes regular appearances in philosophical as well as common-sense discourse. During the first half of the twentieth century psychology tended to focus upon this issue. Young (1943) conceived of emotion as a disturbance of organized behavior and thought; so did Hebb (1949) in his early work. At the same time, the influence of emotions upon the content of beliefs represented one of the dogmas of psychoanalytically inspired thought. Both interpersonal beliefs and scientific views were often seen as the outcomes of emotional responses to the issues or persons at hand. Social views were readily seen as self-serving distortions of available information, as in the studies of the authoritarian personality (Adorno, Frenkel-Brunswik, Levinson & Sanford, 1950) and psychological interpretations of cultural beliefs (Whiting & Child, 1953).

Then the interest in emotional influences upon beliefs receded. In part, this was due to the rise of cognitive psychology. According to this view, many of the biases of judgments, in individuals as well as social groups, could be explained by the operation of general cognitive strategies and principles. In this view, cognitive operations carry the roots of biases within them. One product of this orientation was the work of Kahneman and Tversky (Kahneman, Slovic, and Tversky, 1982) on heuristics in thought; another was the discussion of biases in social judgments by Nisbett and Ross (1980). Indeed, explaining the occurrence of beliefs that deviate from objective evidence in terms of cognitive processes is an alternative to an explanation in terms of emotional factors.

That the role of emotions in judgments and beliefs is nevertheless plausible is brought home by considering a few pertinent facts. One of these is the sheer resistance of beliefs to being modified by information. When it comes to issues of emotional importance, convincing someone to change his or her existing beliefs appears to be a virtually hopeless undertaking. As Abelson (1995: 25–26) wrote,

> Throughout my academic career I have been fascinated by the capacity of holders of very strong attitudes to resist persuasive attempt at change. Public figures and ordinary folk alike often cling tenaciously to beliefs and attitudes that we, as know-it-all academics, are convinced are wrong-headed. Whether the attitudes concern life after death, gay rights, a perceived conspiracy to take over New Jersey, or whatever, we can argue until blue-faced without budging our State Representative or our Uncle Walter an inch.

The near-impossibility of arriving at a mutual understanding when there is disagreement on matters of emotional investment is evident in marital discord and in political and religious conflict. Kosovars and others are horrified by oppression, lack of self-determination, and murder. Serbs are indignant about terrorists who want to tear apart their country, and who lay claims to their own historically sacred ground. Televised discussions between people with opposing views on such issues tend to fall flat because the arguments cherished by one side are regarded as meaningless by the other side, and vice versa.

Why might emotions have these effects on beliefs? These effects are in fact central to the place of both emotions and beliefs in human functioning. It can be argued that they are in no way restricted to belief distortions. They are at the heart of what beliefs are about. The eighteenth-century empiricist David Hume characterized beliefs ("reason," in his terminology) as "perfectly inert" and never able to "either prevent or produce any action" (Hume, 1739/1969: 509). The impulse comes not from reason but from passion, he held. Modern emotion theorists have broken with the tradition of the combat of passion and reason that formed, in part, the context of Hume's ideas. We can nevertheless appreciate the proposition that thinking, no matter how well articulated, is not sufficient for action (Brand, 1984). On the other hand the definition of Alexander Bain and the pragmatist philosophers, that "a belief is that upon which a man is prepared to act," is generally accepted; thoughts without actions are in vain. Although beliefs may guide our actions (Armstrong, 1973), they are not sufficient to initiate action. No matter how rational your thoughts about helping the needy may be, you need an emotional impulse before you actually volunteer to help. Emotions are prime candidates for turning a thinking being into an actor.

The proposed influence of emotions on beliefs is part of the broader issue of the psychological function served by emotions. The general function of emotion is seen as the "management of action" (Oatley, 1992: 24). Not every mental state exercises the same influence on action. We suggest that the link with action is stronger in the case of emotions than it is in the case of beliefs; and that it is stronger in beliefs than it is in knowledge. In the philosophical tradition *belief* is distinguished from *knowledge* by reference to the truth value and claim to objectivity of knowledge: "True" knowledge is distinguished from "mere" belief. Psychology is less interested in this question of *de iure*, the question of the justification of a proposition; it is more concerned about the question of *de facto*, the psychological reality. Thus whether Dracula exists or not is less important for psychology than the fact that Rachel believes and hopes that he will pay her a visit tonight. If there is a difference between knowledge and belief that is of psychological significance, it is the way in which they vary with respect to preparing the individual to act. To have a belief is not so much to claim to have true knowledge as to take a "risk" (see Fiedler and Bless, in this volume) and be prepared to take action. This implies that beliefs should be more emotion-sensitive than knowledge.

These considerations, and the examples given earlier, demonstrate that examining the influence of emotions on beliefs is not merely a matter of academic concern. The influence is important for under-standing action. We suggest that participation in political violence or, at least, support for violent movements by one's votes, one's budget allocations, or one's emotional support, is facilitated by the firmness of one's beliefs regarding the states of the world motivating those actions, and that such firmness of beliefs is fed by the emotions connected to those states of the world. For instance, one would expect an appraisal of the severity of the threat with which one is confronted to be generated and/or enhanced by the degree of fear evoked by the event that elicited the fear in the first place. In our view the way in which beliefs are influenced by emotions is therefore highly relevant to the understanding of socio-political events such as intergroup hostility and violence.

There thus are good reasons for thinking that emotions influence beliefs, and for examining the issue. An important prerequisite for doing so is to define the terms "emotion" and "belief" in such a way that they can be treated as distinct and separate phenomena. This task is not unproblematic, since emotions and beliefs are both mental states. They share certain qualities and they can be distinguished in terms of other attributes but, like all mental states, they are closely intertwined. Mental states evoke other mental states and together they form such an intricate web that distinctions can become blurred. Yet, both emotions and beliefs can be characterized with sufficient clarity to distinguish them. Emotions can be defined as states that comprise feelings, physiological changes, expressive behavior, and inclinations to act. Beliefs can be defined as states that link a person or group or object or concept with one or more attributes, and this is held by the believer to be true. The general proposal thus is that emotions can awaken, intrude into, and shape beliefs, by creating them, by amplifying or altering them, and by making them resistant to change.

There is, however, hardly any empirical research on these issues. As alluded to above, there is much discussion of the effects of cognitions upon emotions, but very little discussion of the effects of emotions upon cognitions. We know little about the scope of such effects: how far they reach, how deep they go. We know almost nothing about the conditions under which these effects occur, or – given what was said above with regard to the cognitive origins of biases in beliefs – whether such effects even exist. To the extent that they do exist, there is little insight into how they come about. "Self-serving beliefs" is a term that has been used quite often by psychologists but, apart from the vacuous lore of repression, there is little theory to account for the phenomenon of beliefs that are self-serving.

These were the major reasons that we as editors had for marshaling this overview of theory and research on the emotion–belief relation. The origins of this volume are to be found in a 1995 workshop organized by the Institute for Emotion and Motivation at the University of Amsterdam, with the support of EPOS and the Kurt Lewin Institute (respectively graduate schools in experimental psychology and social psychology). The contributions to the present volume are for the most part elaborations of contributions to that workshop.

The book begins with two general theoretical treatments of the way in which emotions influence beliefs. The first of these is by Gerald Clore and Karen Gasper. The essence of their argument can be stated quite simply: emotions provide information and guide attention. In general, these two attributes of emotions are functional, but they can also lead the individual astray. Thus when an affective state has no obvious "object," the information provided by the affective state can be misattributed to other, substitute objects. These misattribution effects are most likely to occur in conjunction with mood states, it is argued, precisely because mood states typically lack an obvious "object." However, the informational and attentional effects discussed in the second half of Clore and Gasper's chapter are ones that should (they argue) occur in conjunction with emotions proper. Circumstances that are accompanied by similar emotions, suggest the authors, are likely to be categorized in similar ways, opening up the possibility of conflation of these circumstances. Furthermore, emotional intensity directs the breadth of attentional focus, while emotional quality directs the direction of attentional focus. The general conclusion is that beliefs buttressed by emotion direct attention towards belief-relevant information.

Nico Frijda and Batja Mesquita's chapter is based on the premise that emotions can lead to new beliefs and strengthen existing beliefs. The idea that emotions can create new beliefs arises from the notion that an emotion entails an appraisal based on currently salient concerns. This "temporary" appraisal entailed in an emotion can turn into a long-term belief when an emotion turns into what the authors call a "sentiment." By this they mean a latent representation of someone or something that is of personal concern. For example, someone does something that hurts our interests. To the extent that we are inclined to think that the outcome of the action was intentional, we may form a negative sentiment about the person in question, which in turn will affect the way in which we interpret this person's future behavior. Turning now to the belief-strengthening properties of emotions, the authors point out that strong beliefs are ones that are central to one's concerns; concerns, of course, are deeply implicated in the emotion process. Thus the experience of emotion is a signal to the individual that his or her concerns are at issue, and the more intense the emotion, the more important these concerns are likely to be. In this way all the beliefs that are underpinned by the concerns(s) in question are likely to be strengthened by the experience of emotion. The authors go on to trace these effects of emotions to features of the processes of belief formation in general.

The notion of sentiments is pursued by Keith Oatley in Chapter 4. Like Frijda and Mesquita, he uses this term to refer to relatively long-lasting affective states, mainly dispositions towards other people. Examples are warm affection, despondency, and antipathy. The function of these sentiments, he argues, is to structure our relationships with other people or with certain objects, all the time influencing what we believe about these people or things. These sentiments, he goes on to argue, are the basis of distributed cognition, by which he means cognitions that are distributed socially (i.e., between people), spatially (i.e., between an individual and the external world), or temporally. Much of what we do in our everyday lives, Oatley suggests, involves one or other of these forms of distributed cognition. Each form is facilitated by a sentiment, and this sentiment is associated with certain beliefs. For example, the sentiment of warm affection towards others facilitates socially distributed cognition, but also carries with it an inclination to trust the other person concerned, and to accept what he or she tells us. Without such a sentiment, it is argued, we would not believe sufficiently in the trustworthiness of the other person in order to be able to cooperate.

The next two chapters in the book address the relation between affective states and the processing of social information. In Chapter 5 Joe Forgas draws on his own Affect Infusion Model to argue that the way in which affect influences cognitive processes, including belief formation and maintenance, is dependent on the type of processing that prevails. According to Forgas, it is primarily what he calls "constructive, substantive" processing that allows affectively primed thoughts and associations to be incorporated into the formation of beliefs. One way in which affect influences beliefs is via mood-congruent biases: we are more likely to notice, encode, remember, and make use of information that is congruent with a prevailing mood state. Other forms of processing, which Forgas calls "controlled, directed processing" are impervious to the influence of affect. Such processing is often triggered by having a specific motivational goal, and one such goal might be affect regulation. It is suggested that affect infusion and affect regulation might operate in a homeostatic relation, such that when a certain threshold of affect has been reached via infusion processes, regulation processes are initiated. Thus the critical link, in Forgas's view, between affect and belief is the kind of information processing strategy that is used in a given situation.

In their chapter, Klaus Fiedler and Herbert Bless develop a complementary line of theoretical argument. Starting with Piaget's well-known distinction between assimilation and accommodation, these authors argue that the "top-down" process of assimilation is one that is characteristic of positive, appetitive situations, whereas the "bottom-up" process of accommodation is more typical of negative, aversive situations. Consistent with this reasoning, they go on to suggest that positive affective states are supportive of assimilative tendencies, whereas negative affective states should trigger accommodation processes. Beliefs, goes the next part of the argument, belong to the domain of assimilation, the result being that positive affective states support the formation of new beliefs or the elaboration of existing ones, whereas negative affective states (which stimulate accommodation processes) may encourage the individual to update his or her beliefs in the light of new evidence. The authors report an impressive body of evidence consistent with these theoretical proposals.

Michael Eysenck's chapter is also concerned with information processing, but his focus is specifically on anxiety. He argues that there are several biases associated with anxiety: attentional, interpretive, and memorial. Particularly important, he suggests, is the way in which the emotional disposition of trait anxiety interacts with the emotion of state anxiety. His general argument is that those who are highly trait anxious are cognitively biased in such a way that they believe their environment to be more threatening than it is. Eysenck summarizes the findings of various studies that demonstrate that such biases are especially prevalent when a highly trait-anxious person is also high in state anxiety. Those who are low on trait anxiety but high on a measure of defensiveness are referred to as "repressors." These individuals exhibit a different set of biases that lead them to minimize threat.

In Chapter 8 Eddie Harmon-Jones describes one of the better known theoretical frameworks within which the influence of emotions on beliefs can be explained, namely Festinger's theory of cognitive dissonance. The essence of the theory is that a perceived discrepancy between two or more cognitions gives rise to an uncomfortable tension-like state that motivates the individual to seek ways of reducing this discrepancy. After reviewing the key elements of dissonance theory, Harmon-Jones describes the main paradigms that have been established for testing the theory, before turning to experiments that have explicitly tested the role played by emotion in reducing the discrepancy between cognitions. The reviewed research supports the notion that cognitive discrepancy produces negative affect, and that this in turn motivates attempts at discrepancy reduction. One way in which discrepancy can be reduced is through belief change.

In the final chapter of the book, Margaret Clark and Ian Brissette focus on interpersonal relationships. They argue that we need to take account of the context of a social relationship in order to understand the way in which emotions are experienced, expressed, and interpreted. "Communal" relationships are ones in which emotions are likely to be experienced and expressed to a greater extent than in other forms of relationship. This is a result of the feelings of mutual responsibility that characterize communal relationships. There are some obvious parallels here with Oatley's notion of sentiments that afford cooperative relationships. It follows from Clark and Brissette's argument that if emotions are freely expressed and experienced in the context of social relationships, these emotional expressions and experiences should have an impact on the individual's beliefs about the other person and about the relationship.

We hope that this volume will help to convince those working in the neighboring subdisciplines of cognitive, social, clinical, and emotion psychology that the impact of emotion on beliefs has been unduly neglected in the past, and that the existence of this book will excite their intellectual curiosity and thereby stimulate further theorizing and research on the way in which emotions can influence beliefs.

References

Abelson, R. P. (1995). Attitude extremity. In R. E. Petty & J. A. Krosnick (Eds.), *Attitude strength: Antecedents and consequences* (pp. 25–41). Mahwah, NJ: Erlbaum.

Adorno, T. W., Frenkel-Brunswik, E., Levinson, D. J., & Sanford, R. N. (1950). *The authoritarian personality.* New York: Harper & Row.

Aristotle. *Rethorica.* In *Complete Works*, Book 2, Chs. 2–12. New York: Random House, 1941.

Armstrong, D. M. (1973). *Belief, truth and knowledge.* Cambridge: Cambridge University Press.

Bain, A. (1859). *Emotions and the will.* 4th Ed., 1899, London: Longmans, Green & Co.

Brand, M. (1984). *Intending and acting: Towards a naturalized action theory.* Cambridge, MA: MIT Press.

Hebb, D. O. (1949). *The organization of behavior.* New York: Wiley.

Hume, D. (1739/1969). *A treatise of human nature.* (Ed. E. C. Mossner) Harmondsworth: Penguin.

Kahneman, D., Slovic, P., & Tversky, A. (1982). *Judgment under uncertainty: Heuristics and biases.* New York: Cambridge University Press.

Lazarus, R. S. (1991). *Emotion and adaptation.* New York: Oxford University Press.

Nisbett, R. E., & Ross, L. (1980). *Human inference: Strategies and shortcomings of social judgment.* Englewood-Cliffs, NJ: Prentice-Hall.

Nussbaum M. C. (1994). *The therapy of desire: Theory and practice in Hellenistic ethics.* Princeton, NJ: Princeton University Press.

Oatley, K. (1992). *Best laid schemes: The psychology of emotions.* Cambridge: Cambridge University Press.

Scherer, K. R. (1999). Appraisal theory. In T. Dalgleish & M. Power (Eds.), *Handbook of cognition and emotion* (pp. 637–663). Chichester: Wiley.

Spinoza, B. (1677/1989). *Ethica.* (transl. G. H. R. Parkinson) London: Everyman.

Young, P. T. (1943). *Emotion in man and animal.* New York: Wiley.

Whiting, J. W. M., & Child, I. L. (1953). *Child training and personality: A cross-cultural study.* New Haven, CT: Yale University Press.

2

Feeling is believing: Some affective influences on belief[1]

Gerald L. Clore and Karen Gasper

"Winter Light" is the name of a film by the Swedish film-maker Ingmar Bergman. In it he depicts life in a remote Swedish village in the depths of winter. One of the unhappy characters in this village becomes obsessed with the "Red Chinese" and the inevitability of nuclear war. Throughout the film, the sun barely shines over the horizon, the snowy landscape is barren, and the interpersonal climate is equally cold. There are plenty of reasons for depression very close to home, but this character believes that he is depressed about something thousands of miles away. And in the end, he kills himself, and he does so, he says, because of the "Red Chinese."

Two important attributes of emotional feelings are that they provide information and guide attention. These attributes appear to be generally functional, but they can also go awry. When they do, they produce very different, indeed opposite, effects. The suicide of Bergman's character illustrates both. First, when affective states lack salient objects; the information they provide may be misattributed to substitute objects, and second, when affective states do have salient objects, they may lead one to an overly narrow focus of attention.

In this chapter we discuss the ways in which moods and emotions might influence beliefs. The first half of the chapter discusses seven basic principles underlying our research on general mood, and the second half builds on these principles focusing on how specific emotions may affect beliefs. There is insufficient research on emotions and belief to derive well-supported principles. Instead, generalizing what we have learned from mood research, we propose hypotheses about how the informational and attentional properties of emotion influence the establishment and maintenance of beliefs.

Mood and information

We believe that affective feelings serve an important feedback function (Clore, Wyer, Dienes, Gasper, Gohm, & Isbell, in press; Wyer, Clore, & Isbell, 1999). In the case of general moods, the object about which

10

feelings appear to give feedback depends in part on what is most salient to the experiencer at the time. Bergman's character was depressed because his life was as stark and without warmth as the winter light. But he was not focused on the everyday causes all around him. Instead, he attributed his feelings of despair to news about the nuclear arming of China, a topic about which he gradually became obsessed. Perhaps only so grand a topic as nuclear annihilation was suitable as an object for so profound a depression. In any case, his action illustrates one kind of affective influence on belief, namely attribution effects. Attributions are involved in all emotional states, but the centrality of their role in governing the influences of affect is most easily studied in moods, because they allow attributions to be manipulated.

Emotion and attention

The second process involves attentional effects. Affective influences on attention characterize emotions rather than moods. In our usage, affective states are emotion-like when they have salient objects and mood-like when they do not. For example, when Bergman's character attributed his depressed mood to a specific object, it functioned as an emotion, a dread of "Red Chinese" military strength. Because emotions generally have objects that give them direction, they tend to narrow attention to object-relevant information and emotion-relevant goals.

In his essay on emotion and information processing, Simon (1967) proposed that emotions alter processing priorities, which means that emotion-relevant goals become ascendant. Consistent with that view, we focus on the role of emotion in diverting attention to object-relevant and goal-relevant aspects of the environment and memory. We propose that strong emotion can initiate attentional funneling, a positive feedback loop in which strong feeling narrows attention to goal-relevant information (Easterbrook, 1959). Focusing on only the most goal-relevant aspects of events may then increase their apparent importance, which in turn may intensify emotional reactions to them. An increase in emotional intensity may further narrow attentional focus, making relevant events seem even more important, leading to still greater intensity, and so on in an ever-narrowing circle.

When Bergman's character focused on the nuclear arming of the "Red Chinese," the alarm he would have experienced about this threat would have focused his attention. As his focus narrowed, the threat would loom larger, leading to a greater affective reaction, triggering a further reduction in focus, and so on, resulting in an increasingly extreme view and triggering increased agitation and depression. In this way, affective experience and attentional focus may form an intensity funnel, a positive feedback circuit in which extremity of emotion and intensity of belief might amplify each other through their effects on the mediating factor of attentional focus. The involvement of attentional funneling and related processes on belief maintenance is discussed more fully in Part II of this chapter on Emotion-as-Information and Attentional Effects. We turn first to a discussion of the mediating role of attribution in the influence of affect on belief.

Part I   Mood as information: attributional effects

Much of our research concerns the effects of mood on judgment and belief. We often induce happy and sad moods by showing films or having subjects write a description of a happy or sad event in their recent past. These tasks generally produce subjective experiences of mild happiness or sadness, which often influence subsequent evaluative judgments or beliefs in a mood congruent way.

The role of subjective experiences in this process is particularly important. When evaluating objects or belief statements, people often act as though they ask themselves, "How do I feel about it?" and then use their feelings directly as information for the judgment (Schwarz & Clore, 1988). To have an effect, however, such feelings must be attributed to (or be experienced as caused by) the object of judgment. This account of the process of affective influence is known as the affect-as-information model (Schwarz & Clore, 1983). It holds that affect may influence beliefs because it provides experiential information or feedback about one's appraisal of objects to which the feelings appear to be a reaction.

Traditionally psychologists have assumed that judgments are based exclusively on attributes of the object of judgment (Anderson, 1971; Fishbein & Ajzen, 1975). Consistent with that view, Bower (1981) and Isen (e.g., Isen, Shalker, Clark, & Karp, 1978) hypothesized that mood influences judgment by changing the accessibility in memory of mood-consistent attributes of objects. In other words, mood effects on judgment were assumed to be indirect, being mediated by changes in one's representation of the object of judgment. This position applies when stored representations have both positive and negative features, so that positive mood can make positive features accessible and negative mood can make negative features accessible. However, mood effects also occur when information about an object of judgment is not mixed in valence and hence not subject to selective recall (Schwarz,

Robbins, & Clore, 1985), suggesting a limitation on selective recall as a mediator.

According to the affect-as-information view (Clore, 1992), mood effects may occur without any changes in how objects are represented. Feelings may be experienced directly as liking or disliking, independently of any positive or negative attributes of the object. This hypothesis provides a general account of affective influences on evaluative judgments, decisions, and beliefs. In an effort to formalize those processes, we have proposed a series of principles about affect and information processing (see Clore, *et al.*, in press). One of these is the experience principle.

The experience principle

Moods and emotions have cognitive consequences that are mediated by the subjective experience of affect (affective feelings). One of the most distinctive aspects of moods and emotions is that they are felt, and we focus on the cognitive consequences that appear to be mediated by such feelings. Tests of the experience hypothesis have examined individual differences and situational factors that may moderate the subjective experience of affect. For example, mood effects on judgment are most pronounced among persons who habitually attend to their feelings (Gasper & Clore, in press), among those who are clear about what their feelings mean (Gohm & Clore, in press), and among those instructed to attend to their subjective experience (Gasper & Clore, 1998).

The results of these and other studies implicate the role of conscious affect, or feelings, as one mediator of affective influences. This feeling-based view contrasts not only with explanations based on cognitive priming (e.g., Bower, 1981), as discussed above, but also with explanations based on "unconscious affect" (e.g., Zajonc, 1980).

An impressive body of research shows that emotional stimuli can influence judgment without a judge's awareness of having seen or felt anything (e.g., Bargh, 1997; Murphy & Zajonc, 1993). Rather than being based either on the indirect effects of activated concepts or on the direct effects of conscious feelings, this view emphasizes the effects of "unconscious affect." In studies of subliminal priming, participants are exposed to positive or negative words or to pictures of smiling or angry faces for only a few milliseconds before such a stimulus is masked by a subsequent image. When the subsequent image is a new stimulus to be evaluated, the unconscious prime sometimes exerts an influence, even though people are completely unaware of having seen it. The authors believe that such results show

that emotional influences are really caused by some kind of unconscious affect that does not involve feelings. However, as outlined
elsewhere (Clore & Ketelaar, 1997), we suggest that the effects of
subliminally presented stimuli really depend on cognitive rather than
distinctively affective factors (see also Bornstein, 1992).

If the stimuli used in these studies elicited affective feelings, some
ambiguity might exist about whether the subliminal priming effects
were conceptual or affective. However, there is no evidence that they
do. The words and faces used as stimuli in the best-known studies of
subliminal exposure (see Bargh, 1997; Murphy & Zajonc, 1993) do
have evaluative conceptual meaning but may not give rise to feelings.
Hence, we assume that their influence on subsequent reactions is due
to their evaluative meaning. If so, then they exemplify ordinary
cognitive priming and are not distinctively emotional. Rather than
being noncognitive, emotional phenomena, we believe that they are
best seen as nonemotional, cognitive phenomena.

We are suggesting that the best-known studies of unconscious
affective influence demonstrate the role of affective concepts rather
than of affect *per se*. On the other hand, in many other studies,
affective feelings are elicited. When that is the case, their influence
depends on their information value, which is the subject of a second
principle.

The information principle

The feelings of emotion provide information about the appraisal of
situations with respect to one's goals and concerns. Emotional feelings
are conscious, experiential feedback from appraisal processes that are
largely nonconscious. Feelings make information about appraisals
accessible privately (Frijda, 1986), and facial expressions (Ekman,
1982) make the same kind of information accessible publicly. Affective
feelings are an experiential representation of the personal significance
of situations. The ability to read one's own affective feedback appears
from studies of brain-damaged patients (Damasio, 1994) to be necessary for making everyday judgments and decisions, and it is also a
key ingredient in what has been called "emotional intelligence"
(Salovey, Mayer, Goldman, Turvey, & Palfai, 1995).

Because the causes of moods are generally not obvious, and because
the feelings of mood are not highly differentiated, their information
value is often ambiguous in comparison with that of emotions. For
investigators of affect, this fact has the advantage that feelings and
their apparent meaning can sometimes be varied independently. In
general, the results of relevant research (e.g., Gasper & Clore, 1998; in

press) show that the effective variable is not the feelings themselves, but the experience of their information value. The primary evidence that the information value of feelings is a critical factor comes from misattribution studies in which alternative possible causes for feelings are made salient. These studies are relevant to the attribution principle, to which we turn next.

The attribution principle

The information value, and hence the consequences of affect, depend on how the experience of affect is attributed. In the original studies in this line of research (Schwarz & Clore, 1983), participants were asked in a telephone interview to rate their life satisfaction. Calls were made either on the first warm, sunny days of spring when people were in good moods or on subsequent cold and rainy spring days when they were not. It was found that mood influenced the beliefs of respondents about the degree to which their lives were satisfactory. For some respondents, the interviewers, who pretended to call from another city, asked first about the weather. Answering that question caused them to attribute their feelings to the weather, and the relationship between mood and judgment was eliminated. It is important to note that the attributional manipulation did not change participants' moods; instead it changed the apparent information value of the mood-based feelings for making life-satisfaction judgments. This effect has been shown many times by a number of investigators (e.g., Keltner, Locke, & Audrain, 1993). It suggests that mood effects on judgment involve attributions of affective feelings as reactions to objects of judgment.

We believe that attributional processes play an important role in information processing phenomena regardless of whether they involve feelings. In this regard, consider again demonstrations of unconscious affective priming (e.g., Bargh, 1997; Murphy & Zajonc, 1993). In the usual paradigm, a visual mask is presented immediately after brief exposure to the evaluative stimulus. The mask does not keep aspects of the meaning of the stimuli from being processed, but it does interfere with awareness of having seen the stimulus, and hence with any opportunity to make a correct attribution. As a result, the evaluative meaning that is activated tends to be attributed to the immediately succeeding stimulus. Thus, a neutral stimulus (e.g., a Chinese ideograph) can take on the value of the masked (unconscious) stimulus. In our view, rather than providing a challenge to an attributional view, these results illustrate the importance of attributions (for an extended discussion of this view, see Clore & Ketelaar, 1997; Clore

& Ortony, in press; for a contrary view, see Winkielmann, Zajonc, & Schwarz, 1997).

In keeping with Heider's (1958) original conception, attributions are assumed to be an inherent part of the perception of events. Just as when the movement of a soccer ball is automatically attributed to the foot that kicks it, attributions for affect are usually completely implicit, rather than being explicit, deliberative, or effortful. This automaticity of the attribution is important in the surprising flexibility of attributions that are possible with moods and other affective states lacking a salient object. The key to this flexibility is what we have called the immediacy principle (Clore *et al.*, in press).

The immediacy principle

Affective feelings tend to be experienced as reactions to current mental content. Like other kinds of feeling, affective feelings provide immediate feedback about organismic states of which one might otherwise be unaware. Feelings of physical pain, for example, provide an immediate signal of bodily injury or malfunction that enables prompt and effective damage control. The injury can usually be readily located because the pain generally occurs at the site of the injury. In contrast, affective feelings are often difficult to localize in the body, because their cause is psychological rather than physical. However they are no less immediate, and this immediacy leads to the attribution of affect to whatever is in focus at the time. We assume that the immediacy of emotional reactions underlies the automatic tendency for people to experience their emotional feelings as relevant to their current mental content.

According to the immediacy principle, feelings are experienced as a reaction to whatever is in mind when one attends to them. The feelings of mood generally have a longer duration than those of emotion, so that any situational cause tends to be more remote in time and hence less salient. As a result, the mental content that happens to be salient when the feelings are attended to may not actually have caused them. Moods and mood-like states, such as depression, are notorious for coloring people's beliefs about whatever they focus on. We propose that this is a natural outcome of this more or less automatic tendency for attributions to be guided by the immediacy principle. Such misattributions should be governed in part by whether affective experiences persist over time and whether they already have objects. These considerations highlight the importance of the attributional constraint principle.

Table 2.1. *Object specificity and duration as factors that distinguish affective conditions*

Affective conditions		
	State	Disposition
Object	Emotion	Attitude
Objectless	Mood	Temperament

Attributional constraint principle

Attributions for affect are constrained by the durations of affective conditions and the specificity of their objects. We have indicated that a characteristic of mood states (and of states such as the depression developed by the character in the Bergman film discussed earlier) is that they tend not to have a salient object. Under those conditions, affect may be attributed to whatever one is focusing on at the moment. Because moods last awhile, mood-based affect may be experienced in conjunction with a variety of different stimuli before the feelings fade. Furthermore, because such affect does not already have a salient object, the unassigned feelings are available to be displaced to stimuli that are irrelevant or only partially relevant. According to the attribution principle, the apparent meaning of an affective feeling depends in part on the object to which it is attributed.

We are considering one way in which affect influences belief, namely, through attribution of affect to objects. Such attributions then allow affect to serve as a basis for new beliefs or as validation of prior beliefs about the object. Attribution of affect to an object is necessary for affect to have the kind of information value responsible for affect-as-information effects (Clore, 1992). As illustrated in Table 2.1, affect is generally attributed to a specific object in some affective conditions, whereas affect may not have a specific object for others, making them more subject to misattribution. For example, moods may be distinguished from emotions in part by the specificity of their objects. Moods often begin as emotional reactions to specific events, which become more mood-like as their objects broaden into "things in general."

Affective dispositions are even more enduring than moods, but they may remain latent rather than active. One may have an attitude that remains unexpressed for years. However, attitudes are not liable to misattribution, because their object is fixed. Indeed the attitude may exist only as affect potential dedicated to a specific object or class of objects. Thus, if the source of affect is an attitude, then the occurrence of affect-driven processing should be dependent on the activation by an attitude-relevant stimulus.

Some of the dynamics between dispositional and state affect can be seen in a recent study in which we examined the joint effects of state anxiety and trait anxiety on risk estimation (Gasper & Clore, 1998). Both trait and state anxiety increased judgments of personal risks (e.g., failure) and impersonal risks (e.g., natural disasters). In addition, for some participants we introduced an attribution manipulation to draw attention to the true cause for their current feelings of anxiety, which was risk-irrelevant. In that attribution condition, risk estimates were reduced for participants low in trait (dispositional) anxiety, but not for those high in trait anxiety. Those who reported chronically elevated anxiety tended to reject the experimental procedures as an adequate explanation for their current anxious feelings, and they continued to use them as a basis on which to make risk estimates.

We have not explored whether state affect that is attitude-consistent (as opposed to trait-consistent) would be similarly impervious to discounting explanations. However, everyday observation does suggest that one is less likely to see as valid an excuse for blame-worthy behavior when performed by a disliked person than when performed by a liked person. Such observations suggest that it may be difficult for one to discount the relevance of feelings when they are consistent with a disposition to feel that way, regardless of whether the affective disposition is a personality trait or an attitude.

The attribution principle indicated that whether affect influences belief depends on its being attributed to (experienced as feedback about) a belief-relevant object. Thus, experiencing one's feelings of depression as a reaction to one's shortcomings should influence beliefs about one's future success and other beliefs relevant to oneself as the object of the affect. As such examples suggest, however, the extent to which affect influences belief is a function not only of the object to which it is attributed, but also of the structure of that object. If highly interconnected with other objects, the implications of affect should be broader and more far-reaching than if the object were cognitively more solitary. This relationship is summarized by another principle, not previously proposed, namely, the elaboration principle.

The elaboration principle

The extent of affective influence depends on whether the experience is elaborated or punctuated, and the potential for elaboration depends on the structure of beliefs regarding the object of attribution. According to this principle, the potential for elaborating the meaning of an affective experience depends on the person's conception of the object. A related point was made by Fiske (1982) in her work on schema-triggered affect. She proposed that an object may evoke affect to the extent that the larger cognitive organization of which it is a part evokes affect. The importance of cognitive structure for emotion elaboration was also discussed by Linville (1985), who reasoned that the impact of mood should increase with the degree to which one has a simple (as opposed to a complex) self-conception. A simple self-concept is one in which its various aspects are interconnected as opposed to independent. As in a sinking ship, connections among aspects of the self-conception may allow the apparent implications of an affective event to flood the entire self structure. The control of the apparent implications depends on the connections among relevant beliefs. For example, in marriages of long standing, a single raised eyebrow or particular tone of voice may seem to speak volumes. Whether they do appear to speak volumes or not depends on whether they are punctuated or elaborated, which in turn depends on the structure of the beliefs involved.

Related processes appear to be at work in continuing religious or political struggles around the world (e.g., Ireland, Kosovo, the Congo, and the Middle East). The significance of any one event often depends on whether it is seen as connected to other events in the past, often the distant past. When each side perceives that they are connected, actions and reactions may become more rather than less extreme over time as each one carries the weight of history.

Some of the most extreme cases of individual anger and aggression occur when people believe that their honor is at stake. Nisbett and Cohen (1996), in their work entitled Culture of Honor, trace the prevalence of violent retaliation in the southern United States to the cultural traditions brought by the original settlers of the region. One group were immigrant herders from Scotland and Ireland. They point out that without the benefit of physical boundaries, a herdsman's flock and the area being grazed are only as secure as the reputation of the herdsman for violent retaliation against thieves and intruders. Another element in the old South came from the culture of the French Cavaliers, for whom the concept of honor was especially salient and for whom the reputation for being able and willing to retaliate with deadly force was their keenest weapon.

In clever experiments, Cohen, Nisbett, Bowdle, and Schwarz (1996), showed that whether or not a hostile act by a stranger led to a desire for physical retaliation depended on whether the participants had grown up in the southern or the northern United States. Beliefs about honor were hypothesized to be more accessible to southerners. Presumably their hostile impulses were mediated by perceptions of injury to their honor, which were in turn dictated by their beliefs about honor. In that situation, the anger was presumably caused by the beliefs, but, in addition, we assume that the experience of anger would also serve to reinforce and maintain those beliefs by serving as a kind of experiential evidence that their honor had indeed been implicated.

At the individual level, there also appear to be stylistic differences that make one more or less prone to elaborate or to compartmentalize emotional experiences. Evidence relevant to differences in the tendency to elaborate were obtained in a diary study by Larsen, Diener, and Cropanzano (1987). They found that some individuals had extreme swings in reported affect from one journal entry to the next, whereas others reported only mild swings. The cause of this variation, however, was not differences in the events that they experienced, but differences in how they elaborated those experiences. Some of these stylistic characteristics would also appear to have mental health implications. For example, both tendencies to ruminate (e.g., Nolen-Hoeksema & Morrow, 1993) and to suppress emotional thoughts (e.g., Wegner, 1989) are problematic because both can prevent a person from being able to separate emotional reactions from other thoughts and experiences (as discussed in Clore, 1994a). In contrast, expressing oneself either by writing diaries (e.g., Pennebaker, 1990) or by talking about emotional events is often helpful. One explanation for this fact is that such communication requires framing events in terms of particular times, places, and circumstances, which then constrains the possible meanings and potential attributions for the feelings generated by the event.

Our point here is that the influence of affect depends in part on the object to which the affect is attributed, and also on how one parses or punctuates that object domain. For example, Dweck and Leggett (1988) point out that when a student attributes a poor grade in an exam to a lack of effort, the implications of that attribution depend on the student's implicit theory of effort. A failure to put forth effort could be thought of in multiple ways, as evidence of momentary tiredness, as evidence of general laziness, as ingratitude toward one's family, or perhaps as evidence of one's complete worthlessness as a human being. It depends on whether one's habitual coping style leads one to punctuate the experience or to elaborate its implications. One may either segment such experiences into small units with lots of periods or be prone to run-on sentences with few periods (Newtson, 1973). In that sense, one might think of both depressives and ideological extremists as bad affective grammarians. It is, therefore, the parsing of the object domain that determines whether one "makes mountains out of molehills" or "fails to see the forest for the trees."

The various principles outlined indicate that the information value of affect depends on the object of attribution, which depends in part on what is in mind at the time. The information value also depends on currently active goals. Thus, if one is focused on an object (person, product, idea) with the goal of evaluating it, then positive and negative affect may be experienced as liking or disliking. But if one were focused on a problem with the goal of solving it or on a task with a goal of performing well, then positive and negative affect may be experienced as success or failure feedback. This possibility is summarized in the processing principle.

The processing principle

When one is focused on performing a task or solving a problem, affective feelings may be experienced as feedback about performance or about the value of accessible information. Problem-solving and other information processing tasks involve an interplay of accessible beliefs and new information from the environment. Individuals constantly monitor the adequacy of accessible beliefs, expectations, and abilities versus the need for new information. This assessment is made on the basis of feedback with respect to a hierarchy of small and large goals (Carver & Scheier, 1990). According to the processing principle, the experience of unattributed positive affect during problem solving and other information processing tasks is likely to be experienced as success feedback, leading one to continue relying on currently accessible beliefs and expectations. The experience of negative affect may be experienced as failure feedback, indicating the inadequacy of accessible beliefs and the need for new information. When this is the case, positive moods should lead to reliance on one's own impulses, habits, prior beliefs, or expectations, and negative moods should lead one to inhibit their use, to focus on new information from the environment, and to learn (Clore *et al.*, in press; Wyer, Clore, & Isbell, 1999).

Relevant research has examined the role of happy and sad mood in the use of stereotypes (Isbell, Clore, & Wyer, 1998). To induce moods, participants were asked to recall and describe in detail a happy or sad event in their recent past. Then they read a story about a day in the life of a woman described either as an introverted librarian or as an extraverted sales person. This initial information was intended to activate stereotypic beliefs about persons in such roles. However, the story contained an equal number of introverted acts and extraverted actions by the woman.

After reading the story, participants rated the woman on personality dimensions that were correlated with extraversion and introversion. The results were highly consistent with predictions based on the processing principle. The ratings showed dramatically that individuals made to feel happy had focused more on general stereotyped beliefs about librarians and salespersons, whereas individuals made to feel sad had focused more on the specific actions of the woman as described in the story.

To determine whether the results were in fact due to the information value of the feelings, the cause of their affective feelings was made apparent for some participants by asking them to rate how happy or sad the event description task had made them feel. In such an attribution condition, participants should experience their affect as a reaction to the mood induction task rather than as feedback about their beliefs. Consistent with the attribution principle, mood no longer showed the same effects. In fact they were now reversed, suggesting that whether greater weight is placed on stereotype-based expectations or on actual behaviors depends on whether participants experience the affect as feedback about their beliefs or as due to extraneous sources.

Similar results have been obtained when the accessible beliefs consisted of expectations based on scripts for behavior in common situations, such as the restaurant script (Bless, Clore, Schwarz, Golisano, Rabe, & Woelke, 1996). In a related vein, the political scientist Gregory Marcus has shown that voters in positive moods are more likely to rely on party identification, whereas those in negative moods are more likely to rely on what political candidates actually say (Marcus & McKuen, 1993).

The reliance on stereotypes of others, political party identification, and other prior beliefs would seem to be potentially relevant to the role of belief in trouble spots around the world. Does this research have implications for such situations? Surely, the problems in Kosovo, Palestine, Ireland, and the Congo are not due to the fact that the disputants are too happy! As it happens, several studies have recently reported that individuals in angry states react to these kinds of information processing tasks in the same way that individuals in happy moods do (e.g., Bodenhausen, Sheppard, & Kramer, 1994). That is, individuals in angry as well as happy moods give precedence to prior beliefs and expectations rather than to observation and learning. Bodenhausen *et al.* (1994) found that individuals in angry moods as well as those in happy moods show a heightened likelihood of relying on an ethnic stereotype to judge a defendant in a mock trial. Although both happy and angry moods might be expected to have elevated arousal, Bodenhausen ruled out arousal as the critical factor.

It should be noted that the relation between anger and category-level processing is also not peculiar to situations involving stereotypes or judgments of blame or guilt. Similar effects have been found for judgments of movie preferences (Kaplan, Kickul, & Reither, 1996). Results showed that individuals in both angry moods and happy moods based their judgments of films on their general preferences for particular genres of film (comedy, horror, adventure), whereas those in sad moods attended to the quality of the specific films within each genre. From an informational perspective, we assume that the key lies in the similarity of information about self provided by the feelings of happy and angry states. Anger, like happiness, implies that the person's own beliefs are valid. Indeed, anger appears to be an emotion aimed at asserting one's own belief and perspective. Thus, we might expect individuals who feel aggrieved to engage in belief-driven rather than data-driven processing. In any case, it seems plausible to suppose that anger does play a role of the kind we propose in Kosovo, the Middle East, and other settings of intergroup conflict.

In summary, we have argued that the information conveyed by such mood-based feelings is simply that something is good or bad. However, by themselves, the feelings specify neither what object is good or bad, nor in what way. In the previous discussion of mood and processing, we suggested that when engaged in problem solving or some other performance task, positive mood is often experienced as success feedback, leading one to rely on the most accessible information. Conversely, negative mood is often experienced as failure feedback, leading one to doubt the adequacy of accessible (internal) information and to a focus on acquiring new (external) information. However, some research suggests that not only happy moods but also anger increases belief-driven processing. Such data suggest that the important factor is not the feelings *per se*, but the information they convey. Both anger and happiness convey information that the perspective of the emotional person is valid, which leads to a general tendency for them to rely on whatever information is currently accessible. That idea is consistent with a view explored in the second half of this chapter, namely, that the influence of specific emotions on processing should reflect the model of the situation inherent in a given emotion type. The situational model for a given emotion is given in the cognitive eliciting conditions for that emotion, as specified in appraisal theories (e.g., Ortony, Clore, & Collins, 1988).

Part II Emotion as information: attentional effects

At the beginning of this chapter, we alluded to a 1960s film by Ingmar Bergman in which a depressed character committed suicide, because he believed that nuclear war with the "Red Chinese" was inevitable. We used this strange behavior to differentiate the affective influences of moods and emotions. We argued that, like the character's depression, feelings of mood often have no salient object, so that they can be misattributed to whatever plausible objects are cognitively accessible at the time. In contrast, the feelings of emotion do have objects as well as inherent structure, both of which limit problems caused by misattribution, but which may create other problems related to a narrowing of attentional focus. An overly limited focus can lead to extreme belief and rash action, as in the case of Bergman's character. Once his general feelings of depression were attributed to a specific object (the nuclear arming of the "Red Chinese"), they behaved more like a specific emotion of dread, focusing attention on belief-consistent evidence until he lost all sense of proportion.

In this second half of this chapter, we address the effects of emotion on belief. We begin by applying to emotion the affect-as-information principles discussed earlier in relation to mood, and then we turn to two attentional effects specific to emotion. The section is therefore divided into three parts: (1) Emotion as information – the direct informational effects of emotion on belief; (2) Emotion and attention – the role of feeling-enhanced belief in producing belief-consistent evidence through selective attention, and (3) Intensity and goal focus – the role of intensity of feeling in reducing the active goal space and increasing apparent belief importance. In this section, we apply what we have learned from our research on mood and belief to emotion and belief. However, the research literature on emotion provides less guidance for deriving principles than does the mood literature. Consequently, we extend the principles to several tentative hypotheses about emotion and belief.

Emotion as information

Knowing something directly from first-hand experience (experiential knowledge) is a different form of knowledge than knowing about the same thing indirectly (propositional knowledge). On the street, as well as in departments of philosophy, the importance of making such a distinction is well recognized. Of these two forms, experiential knowledge often has priority. One can debate propositional knowledge and one can even be convinced by argumentation that one's own view is mistaken, but this is not so readily done with experiential knowledge. To disbelieve what we experience is uncommon. Indeed, if it were to happen often, we might begin to think that we were losing our minds. Inconsistency between beliefs and reality suggests ignorance, but inconsistency between experience and reality suggests insanity.

We assume that people are constantly engaged in integrating subjective and objective information, and that a mismatch between them tends to elicit processes focused on bringing them into line (Heise, 1979). Another way of saying this is that affect provides constraints on beliefs and vice versa. Highly evaluative beliefs about something are usually capable of eliciting strong feelings, and strong feelings tend to elicit a search for supporting beliefs. For example, when retelling humorous, frightening, or angering incidents, factual details are often shaped and molded so that the incident more fully justifies one's reactions of humor, fear, or anger. In a similar manner, persons in love generally believe that their romantic partner has wonderful attributes, whereas if the relationship turns bitter, they may develop highly negative beliefs about the partner. Deep feelings of love or hate simply cannot be maintained by focusing on beliefs about moderate virtues or common foibles.

We are suggesting that beliefs are adjusted to be compatible with internal evidence in the form of feelings, just as they are adjusted to be compatible with external evidence from perceptual experience. Even in the case of purely logical argumentation, people need to feel that the case against their position is compelling before they change their minds. Such observations lead us to suggest a *feelings-as-evidence hypothesis*. Specifically, the feelings-as-evidence hypothesis is that belief-consistent feelings may be experienced as confirmation of those beliefs. Evidence from the sensations of feeling may be treated like sensory evidence from the external environment, so that something both believed propositionally and also felt emotionally may seem especially valid. In this sense, we assert that feeling is believing.

This hypothesis is based on the information and attribution principles discussed earlier in the section on mood research. If moods influence belief when the feelings appear to provide information relevant to the object of belief, then the same process should be evident in emotions. However, instead of providing generalized positive and negative feelings that can be attributed to whatever is salient at the time, emotions already have objects and involve activation of a specific causal schema. Thus, specific emotions already implicate particular beliefs, so that the sensory feelings involved in the emotion may act as evidence of the truth of that belief and of others consistent with it.

A related process is also evident in nonemotional feelings. For example, "cognitive feelings" (Clore, 1992) are feelings about knowing, such as surprise, familiarity, and insight. Other examples are the subjective experience of coherence or consistency and the experience of ease or difficulty when retrieving something from memory (Schwarz, Bless, Strack, Klumpp, Rittenauer-Schatka, & Simons, 1991). In that regard, belief in a proposition is enhanced when it is easy to retrieve confirming instances (Tversky & Kahneman, 1973). For example, Schwarz *et al.* (1991) showed that people asked to recall six examples of assertive behavior rated themselves as more assertive than those recalling twelve, because the recall of six was experienced as easier. Such phenomena show one role that feelings can play as apparent evidence for the validity of a belief.

In summary, we have differentiated experiential and propositional forms of knowledge, and noted that experiential forms often have priority. We proposed a feelings-as-evidence hypothesis, which says that cognitive and affective feelings, despite the fact that they are self-produced, may be experienced as internal evidence for beliefs that rivals the power of external evidence from the environment. However, in keeping with our informational approach, the ability of emotional feelings to bolster beliefs in this way depends on their information value. We now turn to examine the beliefs inherent in emotions, which are also the beliefs for which emotions provide the most direct evidence.

The information in emotional feelings

The information value of emotions is more constrained than that of moods. Emotions have inherent cognitive structure that moods do not have. In addition to the specificity imposed by its object, an emotion represents a particular model of the situation to which it is a reaction. This structure means that the information value of emotional feelings is specific rather than general. Appraisal theorists (e.g., Frijda, 1986; Ortony *et al.*, 1988; Roseman, 1991) have specified some of the eliciting conditions for common emotions. For example, the eliciting conditions of twenty-two emotion types are outlined in Figure 2.1. According to Ortony *et al.* (1988), there are three sources of value (goals, standards, attitudes) which give rise to three kinds of affective reactions (desirability, approval, liking), which are differentiated into specific emotions. Thus emotions can represent the desirability or undesirability of outcomes of events relative to goals (implicated in such emotions as joy or sadness and hope or fear), the praise or blameworthiness of an agent's actions relative to standards (implicated in such emotions as pride or shame), and the appealing or unappealingness of attributes of

ORTONY, CLORE, AND COLLINS' TYPOLOGY OF EMOTIONS

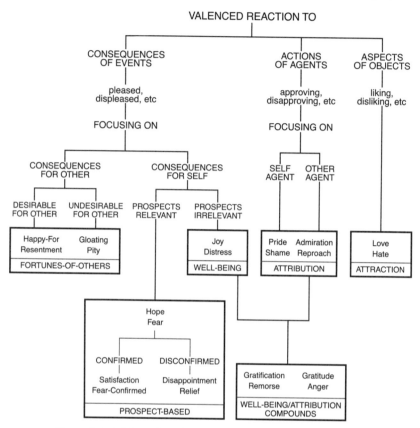

Figure 2.1 A hierarchy of cognitive eliciting conditions in which three sources of value (goals, standards, attitudes) yield three affective reactions (desirability, approval, liking), which are differentiated into twenty-two specific emotion types (Ortony, Clore, & Collins, 1988).

objects relative to attitudes and tastes (implicated in such emotions as love or disgust).

The specific emotion types occur when these affective reactions are further differentiated by appropriate cognitive distinctions such as whether an outcome is relevant to oneself (e.g., sadness) or others (e.g., pity) and whether it is past (e.g., sadness) or prospective (e.g., fear). Whereas the feelings of mood indicate that things in general are good or bad, feelings of emotion indicate that something in particular is good or bad and in what way.

We have emphasized that emotional feelings provide internal, felt evidence that an object or situation has the attributes implied by the emotion. One implication of this process is that when two situations elicit similar emotional reactions, one may infer that the situations themselves are similar, that is, that similar beliefs apply to both. This idea is summarized in the Emotion Categorization Hypothesis.

The *emotion categorization hypothesis* is that similarity of emotional reactions promotes inclusion of different situations into a single belief structure. Affect has recently been proposed as an element in categorization by Niedenthal, Halberstadt, and Innes-Ker (1999) who found evidence that affective states lead to increased weighting of emotional dimensions in multi-dimensional scaling studies. Building on this idea, we suggest that similarity of emotional reactions to two situations should contribute to perceptions that the situations are inherently similar. In other words, to the extent that subjective similarity is taken to imply objective similarity, then beliefs relevant to one situation may be applied to another situation that elicits a similar emotion.

This problem is illustrated by the case of a historian known indirectly to the first author. This historian, whom we shall call Professor Bitterman, had not published enough to flourish professionally, leaving him feeling disaffected and embittered about his standing in his department and his field. His speciality happened to be Western European history, a once dominant area in departments of history that had waned in popularity with the rise of feminism and multi-culturalism in American universities. This fact is important, because Professor Bitterman not only felt personally underappreciated, but also felt that his area of study was underappreciated. Both engendered anger and resentment, and the emotional categorization idea is that similarity of emotional reactions might contribute to forming the category.

Once the situations were categorized together, the conflation of beliefs about these two domains also provided secondary gains for the professor. For example, he identified his local, personal situation with the decline of Western Europe as a focal area among American historians. As a result, he could entertain an image of himself as a valiant figure engaged in a high-minded, if doomed struggle in defense of the Western intellectual tradition. We suggest that the inclusion of different situations in a common category results in the co-mingling of beliefs relevant to each. Since emotions may be triggered by relevant beliefs, this categorization-based co-mingling of beliefs, which itself had emotional causes, can also have emotional consequences, as seen in the emotional misattribution hypothesis, which is an implication of the elaboration principle discussed in the section on mood.

The *emotion misattribution hypothesis* is that when multiple situations are categorized together, one may be unable to allocate accurately the affect appropriate to any one of them. In such situations, affect appropriate to the most urgent category member may be elicited by any member of the category, making all members seem similar in significance. For example, Professor Bitterman began to respond with the same anger and resentment to an increasingly wide range of ideas and individuals that he perceived as related either to his own low status or that of his subdiscipline.

Of course, it is reasonable for a person to be more upset by two causes of woe than by one. Thus, it is not surprising that Bitterman was more depressed by the combination of personal failure and the demise of his subdiscipline than to either alone. Our point, however, is that the co-mingling of beliefs about the two situations should also make it difficult to distinguish the feelings of resentment elicited by his low personal status from the resentment elicited by the declining status of his field of study. Such conflation may have had two kinds of effects. First, emotional reactions to his personal situation that might otherwise seem petty and defensive could then be justified by being attributed as reactions to his concern with lofty academic and cultural issues. Anger and resentment about his personal lack of effectiveness could thus be made not only acceptable but noble and high-minded. A second effect was that academic and social issues he believed to be relevant to the decline of his field came to elicit a disproportionate level of passion. He believed that the study of Western Europe had declined in status because of the rise of feminism and multi-cultur-alism. The co-mingling of beliefs about the two domains meant that feelings of personal threat, an emotion appropriate to the most urgent of the activated beliefs, would then be experienced as a reaction to abstractions such as feminism. He acted as though he felt personally affronted by the idea of feminism and multi-culturalism, and indeed, owing to the misattribution of emotion, he literally did feel as though his personal honor was at stake. Moreover, to bring the process full circle, it is also likely that, in the face of the intense feelings apparently elicited by feminism, he would be led to entertain more extreme beliefs about feminism to achieve congruence between his feelings and his beliefs.

Thus, the emotion categorization hypothesis proposes that having the same emotional reaction to two different but related events may help weld them into one category so that the beliefs relevant to each become fungible or transferable from one account to the other. And the related emotion misattribution hypothesis is when multiple beliefs give rise to similar emotions, it may be difficult to attribute them accurately to their respective sources.

In summary, in this section we argued that specific emotions are relatively rich in information, because they have objects and distinctive patterns of feelings. These objects and qualities of feeling provide experiential representations of specific kinds of situations. With respect to beliefs relevant to a given emotion, feeling a relevant emotion may be experienced as evidence, confirming the validity of the beliefs. For example, anger involves a belief that undesirable outcomes have been caused by someone's blameworthy behavior. To the extent that relevant feelings serve as evidence of the validity of that or related beliefs, emotional feeling can then increase certainty or commitment. In the next subsection, we note that perception can be described as a cyclical interaction between belief (which guides attention), attention (which samples available information), and information (which modifies belief). The relative priority of belief-driven processing versus experience-driven processing in this cycle depends on how strong or compelling the belief is. By strengthening a particular belief, emotional feelings create conditions for belief-driven processing in which the likelihood of maintaining and using that particular belief should be increased.

Emotion and attention

Organisms ordinarily attend to sensory stimuli that are intense and changing, so that flashing lights and loud noises reliably attract attention. Similar factors may also underlie the attention-grabbing aspects of emotion. The main difference is simply that in the case of emotion, the sensory stimulation is internally generated. This internal stimulation is in the form of emotional feelings, and it attracts attention just as external stimuli do. And, as with other sensory cues, the more rapid the onset and the greater the magnitude of affective feelings, the more completely they should command attention (Clore, 1994b). These observations suggest an attention hypothesis that intensity of feeling activates attentional processes, which are then guided by accessible concepts or beliefs toward concept-relevant information.

The *attention hypothesis* concerns the role of the informational components of emotion (their object and the qualitative aspects of feeling) in attention. It is related to the immediacy principle discussed in the section on mood. That is, both concern the fact that feelings are experienced as being relevant to what is in one's attentional space. The only difference is that emotions guide attention to the existing object, and moods, which may have no salient object, are often attributed to whatever is in attentional space.

The role in attention of the object and quality of emotional feeling can be appreciated by analogy with feelings of physical pain. In addition to its motivating function, pain also attracts attention and provides information about the nature of an injury or malfunction. It is possible for pain to serve these functions to the extent that it has a distinctive quality and a specific object or location (e.g., a sharp pain in one's knee). However, when coming down with a cold, one may be aware simply of feeling under the weather, without being able to localize it. Such conditions are problematic because, in the absence of information about the locus of the disturbance, one is unable to take remedial action. In a similar manner, because moods are relatively undifferentiated feeling states that lack salient objects, they also provide few constraints on attention and hence on possible attributions for the experience.

Emotional feelings guide attention, not so much to themselves, but to what they signify. In a similar manner, flashing lights on a police car do not necessarily make one look at the lights alone, but draw one's attention to aspects of the situation that make them meaningful. We have said that the meaning or information value of emotional feelings (e.g., fear) lies in their apparent source or object and in the situation represented by their quality (e.g., the prospect of an undesirable outcome). To the extent that this potential information activates relevant concepts and beliefs, attention may be guided by these concepts toward belief-relevant aspects of memory or the environment.

The roles of belief, attention, and experience in perception have been usefully conceptualized by Neisser (1976) in his discussion of what he called "The perceptual cycle." His framework reconciles top-down, cognitive accounts of perception with bottom-up, experience-based approaches (Gibson, 1976). He proposed that perception is a process involving a continuous interplay of schema-driven and data-driven processing. Specifically, the perceptual process involves a schema of a situation, which directs exploration, which influences the sampling of available information, which in turn modifies the schema. To the extent that one is willing to equate "schema" with "belief," and "exploration" with "attention," this idea may be helpful in the present discussion. We envision a continuous three-part cycle with belief directing attention, attention guiding the sampling of information, information modifying belief, and so on.

In Neisser's model, a current schema acts like an hypothesis in an experiment, guiding (or placing constraints on) an active search for relevant evidence from the environment. But in addition to such top-

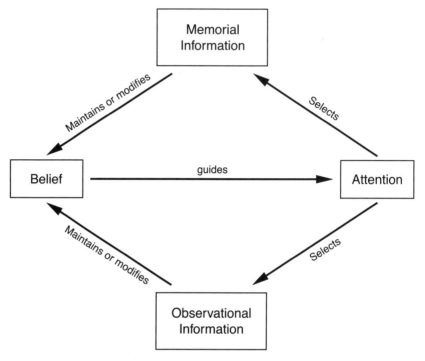

Figure 2.2 Two alternative perceptual cycles involving a single belief, which guides attention to internal (memorial) and external (observational) data sources.

down activity, one's schemata or hypotheses are also informed in a bottom-up way by the unanticipated content of the data sample. As one moves through time, sensation and cognition engage in a kind of perceptual dance, the direction of each being dependent on changes in the other. One could apply this idea either to environmental search, as Neisser did, or to memory search. In either case, an active idea serves as a frame or hypothesis, data are collected, the hypothesis is modified, and so on. Figure 2.2 illustrates this idea by showing two alternative perceptual cycles involving a single belief, which guides attention to both internal and external data sources in similar ways.

How is affect relevant to this process? We propose that beliefs that are buttressed by feeling have greater weight in the perceptual process. According to the feelings-as-evidence hypothesis, feelings may be experienced as a form of internal data that validates or seems to provide evidence for the belief, or in some other way feelings may commit one to the belief. Whether feelings serve as evidence of a belief, leading indirectly to commitment, or are experienced as commitment, one can see that feelings might lead to belief-guided attentional focus.

In Neisser's account of perceptual processes, an active schema guides the sampling of data from the environment, just as hypotheses guide the data collection of experimenters. But instead of an even-handed interaction of schemas and sensations, a belief associated with strong feeling may serve more as dogma than as an hypothesis. One need only try to reason with a fearful or an angry person to observe such commitment. Emotions of love, jealousy, anger, and fear represent commitments to particular beliefs, which the person "tests" through selective attention to data. For example, being in love represents a commitment to the belief that the loved one has wonderful attributes, being jealous is a commitment to the belief that one's relationship is in jeopardy, being angry is a commitment to a belief that someone's actions are blameworthy, and being afraid is a commitment to a belief that one is in danger.

Once an emotion is experienced, the system no longer operates as a scientist carefully weighing the pros and cons of the belief implied by the emotion. Instead, the emotional person acts like a prosecutor or a defense lawyer seeking by any means to find evidence for the belief. Presumably, the experiential aspect of the emotion is itself responsible for this process of interrupting the flow, providing information, and, through associated beliefs, guiding attention.

In relevant research, states of anger have been found to lead to a focus on blameworthiness, and fear to a focus on risk (Gallagher & Clore, 1985; Keltner, Ellsworth, & Edwards, 1993). We are proposing that beliefs and concepts rather than feelings provide the steering for attentional processes. Research by Niedenthal and Setterlund (1994) found support for this hypothesis. They examined both concept-related and feeling-related information, and they found that attention was drawn only to semantic or descriptive content of the emotion, and not merely to information of similar valence as the feelings.

If it is true that the guidance of attribution depends on concepts rather than feelings, then the same should hold for the influence of concepts versus feelings on memory. However, a great deal of research and theory in the past twenty years has implied that the feelings lead to the retrieval of feeling-congruent material from memory (e.g., Bower, Monteiro, & Gilligan, 1978; Isen, Shalker, Clark, & Karp, 1978). Despite such expectations, a reliable relationship between mood and memory has often been difficult to find (see Blaney, 1986), and when such relationships have been found, they seem likely to have been due to cognitive rather than affective components of experimental situations. A review of the relevant literature (Wyer, Clore, & Isbell, 1999) shows that many of the methods of inducing moods include instructions in which the desired state is labeled. Moreover, in situations in which such labeling is unlikely, mood congruence tends not to be found (Parrott & Sabini, 1990). We are not suggesting that moods cannot lead to mood-congruent recall. Indeed, in everyday life, they presumably do so frequently. However, when they do, we believe that the descriptive content (the concept of the mood and cognitive concepts about the inducing situation) primes concept-congruent memories. We think it unlikely that the feelings of mood prime feeling-congruent memories.

Evidence supporting this interpretation comes from Garvin (in preparation), who crossed ordinary cognitive priming (making sentences from word strings containing the emotional concepts 'happy' or 'sad') with incidental mood (induced by listening to happy or sad music). While in the mood state, participants read a story containing an equal number of happy and sad events (Bower, Gilligan, & Monteiro, 1981). Consistent with the attention hypothesis, the results showed that cognitive priming produced concept-congruent recall, and that, by themselves, the feelings induced by the music did not influence recall.

In summary, we have said that emotional intensity, because it signifies urgency, governs the breadth vs. narrowness of attentional focus (Easterbrook, 1959). In addition, the quality of experience, when represented as a belief, governs the direction of attention. When the presence of feelings indirectly increases commitment to a belief by appearing to serve as evidence for the belief, or by being experienced directly as commitment, then the perceptual cycle may be weighted in favor of top-down processing. This hypothesis explains how emotion may produce emotion-consistent perceptual evidence by directing attention to emotion-consistent data. These processes may create consistency between emotions and beliefs by guiding attention to observable data that the believer can point to. We have focused primarily in this subsection on the role of belief in guiding attention, and on the role of intensity of affect as an indication of the urgency of situations. It remains to examine the reciprocal effects of intensity and goal focus.

Intensity and goal focus

Simon (1967) proposed that a primary function of emotion is to reset the processing agenda so that one attends to urgent things first. Presumably this process involves changes in the priority of goals. For example, the goal of winning a chess game should be diminished if one suddenly hears a smoke alarm, and the goal of making one's point

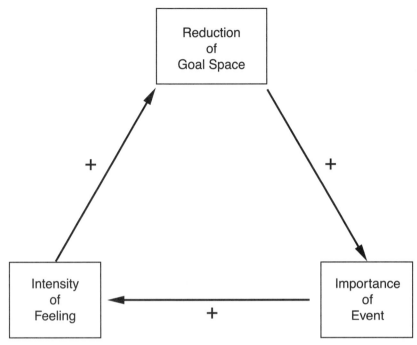

Figure 2.3 An attentional funnel in which attentional focus produced by intense feeling reduces the active goal space, which increases the apparent importance of goal-relevant events, which in turn intensifies feeling.

in an argument should fade if the other person bursts into tears. Emotional events take precedence, especially if they involve surprising events and intense reactions. That is, as implied in the attention principle, the intensity of feeling should govern the exclusivity of goal focus. This exclusivity may then have other consequences that constitute an attentional funnel (see Fig. 2.3)

An attentional funnel is a positive feedback loop that may be created when the attentional focus produced by intense feeling reduces the active goal space, which increases the apparent importance of goal-relevant events, which in turn intensifies feeling. It is easy to see how emotion and the progressive funneling of attention might promote a single-mindedness that increases the apparent urgency of a situation and therefore the intensity of affective and behavioral responses to it. For example, the elicitation of anger should make one focus on the blameworthiness of actions, but the more one focuses on that aspect, the less salient other aspects would be and therefore the more important the blameworthy action may seem. In turn, the more important the action seems, the more intensely one is likely to feel anger, which should narrow one's focus still more, increasing the relative importance of the action, and so on. Later, after the intensity of affect has subsided and other goals have come into view, one might see oneself as having been short-sighted and react with embarrassment at one's own behavior. That process seems to be a direct result of the fact that strong feeling reduces the active goal space, and a reduction in strong feeling reverses the process.

Evidence comes from a study of sports fans (Clore, Ortony, & Brand, unpublished). Investigators studied a hundred individuals who regularly went to basketball games played at the University of Illinois. For a whole season, the fans reported on the nature and intensity of their emotional reactions during and after each basketball game. In addition, other questions were asked before the season began. Among those was a question about the relative importance of Illinois basketball to their life as a whole. As might be imagined, the success of the team was of little importance in the context of their primary life goals. Despite this fact, the fans generally reported that they experienced intense emotion during the games, often involving shouting and yelling.

This result presents a theoretical problem, because a central assumption of cognitive approaches to emotion is that there should be a strong relationship between the intensity of emotion and the perceived importance of relevant goals. However, the rating data showed intense emotional responses to events that were judged as unimportant. We conclude that it may not be the absolute importance of a goal that gives events emotional potency, but rather the momentary importance of affected goals relative to other goals that are active and salient in the moment. These considerations suggest a more general hypothesis about momentary goal importance.

A *goal importance hypothesis* is that the momentary importance of goal-relevant events and the intensity of resulting emotions may increase as the salience of potentially competing goals decreases. This hypothesis suggests that the abstract importance of a goal to which an event is relevant is not as important as the total impact of the event on whatever goals are active and salient at the time. Of course, more than one factor governs the impact of a given event. For example, research shows that events that have implications for multiple goals may lead to more intense or long-lasting emotions than those with implications for only one goal (Frijda, Ortony, Sonnemans, & Clore, 1992). However, our current focus is on the role of attentional focus in reducing the moderating influence of potentially competing goals. Thus, the more intently one focuses on a single goal, the less the likelihood that action or inference relevant to that goal will be constrained by other, competing goals.

This hypothesis explains why sporting events can elicit such extreme emotion from spectators even though they are low in general importance. When fans enter the stadium they enter a world with a very simple goal structure. Because they have a goal to win, things that promote winning are good, and things that promote losing are bad. With such a sparse goal space, a winning shot can completely satisfy one's active and salient desires, and a missed shot can completely thwart them. This is surely a condition that should promote intense emotion, however short-lived. Such a singular focus can also lead to extreme action, as can be seen in soccer riots.

We are suggesting that going to sporting events can be an intense experience for fans who care because of their relatively simple goal structure. Paradoxically, it may be a relaxing experience for the same reason. An absorbing sporting event allows a vacation from the burden of everyday goals and concerns into a world of singular and clear goals. Also, a winning performance by one's team allows all of one's momentarily active goals to be completely and immediately satisfied, an inviting prospect in a world of unfinished tasks and small steps toward distant goals.

Other evidence that simpler mental structures lead to more intense emotional reactions has been reported by Linville (1985). As indicated earlier, she showed that recalling emotional events has a larger impact on the moods of individuals with simpler self-concepts. And she showed that evaluations of anything tend to be more extreme the fewer the dimensions on which they are considered. More complex structures are likely to include material that is either irrelevant to a particular inference or contradictory.

One way to view the results of Linville's research and the proposals we have made is that emotional intensity and simple-mindedness are related. She showed that a simpler cognitive structure affords fewer competing or moderating considerations, so that elaboration of the possible implications of an emotional event is relatively unconstrained. In contrast, we have emphasized the other side of the process. That is, that being emotional creates a sort of simple-mindedness in the sense that as emotions focus attention on relevant goals and information, the accessibility of competing goals and concerns is reduced, simplifying current mental structure.

Summary

This chapter was divided into two parts that focused on two different kinds of feeling, moods and emotions, and on two different functions of affect, to provide information and to guide attention. Much of the research on informational effects has been done by inducing general moods. Since moods tend to be unconstrained by their own objects, they are easily misattributed to substitute objects. Experiments involving attribution manipulations suggest that the critical variable in affective influences on belief is often the information conveyed by feelings. On the basis of prior research, seven principles were presented and discussed. These are as follows:

(1) The experience principle. Moods and emotions have cognitive consequences that are mediated by the subjective experience of affect (affective feelings).
(2) The information principle. The feelings of emotion provide information about the appraisal of situations with respect to one's goals and concerns.
(3) The attribution principle. The information value, and hence the consequences of affect, depend on how the experience of affect is attributed.
(4) The immediacy principle. Affective feelings tend to be experienced as reactions to current mental content.
(5) The attributional constraint principle. Attributions for affect are constrained by the duration of affective conditions and the specificity of their objects.
(6) The elaboration principle. The extent of affective influence depends on whether the experience is elaborated or punctuated, and the potential for elaboration depends on the structure of beliefs regarding the object of attribution.
(7) The processing principle: When one is focused on performing a task or solving a problem, affective feelings may be experienced as feedback about performance or about the value of accessible information.

In the second half of the chapter, we focused on the informational properties of emotion rather than mood and on the role of beliefs, especially those fueled by emotion, to guide attention toward belief-relevant information. In the absence of plentiful research, our discussion of emotional effects on belief was guided by five hypotheses, which are as follows:

(1) The feelings-as-evidence hypothesis is that belief-consistent feelings may be experienced as confirmation of those beliefs.

(2) The emotion categorization hypothesis is that similarity of emotional reactions promotes inclusion of different situations into a single belief structure.

(3) The emotion misattribution hypothesis is that when multiple situations are categorized together, one may be unable to allocate accurately the affect appropriate to any one of them.

(4) The attention hypothesis is that intensity of feeling activates attentional processes, which are then guided by accessible concepts or beliefs toward concept-relevant information.

(5) The goal importance hypothesis is that the momentary importance of goal-relevant events and the intensity of resulting emotions may increase as the salience of potentially competing goals decreases.

In conclusion: we touch on several of the properties of affect embodied in these principles and hypotheses that are directly relevant to belief development and maintenance. The first is the fact that emotions are informative. One of their prime functions is to provide immediate, attention-getting feedback about aspects of situations appraised as goal-relevant. Emotional feelings are automatically experienced as feedback relevant to current perceptual and mental content. Therefore, according to the immediacy principle, even feelings arising from completely endogenous causes will tend to be experienced as information about whatever is currently in focus. An implication of this research, therefore, is that the range of beliefs susceptible to influence by mood (including depression and anxiety) is limited only by the attributions that people make for such feelings.

A second property with relevant implications is that emotions are believable. Because emotional feelings are directly experienced, and arise from within, the personal validity of the information they appear to convey seems self-evident to the person experiencing them. One can argue with logic, but not with feeling. When feelings have no fixed object and little inherent structure, as in the case of moods, their information value is unconstrained. Thus, the feelings arising from moods can become universal donors of credibility to any associated beliefs.

A third important fact is that implicit in each emotion is a model of situations in which such emotions are experienced. Thus, fear necessarily involves an implicit assumption that something in the current situation poses a threat. Unlike moods, which imply only that things are generally positive or negative, specific emotions implicate a more complex schema or set of beliefs about a situation. Thus, one of the most obvious and important implications of emotion for belief is that the occurrence of an emotion already means that the emotional person is committed to particular beliefs about that situation. As indicated earlier, being jealous is already a commitment to a belief that one's relationship is in jeopardy, being angry is a commitment to a belief that someone's actions are blameworthy, and being afraid is a commitment to a belief that one is in danger.

A fourth property that is important in emotional effects on belief is that emotion guides attention to object-relevant information. We suggested that the attention is activated (and narrowed) by intensity of feeling (the quantitative aspect), whereas attention is directed by the object of feeling (the qualitative aspect). We argued that emotions could be expected to guide attention to belief-relevant information because they have objects, whereas moods would not be expected to guide attention because they tend not to have objects. Intense moods might result in vigilance combined with difficulty sustaining and directing attention. The proposed differences in the effects of mood and emotion on attention to external perceptual information should also hold for attention to internal information in memory. Thus, we predict that emotions, but not moods, should elicit belief-consistent recall.

Each of the above properties individually have implications for the influence of mood and emotion on belief, but some may also act in tandem. For example, in the perceptual cycle (Neisser, 1976), the credibility conferred by emotional feelings may complement the direction of attention provided by emotional objects. Together they may give priority to belief-consistent information. We assume that perception involves a constant interplay of top-down (belief-driven) and bottom-up (data driven) processing in which beliefs about the current situation guide the sampling of available information, which in turn may modify beliefs. If feelings provide their own apparent validation for beliefs, selective data-sampling and resistance to bottom-up modification of the belief may lead to inappropriate belief maintenance.

Note

[1] The authors wish to acknowledge Michael Robinson and the members of the Affect Group for their advice on this project. This project was supported by NSF Grant SBR 96–01298, NIMH Grant MH 50074, and by a John D. & Catherine T. MacArthur Foundation Grant (32005–0) to the Center for Advanced Study in the Behavioral Sciences. Correspondence should be addressed to Gerald L. Clore, Department of Psychology, 603 East Daniel Street, Champaign, IL 61820. Electronic mail to gclore@s.psych.uiuc.edu.

References

Anderson, N. H. (1971). Integration theory and attitude change. *Psychological Review, 78*, 171–206.

Bargh, J. A. (1997). The automaticity of everyday life. In R. S. Wyer (Ed.), *Advances in social cognition* (Vol. 10, pp. 1–61). Mahwah, NJ: Erlbaum.

Blaney, P. H. (1986). Affect and memory: A review. *Psychological Bulletin, 99*, 229–246.

Bless, H., Clore, G. L., Schwarz, N., Golisano, V., Rabe, C., & Woelke, M. (1996). Mood and the use of scripts: Does being in a happy mood really lead to mindlessness? *Journal of Personality and Social Psychology, 71*, 665–679.

Bodenhausen, G. V., Sheppard, L. A., & Kramer, G. P. (1994). Negative affect and social judgment: The differential impact of anger and sadness. *European Journal of Social Psychology, 24*, 45–62.

Bornstein, R. F. (1992). Inhibitory effects of awareness on affective responding: Implications for the affect-cognition relationship. In M. S. Clark (Ed.), *Emotion* Vol. 13 *Review of personality and social psychology* (pp. 235–255). Newbury Park, CA: Sage.

Bower, G. H. (1991). Emotional mood and memory. *American Psychologist, 36*, 129–148.

Bower, G. H., Monteiro, K. P., & Gilligan, S. G. (1978). Emotional mood as a context of learning and recall. *Journal of Verbal Learning and Verbal Behavior, 17*, 573–585.

Bower, G. H., Gilligan, S. G., & Monteiro, K. P. (1981). Selectivity of learning caused by affective states. *Journal of Experimental Psychology: General, 110*, 451–473.

Carver, C. S., & Scheier, M. F. (1990). Origins and functions of positive and negative affect: A control-process view. *Psychological Review, 97*, 19–35.

Clore, G. L. (1992). Cognitive phenomenology: Feelings and the construction of judgment. In L. L. Martin & A. Tesser (Eds.), *The construction of social judgment* (pp. 133–164). Hillsdale, NJ: Erlbaum.

Clore, G. L. (1994a). Why emotions are felt. In P. Ekman & R. J. Davidson (Eds.), *The nature of emotion: Fundamental questions* (pp. 103–111). New York: Oxford University Press.

Clore, G. L. (1994b). Why emotions vary in intensity. In P. Ekman & R. J. Davidson (Eds.), *The nature of emotion: Fundamental questions* (pp. 386–393). New York: Oxford University Press.

Clore, G. L., & Ketelaar, T. (1997). Minding our emotions: On the role of automatic, unconscious affect. In R. S. Wyer (Ed.), *Advances in social cognition* (Vol. 10, pp. 105–120). Mahwah, NJ: Erlbaum.

Clore, G. L., & Ortony, A. (in press). Cognitive in emotion: Never, sometimes, or always? In L. Nadel & R. Lane (Eds.) *The cognitive neuroscience of emotion.* New York: Oxford University Press.

Clore, G. L., Ortony, A., & Brand, S. (unpublished). The joy of victory and the agony of defeat: The emotions of sports fans. Champaign, IL: University of Illinois.

Clore, G. L., Wyer R. S., Dienes, B., Gasper, K., Gohm, C., & Isbell, L. (in press). Affective feelings as feedback: Some Cognitive Consequences. In L. L. Martin & G. L. Clore (Eds.). *Mood and social cognition: Contrasting theories.* Mahwah, NJ: Erlbaum Associates.

Cohen, D. Nisbett, R. E., Bowdle, B. F., & Schwarz, N. (1996). Insult, aggression, and the southern culture of honor: An "experimental ethonography." *Journal of Personality and Social Psychology, 70*, 945–960.

Damasio, A. R. (1994). *Descartes' error*. New York: Putnam & Sons.

Dweck, C. & Leggett, E. (1988). A social cognitive approach to motivation and personality. *Psychological Review*, 95, 256–273.

Easterbrook, J. A. (1959). The effect of emotion on cue utilization and the organization of behavior. *Psychological Review, 66*, 183–201.

Ekman, P. (1982). *Emotion in the human face*. New York: Cambridge University Press.

Fishbein, M., & Ajzen (1975). *Belief, attitude, intention an behavior*. Reading, MA: Addison-Wesley.

Ekman, P. (1982). *Emotion in the human face*. New York: Cambridge University Press.

Fiske, S. T. (1982). Schema triggered affect: Applications to social perception. In M. S. Clark & S. T. Fiske (Eds.), *Affect and cognition: The 17th annual Carnegie symposium on cognition* (pp. 55–78). Hillsdale, NJ: Erlbaum.

Frijda, N. H. (1986). *The emotions*. New York: Cambridge University Press.

Frijda, N. H., Ortony, A., Sonnemans, J., & Clore, G. (1992). The complexity of intensity: Issues concerning the structure of emotion intensity. In M. S. Clark (Ed.), *Review of Personality and Social Psychology* (Vol. II, pp. 60–89). Beverly Hills, CA: Sage.

Gallagher, D., & Clore, G. L. (1985). Effects of fear and anger on judgments of risk and evaluations of blame. Paper delivered at the Midwestern Psychological Association, Chicago, May.

Garvin, E. (in preparation). Mood and memory? Forget about it. Unpublished Master's thesis, University of Illinois.

Gasper, K., & Clore, G. L. (1998). The persistent use of negative affect by anxious individuals to estimate risk. *Journal of Personality and Social Psychology, 74*, 1350–1363

Gasper, K., & Clore, G. L. (in press). Do you have to pay attention to your feelings to be influenced by them? *Personality and Social Psychology Bulletin*.

Gibson, J. J. (1976). *The ecological approach to visual perception*. Boston: Houghton Mifflin.

Gohm, C. & Clore, G. L. (in press). Individual differences in emotional experience: A review of scales. *Personality and Social Psychology Bulletin*.

Heider, F. (1958) *The psychology of interpersonal relations*. New York: Wiley.

Heise, D. R. (1979). *Understnding events: Affect and ahte constsuction of social action*. New York:: Cambridge Universty Press.

Isbell, L. M., Clore, G. L., & Wyer, R. S. (1998). Mood-mediated uses of stereotyping in impression formation. Unpublished manuscript, University of Illinois at Urbana-Champaign.

Isen, A. M., Shalker, T. E., Clark, M. S., & Karp, L. (1978). Affect, accessibility of material in memory and behavior: A cognitive loop? *Journal of Personality and Social Psychology, 36*, 1–12.

Kaplan, M., Kickul, J., & Reither, A. (1996). Mood and extent of processing plot and visual information about movies. Paper delivered at the Midwestern Psychological Association, Chicago, May.

Keltner, D., Ellsworth, P., & Edwards, K. (1993). Beyond simple pessimism: Effects of sadness and anger on social perception. *Journal of Personality and Social Psychology, 64*, 740–752.

Keltner, D., Lock, K. D., & Audrain, P. C. (1993). The influence of attributions on the relevance of negative feelings to satisfaction. *Personality and Social Psychology Bulletin, 19*, 21–30.

Larsen, R. J., Diener, E., & Cropanzano, R. S. (1987). Cognitive operations associated with individual differences in affect intensity. *Journal of Personality and Social Psychology, 53*, 767–774.

Linville, P. (1985). Self-complexity and affective extremity: Don't put all your eggs in one cognitive basket. *Social Cognition, 3*, 94–120.

Marcus, G. E., & Mackuen, M. B. (1993). Anxiety, enthusiasm, and the vote: The emotional underpinnings of learning and invlvement during presdiential campaigns. *American Political Science Review, 87*, 672–685.

Murphy, S., & Zajonc, R. B. (1993). Affect, cognition, and awareness: Affective priming with optimal and suboptimal stimulus exposures. *Journal of Personality and Social Psychology, 64*, 723–739.

Neisser, U. (1976). *Cognition and reality.* San Francisco: W. H. Freeman & Co.

Newtson, D. (1973). Attribution and the unit of perception of ongoing behavior. *Journal of Personality and Social Psychology, 28*, 28–38.

Niedenthal, P. M., & Setterlund, M. B. (1994). Emotion congruence in perception. *Personality and Social Psychology Bulletin, 20*, 401–411.

Niedenthal, P. M., Halberstadt, J. B., & Innes-Ker, A. H. (1999). Emotional response categorization. *Psychological Review, 106*, 337–361.

Nisbett, R. E. & Cohen, D. (1996). *Culture of honor: The psychology of violence in the South.* Boulder, CO: Westview Press.

Nolen-Hoeksema, S., & Morrow, J. (1993). The effects of rumination and distraction on naturally occurring depressed moods. *Cognition and Emotion, 7*, 561–570.

Ortony, A., Clore, G. L., & Collins, A. (1988). *The cognitive structure of emotions.* New York: Cambridge University Press.

Parrott, W. G., & Sabini, J. (1990). Mood and memory under natural conditions: Evidence for mood and incongruent recall. *Journal of Personality and Social Psychology, 59*, 321–336.

Pennebaker, J. W. (1990). *Opening up: The healing power of confiding in others.* New York: William Morrow.

Roseman, I. J. (1991). Appraisal determinants of discrete emotions. *Cognition and Emotion, 5*, 161–200.

Salovey, P., Mayer, J. D., Goldman, S. L., Turvey, C., & Palfai, T. P. (1995). Emotional attention, clarity, and repair: Exploring emotional intelligence using the trait meta-mood scale. In J. Pennebaker (Ed.), *Emotion, disclosure, and health.* Washington, DC: American Psychological Association.

Schwarz, N., Bless, H., Strack, F., Klumpp, G., Rittenauer-Schatka, H., & Simons, A. (1991). Ease of retrieval as information: Another look at the availability heuristic. *Journal of Personality and Social Psychology, 61*, 195–202.

Schwarz, N., & Clore, G. L. (1983). Mood, misattribution, and judgments of well-being: Informative and directive functions of affective states. *Journal of Personality and Social Psychology, 45*, 513–523.

Schwarz, N., & Clore, G. L. (1988). How do I feel about it? Informative functions of affective states. In K. Fiedler & J. Forgas (Eds.), *Affect, cognition, and social behavior* (pp. 44–62). Toronto: Hogrefe.

Schwarz, N., Robbins, M., & Clore, G. L. (1985). Explaining the effects of mood on social judgment. Paper read at the Midwestern Psychological Association, Chicago, May.

Simon, H. A. (1967). Motivational and emotional controls of cognition. *Psychological Review, 74*, 29–39.

Tversky, A., & Kahneman, D. (1973). Availability: A heuristic for judging frequency and probability. *Cognitive Psychology, 5*, 207–232.

Wegner, D. M. (1989). *White bears and other unwanted thoughts: Suppression, obsession, and the psychology of mental control.* New York: Penguin Books.

Winkielman, P., Zajonc, R. B., & Schwarz, N. (1997). Subliminal affective priming resists attributional interventions. *Cognition and Emotion, 11*, 433–465.

Wyer, R. S., Clore, G. L., & Isbell, L. (1999). Affect and information processing. In M. Zanna (Ed.), *Advances in experimental social psychology* (vol. 31, pp. 1–77). New York: Academic Press.

Zajonc, R. B. (1980). Feeling and thinking. Preferences need no inferences. *American Psychologist, 35*, 151–175.

3

Beliefs through emotions[1]

Nico H. Frijda and Batja Mesquita

Emotions influence beliefs. This is a classical assumption. People's emotions, according to this assumption, determine what they think, and what they think is true. We use the word "belief" for a proposition that a person considers to be true. The truth of most propositions is not objectively fixed. Most propositions affirmed in beliefs go beyond the mere occurrence of observable facts. They extend to the causes or intentions behind events, their likely consequences, and the enduring properties of things or persons that make them behave in a particular manner. That some harm was due because a particular individual caused it, that he caused it because he intended to effect that harm, that he did so because he has an evil nature – all are beliefs in this sense.

Thus the thesis that this chapter examines is that emotions influence beliefs. We will first present some evidence for this thesis. We will then try to show that it is of the nature of emotions to have this influence, particularly when those emotions have certain properties or arise under certain conditions, owing to the properties of emotional thinking generally. These properties and conditions are able to influence beliefs because of the properties of belief formation in general.

Emotions influence beliefs in basically two ways. They may give rise to beliefs where none existed, or change existing beliefs; and they may enhance or decrease the strength with which a belief is held.

The notion of "belief strength" is being used to refer to a number of phenomena that may or may not occur together; we do not know. Some beliefs are extreme, and without nuance. A particular political view is considered just bad, and all its consequences very harmful. Also, some beliefs are being firmly held, even in the face of weak evidence. One may be convinced of their truth, whatever the strength of the evidence. A belief may persist in the face of evidence that contradicts it. The belief renders that evidence powerless. It is ignored or dismissed; arguing appears useless. Furthermore, a person holding a belief may accept information as credible that would appear doubtful to other people or, by contrast, is considered as not worth believing when it appears convincing to others. In the heat of the Kosovo conflict, American radio interviewed a Belgrade citizen and suggested that Milosevich had selfish motives. The interviewer confronted the man with the fact that Milosevich had never shown any interest in the fate of the Serbian soldiers in the Bosnian conflict, and had never visited them. The Belgrade citizen responded: "I do not think that that is true. But even if it were true, I am sure he received those soldiers."[2] Hopes emerge on slight foundations. One tends to believe rumors that are consonant with one's prevailing emotional attitude, as when the mob decried the commander of the Bastille as a tyrant and killed him, when in fact he had instituted humane reforms (Schama, 1989: 595). All this has consequences for action. Beliefs have been defined as "that upon which a person is prepared to act" (Bain, 1859). Beliefs may facilitate readiness to engage in actions relevant to them, and to endorse such actions by others. One is prepared to fight for a cause one believes in, and to vote for credits that allow others to fight. Presumably, this is the more so when emotions have strengthened the beliefs.

Conviction, extremity, resistance to change through incompatible information, acceptance of consonant information, and endorsement of actions: they are aspects of durability and impact on behavior and information processing that operationalize the notion of strength of beliefs, as they also do of "attitude strength" (Krosnick & Petty, 1995: 3–4).

Emotion-instigated beliefs illustrated

Although an influence of emotions upon beliefs is widely accepted and ancient wisdom, there is little research proving this. Little is known about the scope or power of this influence, or the precise conditions under which it occurs. From the perspective of systematic study, it is no more than an assumption. It is, moreover, hardly discussed in emotion theory, although it is with respect to moods (Clore and Gasper, this volume; Fiedler, this volume; Forgas, this volume) and attitudes (Krosnick & Petty, 1995).

An influence of emotions upon beliefs is, however, being accepted as a fact on the basis of massive informal evidence. True enough: the observations and anecdotes forming that evidence are open to different interpretations. Emotional events may instigate or strengthen beliefs independently of their being emotional (e.g., Nisbett & Ross, 1980). Some influence of emotional factors upon beliefs is, however, well established experimentally (Kruglanski & Freund, 1983; Kunda, 1990; Pyszczynski & Greenberg, 1987). The scope of those influences is strongly suggested by anecdotal evidence. On the basis of that evidence, it appears very plausible that emotional meaning adds to belief strength, in its various manifestations and consequences; that such strength would be less if the events merely represented contingent facts; and that the influence may be of considerable magnitude and social consequence. The evidence covers a large variety of domains. We will draw some examples from political beliefs, personal relationships, addiction, and religion.

First, political beliefs. The use of emotions to instill beliefs is prevalent in political propaganda. Depicting individuals, groups, or issues from an emotional perspective, or as actors in emotional events, evokes emotion. It thereby slips the belief that the emotion is about into the listener's mind. Presumably, it slips the beliefs into the listener's mind more easily, smoothly and unquestioned than would happen when the information alone was transmitted. In the Yugoslavian crisis of the early nineties, Serbian propaganda aroused nationalistic sentiment and fervor in the Serbs through the anger evoked by recalling Croatian crimes from the forties during Nazi terror. It evoked fear by focusing attention on the fact that contemporary Croatian Ustashas carried the same regalia as fifty years before. It also aroused pride by reminding the Serbs how valiantly they had opposed Turkish onslaughts in Kosovo 600 years before. All this presumably enhanced acceptance of messages about what contemporary Croats were wanting to do to them, and gained support for the government policy of increasing the defense budget. Croatian propaganda ran similar courses, and one may well believe that both propaganda sources made the belief in the enemies' evil nature and intents next to indubitable. The journalist Glenny (1992) called both the Croatian and Serbian television systems the greatest criminals of the 1989–96 Yugoslavian war.

In the recent Rwanda conflict, anti-Tutsi propaganda made similar use of emotions. When the genocide began in 1994, the Hutu radio station Radio Mille Collines had been incessantly pouring out descriptions of the Tutsis as "cockroaches that needed destruction." The propaganda received additional body from people's recollections about the Tutsi oppression of Hutus prior to 1959, from the radio station reminding them of that, and asserting that the Tutsis tried to make those times come back. It all resulted in firm beliefs about the Tutsis' evil nature, just as forty years earlier many Tutsis (and Belgians and Germans) firmly believed the Hutus' inferior status justified their domination of them. Hutu beliefs in Tutsi evil presumably were enhanced by the fear of losing current advantages and the attractions of sharing in the Tutsi riches (Prunier, 1995), because generally we think evil of those whom we fear. As the journalist Keane reported an interview with Hutu soldiers at a roadblock:

> "The Tutsis don't want to share this country with another race. They want us to be their slaves again like in the old days." Another voice spoke up: "They want to colonize other people. But you must remember, we are human beings too." These last words struck me as ironic, even sad in a way. The man who spoke them was dressed in rags and was barefoot. He looked frightened and worn out. It was quite possible that he had been involved in the killing. *We are human beings too.* The words of the men at the roadblock were almost word for word a recitation of the government's line. These men really did believe that they were about to be returned to the dark ages of Tutsi autocracy. All the stories of oppression and humiliation that had been handed down from their parents, all the conspiracy theories of the government and all the fear caused by the RPF (Rwanda Patriotic Front) incursions since 1990 had been whipped up by extremist politicians to produce pathological hatred of the Tutsis. I asked one of the men what would happen if a Tutsi came up to the roadblock. He simply smiled. (Keane, 1995: 165–166).

Scapegoating is a variant of belief formation, stemming from lore, from propaganda, and due to the common human propensity to find a culprit for one's distress. The famous medieval composer and poet Guillaume de Machaut wrote, in his poem "The judgment of the King of Navarra":

> After that came a scoundrel,
> False and treacherous,
> It was the shameful Jew,
> The evil and disloyal one,
> Who says good things but loves all bad things,
> . . .
> Who next poisoned various places
> And rivers and springs
> That were clear and healthy,
> By which many lost their lives,
> Because those who used it
> Died rather suddenly,
> Sometimes by tens of hundred thousands
> Died in the fields or the towns

This was intended to explain the great plague of 1349 and 1350 (quoted from Girard, 1982). Blaming the Jews for losing World War I and the economic crisis thereafter led to similar beliefs being accepted by a very large number of Germans during the 1930s – perhaps a majority (Goldhagen, 1996). In Lithuania, much of the civilian population enthusiastically took part in the destruction of Jews after the German incursion in 1941, as a revenge for the Soviet oppression of the previous years for which they were held responsible (Bregstein, 1995).

Of course, emotions that induce belief changes do not result from propaganda or preconception only. They also result from actual emotional conditions. Prior to the NATO bombing of Serbia in the Kosovo war, many Serbians were critical of Milosevich. After its onset, they gave him their enthusiastic support (or so at least it seems), and, foreseeably, became ready for unflinching and long-lasting resistance fed by the conviction of their cause being just.

Beliefs may be shaped or stabilized by emotions in subtle fashions. One of these is the use of concepts that carry emotional valence. Some concepts better fit a given emotional judgment than others. These concepts then may lead a life of their own. They have their own implications and turn into beliefs that in their turn support emotions. The Hutu radio reference to the Tutsi as cockroaches implied that they were disgusting and had to be eradicated. Israelis called their guerrillas of the 1940s freedom fighters, and the Palestine guerrillas terrorists (Fisk, 1991). The first are with justification to be honored, the second with justification to be defiled. The term "terrorist," of course, carries fearsome overtones that played upon the efforts and attitudes of those fearing them and gave support to those who fought them, in Israel as well as in the various nations coming out of Yugoslavia (Glenny, 1992). Emotions thus generate the use of concepts that sustain certain beliefs, which in their turn further support emotions: the emotion-belief spiral.

Beliefs about political events are also colored by emotion on a smaller scale. One of us (NHF) as a young boy could not believe that the Duke of Alva, the Spanish governor in charge of quenching the revolt of the Netherlands at the end of the sixteenth century, was one of the most cultured men of his time. Compared to him, freedom-hero William of Orange was a boor. During World War II, we in the Netherlands believed the Allied war bulletins about objects destroyed by air attacks and not those of the Germans on the number of planes shot down. We thought the bombing of Dresden justified, and that of Rotterdam abhorrent. By and large, we shared the view of the Japanese as virtual animals, propounded by American propaganda (Dower, 1986).

Second, emotions shape beliefs in personal relationships. Examples can easily be found. In jealousy, one is not only suspicious. At times one is convinced of one's partner's infidelity. One perceives clear evidence in stray handkerchiefs, in the drifting away of one's partner's attention, in his or her novel ideas, interests or possessions. In envy, the object of envy is denigrated and devalued, and the actions that have led to the acquisition of envied honors or goods are devalued or despised. The propensity of envy to come to such belief changes is manifest in the eager acceptance of gossip, itself glaringly evident in the sales of gossip magazines.

Strong desires in general tend to induce or influence beliefs. In infatuation, as in other desires, beliefs often are playthings in the hands of the emotions. When in love, at one moment one believes one is loved in return; at the next moment one is certain not to have evoked any interest. Books, music, clothing, and political views that the object of one's love likes are believed to be good. When the object declares not to be interested in one's person, one may find the excuse that he or she does not dare to admit the love felt, or does not dare to admit it to him/herself. When a girl says "no," the boy may think she means something different. Also, one tends to be convinced of the object's charm or beauty. One sees them as objective characteristics, and not as subjective views. Those beliefs are perhaps even clearer in the parents of a newborn baby. Many a parent feels to have lucked out with such an exceptional baby. The emotion of love is transformed into the belief that the infant itself is most loveable.

Addictions provide similar illustrations. There tends to be undervaluation of health risks of substance use and undervaluation of the relations between the addiction and social or intellectual consequences. The estimates tend to be considerably lower than those by non-users (Elster, 1999b for a review). The finding applies to all sorts of addictions: smoking, drinking, drug use, bulimia, and gambling. Also, in all kinds of addiction one frequently finds illusionary thoughts like "this will be my last one," "this one more makes no difference," "just this one is no real infringement of my decision to stop." Maybe this is an instance of people's belief being more capable than others at controlling dangerous outcomes, which has widespread occurrence (Klein & Kunda, 1994).

Religion provides a further major domain of emotion-inspired beliefs. William James (1902/1982), in his analysis of religious experience, avows himself impressed by how much the beliefs and the emotional value of their object are intertwined. The two tend to go together. To the believer, God's glory and greatness are facts, not feelings. The feelings are seen as natural responses to these facts. One's feelings of awe are proof of His glory and greatness. Everything said by the prophet or said to be said by the Godhead is unassailable truth, even if the nature of that truth is sometimes unfathomable. The acceptance of His pronouncements as truth itself is in large measure an outcome of emotion: belief is a demonstration of loyalty and a proof of love. The intertwining of belief and emotion is most evident in conversion experience, in which an emotionally overwhelming experience vouches for the truth of the acquired belief and constitutes it as a conviction.

Basic to this is the conviction of the "reality of the unseen," as James called it (James, 1902/1982: Ch. 2). It is a conviction for which arguments are felt to be irrelevant or secondary. It includes feelings of the objective presence of the unseen Power, as well as a factual emotional relationship with that Power: one of veneration, of submitting to an existence appraised as holy, or of the endeavors to fuse with it, as these occur in certain forms of mysticism.

Religious conviction sometimes originates in an emotional turmoil; this is again most notable in conversion experiences. Many conversion accounts refer to prior suffering from a sense of sin, and despair from inability to escape from sin. The conversion experience comes as a revelation linked to the relief from sin. It engenders violent emotions of redemption, of being accepted and being saved that in turn confirm the truth of the revelation. Religious belief often satisfies profound emotional needs such as those for submission, for losing the self, and for fusing with others or the world as a whole, all of which may be variants of the need to belong (Baumeister & Leary, 1995), whether to the world as a whole, the Godhead, or the Community of the Faithful. Who will not, if at all possible, firmly believe what provides so much consolation?

James explains the conversions by shifts in "emotional focus." New domains of experience and information enter the person's mind. They focus and support the new belief, in the same way that a standing belief is rendered indubitable by the network of detailed beliefs, social habits and modes of interpersonal interaction in which it is embedded. Acceptance of such a belief is supported by living according to the entire network.

Beliefs as parts of emotions

The examples given suggest links between emotions and the occurrence or the strength of beliefs. The examples of course leave open to what extent those links are indeed causal ones, going from emotions to beliefs. As we remarked before, there are plausible alternative explanations. Beliefs are among the emotion antecedents. And the events that elicit emotions may fix beliefs at the same time, and often solid ones at that. When a dog bites you, that precipitates the undeniable knowledge that dogs can do so, in addition to precipitating fear and distress.

Do emotions indeed influence beliefs and, if so, how can they do so? There are several key issues. Can emotions give rise to beliefs or belief changes? How and what circumstances cause emotions' resistance of beliefs to change, and other forms of belief to strengthen?

How, and in what way, might emotions influence beliefs? One could view them as two discrete classes of psychological events. Hume (1740) certainly did so. However, how one might influence the other is in principle not too difficult to understand. A basis for explanation lies in the very nature and structure of emotions. The relationship between emotions and beliefs is intimate. Emotions involve beliefs; they include the formation of beliefs, and they often stimulate the elaboration of those beliefs (Frijda, 1993). Let us specify.

Emotions involve beliefs

Beliefs are a part of emotions. They are part of emotional experience, as they constitute the meaning attached to events. The beliefs that are part of emotions, usually called cognitive appraisals (e.g., Lazarus, 1991), stem from the relevance of the eliciting event to one or several of the individual's concerns. They consist in the perception or evaluation of the eliciting object as beneficial or harmful for one's person or for those concerns. Those beliefs form much of one's emotional experience, together with the concomitant feelings of pleasure and pain (Frijda, 1986).

In that experience, the belief is projected upon the object or event, as one of its properties. One perceives wonderful and beautiful people, not people who evoke feelings of delight and enjoyment. Holy words are heard or read as venerable words, rather than as words that inspire veneration; that is why some of them are spoken softly, or not at all. We also feel that prophets and political leaders generate admiration because they are admirable, and not vice versa.

Emotions involve belief formation

These beliefs are the product of appraisal processes that include activation of pre-existing beliefs relevant to the event, or create novel beliefs about its meaning. That is, sometimes the belief that forms the core of the emotion was formed long ago. Riding the city bus without a ticket and seeing the controller enter activates the pre-existing belief that this makes you lose face as well as money. Sometimes the belief is formed on the spot, during explicit cognitive appraisal, for instance when the meaning and implications of the event slowly dawn, or when the agency for an event is attributed to a particular person.

These beliefs created on the spot are in principle temporary beliefs. They result from the way the event is appraised and are creations of the moment. They are part of the emotional response itself. You may get angry with the ticket controller because you feel caught. The extent to which beliefs are parts of emotional responses is evident in love. When falling in love, one often considers the love object to be beautiful and attractive. When afraid of spiders, a spider close by looks frightening. During a marital quarrel, one may wonder what one saw in one's partner. But the beliefs usually are temporal. They last for as long as the emotion lasts. They fade when the emotion is over. Perception of beauty and attractiveness tend to fade when love has faded, just as one may in vain seek the attractiveness perceived during desire when sexual intercourse is over. The grizzly looking spider turns into a fairly harmless insect as soon as it has crept to the other side of the table. After the quarrel, one may be amazed at the evil things one thought and said about one's partner, and the contempt and suspicions that crossed one's mind.

Emotions stimulate elaboration of beliefs

The beliefs constructed in emotions may go further than turning an emotional impression (beauty, nastiness, grizzliness, causal agency) into the belief about a true property. Such information may serve as a starting point for elaboration by the evoked emotion. Take startle. You hit your head on the kitchen shelf, and you strike out at it, thus treating it as a blameworthy actor. Or, if you are a hyperstartler, somebody may merely touch you unexpectedly and you strike out at him or her (Simons, 1997). Startle turns into anger by identifying a culprit even if there is none. It may not merely do so in a flash. A self-reported anger incident reported by Stanley Hall (1899) tells of a man stumbling over a coil of barbed wire near his doorstep. He picks up the coil and dumps it into the nearby river, some ten-minute walk away. In another *reported* incident, a man hurt himself on a boulder, went into his barn, came out with a sledgehammer and smashed the boulder. There was a belief of coil, boulder, or kitchen-shelf as blameworthy actors. The pain or the startle created it.

The construction of beliefs can be yet more extensive. Many beliefs are created to fill out the picture of the emotional situation. Others are formed to justify or explain one's emotional appraisal. Distress of any kind may lead to blaming. People despise those whom they humiliated (Miller, 1993), thus starting a cycle of further humiliation. As the old Latin saying goes: *Propium ingenii humani est odisse quem laesis*, (It is proper to the human mind to hate whom we hurt).

These belief elaborations illustrate that emotions are usually not one-shot reactions to antecedent perceptions or beliefs. They usually

are processes over time that involve cyclical processes in which information generates emotional responses that generate new information,
and so on (Lewis, 1996). They may include protracted thought activity:
that of rumination (Nolen-Hoeksema, 1987; Rimé, 1995). Rumination is
explained to a large extent by the actualization of cognitive schemas,
since schemas on emotional issues tend to be particularly well developed (Tesser, Martin, & Mendolia, 1995), and acute emotions may be
expected to activate them strongly. When walking home after an angry
interchange, thoughts continue which carry the angry action readiness
further and find novel faults with one's antagonist. Thoughts ramble
on and on. Self-blaming sadness likewise continues in finding novel
failures and seeing one's faults as encompassing (Nolen-Hoeksema,
Morrow & Fredrickson, 1993) multiplying the "dysfunctional beliefs"
(Beck, 1976) of depression. These beliefs wax and wane with the
depression (Coyne & Gotlib, 1983), and thus are the product of the
depression rather than its antecedents. Illustrations can be multiplied.
In shame, the pains of rejection and ridicule motivate agreement with
the mocking or disapproving audience, which often is an element of
shame (Frijda, 1993). In guilt emotion,[3] one believes one is to blame
even when knowing that this is not actually the case. Having inadver-
tently caused harm, and feeling impelled to make amends, one racks
one's brain to find what one could have done differently; and often
one finds something (Frijda, 1993).

All this cognitive activity is motivated by the state of action readiness that forms the core of emotions (Frijda, 1986). It tends to amplify
the emotion. This appears from anger self reports: walking home after
a quarrel, you get angrier and angrier. Such amplification has also
been noticed in anxiety maintenance – fear makes you detect more
fearful stimuli, which increases fear – and vicious cycles in depression
– depression stimulates thoughts of worthlessness that enhance depression. It further explains the phenomenon of attitude polarization
after discussions (Judd & Brauer, 1995; Petty, Haugtvedt, & Smith,
1995; Tesser *et al.*, 1995). Rumination and amplification help to prolong
the life of the temporary beliefs. The longer and more extensive
rumination and other thoughts continue, the more solid the relevant
schemas become, and the more persistent the beliefs. For this there is
consistent evidence in the attitude literature (Petty, Haugtvedt, &
Smith, 1995; Tesser *et al.*, 1995).

Features of emotional beliefs

The beliefs that are part of emotions have three important features.
First, they tend to involve generalizations. They are about stable and

intrinsic properties of the object; they refer to what the object is capable of. One's perception of an animal as frightening or dangerous because it barks or bites obtains the shape of a belief that that dog is dangerous, or that dogs in general are. One's delight with the sweet behavior of a person may turn into the belief that this person is sweet and delightful. A man who has been abandoned by a woman may take this as evidence of the untrustworthiness of women generally. One's anger with an individual may generate an attitude of hate, that is, of rejection of the person as such. Having categorized the emotional object, as a woman, a Tutsi, or a Croat, is one of the conditions prompting such generalization.

Second, even if temporary, these beliefs make a claim to temporal persistence. Since they pertain to intrinsic properties of the emotional object, they are about things that persist. The thoughts that cross one's mind during a marital quarrel include thoughts like "I never knew that he is so insensitive," or cold, or cruel, or, indeed, capable of any of those.

Third, for the time they are held, they are strong beliefs, in the sense of appearing to have a high likelihood of being true, or they are felt to be true, period. During jealousy, one is certain that one's suspicion is justified, and that a given sign implies unfaithfulness. During an angry interchange, there is no doubt about evil intent. When in love, there is no doubt about the deep and intrinsic sweetness and devotion of the loved one.

Sentiments

Temporary beliefs entailed in emotions may, however, turn into generalized long-term beliefs. When this happens, an emotion turns into a sentiment.

What we call a sentiment (following Shand, 1922, and Arnold, 1960) consists of an appraisal structure that includes concern relevance of its object. Sentiments thus are dispositional emotions. They are schemas ("affective schemas," Fiske, 1982) with the same structure as emotions. They consist of the latent representation of some object as being relevant to one's concerns, and as suggesting what kind of action might be desirable in relation to them. In emotion, a perception takes the place of a latent representation or a mere thought, and action readiness that of the knowledge of what action might be desirable. Sentiments turn into actual emotions when their objects are encountered with sufficient urgency or proximity. All this is part of general emotion theory (Frijda, 1986; Frijda, Mesquita, Sonnemans, & Van Goozen, 1991).

"Sentiments" is the name for attitudes one cares about. They are attitudes towards what touches upon one's concerns. They are not fully equivalent to what are called "strong" attitudes (Eagly & Chaiken, 1993; Krosnick & Petty, 1995). A sentiment can be weak, but still involve personal or value-related relevance, whereas an attitude may merely be strong and its inherent belief convincing because of the solidity of cognitive elaboration (Abelson, 1988). Sentiments have emotional force, by definition. On occasion, they may engender "passions," that is, long-term goals with a highly emotional content, such as love or desire for revenge (Frijda *et al.*, 1991).

When emotions lead to sentiments

Emotions result in sentiments only under certain conditions. They are conditions that make the transformation of temporary beliefs into permanent ones understandable, and often meaningful. One such condition is that the emotional event lends itself to dispositional attribution; personality dispositions are permanent attributes. Such attribution, and thus also the fundamental attribution error, is made more readily when agent properties are salient (Jones & Harris, 1967). When a dog has bitten without provocation, he is likely to have a propensity for doing so. A given act of indifference reveals a capacity for being inconsiderate and loss of affection that can be forgiven but not forgotten. An important variety of dispositional attribution is recognizing the fitness of an object for satisfying a particular concern, or of its unfitness for such satisfaction. Falling in love may be triggered by physical attractiveness, manifest gentleness, sympathetic reciprocating of self-disclosure – all conditions that involve recognition of fitness as a property of the love object.

Another likely condition is pertinence of the belief to an ongoing situation, and its usefulness for dealing with it. This is the case with emotional situations of long duration, such as a deteriorating marital relationship, political oppression, and an ongoing fight that may receive support from the belief. In all of these, hate may develop, and aversion or fear for the antagonist as such. Some events have permanent effects even if the events are brief. This is so for damage to self-esteem or feelings of identity, and for loss of perceived or actual respectability, social status or position of an individual, or of the group to which one feels one belongs.

A third condition is the presence of social encouragement or example for the belief. When offended by a member of a minority group, existing stereotype provides both the generalization and the permanence.

Other sources of sentiments: emotion anticipations

This last condition points to sources of sentiments other than emotions. These sources have been discussed at length in the attitude literature (e.g., Eagly & Chaiken, 1993). Many sentiments are acquired by social example, by hearing emotionally charged speech, by just adopting affective schemas current in schoolbooks and other media, and by witnessing the emotional behavior of others. The acquisition of animal phobias and food preferences and aversions provides examples. Animal phobias are strongly correlated with parental animal aversions (Merkelbach, 1989). It is likely that most fears of spiders in northern countries are acquired by seeing one's parents shrinking back from them. Cultural transmission of likes and dislikes for snails, fried grasshoppers, offal, and hot peppers probably proceed partly by mere habit, and partly by the gusto or aversion witnessed in the social surroundings (Rozin & Fallon, 1987).

Sentiments may also arise because events or issues are indirectly relevant to concerns. Individuals may feel unable to remain critical or aloof with respect to them, because this may imply placing oneself outside one's group. One may not want to break with accepted ideology or group conformity (Abelson, 1995; Boninger, Krosnick & Berent, 1995). Sentiments may result from their relevance to the concern of belonging to one's group. Few Serbians can afford to feel strongly about injustice being done to the Albanians in Kosovo, or not to feel strongly about what they believe to be NATO aggression. Similarly, few Hutus, back in 1994, could afford to consider the Tutsis as human beings.

In all these cases, there was, moreover, external pressure to side with the majority, or with official ideology. Agreeing with dominant group ideology certainly was less dangerous than remaining silent, and probably less dangerous than merely expressing group ideology without acclaiming the actions. But emotional pressure not to abandon loyalty to the group will have been as potent, or more, than external pressure. Similar emotional pressure explains other sentiments. James (1902/1982) explained the violent defense of religious leaders and their views as serving one's loyalty and devotion to them, or to one's religious group. The emotional content of sentiments thus, we think, may stem from the concerns for remaining within the group and close to its members, and the emotions that threat to that concern evokes.

Sentiments may originate in the concern for remaining true to oneself, the concern for personal identity, so often mentioned as a source of ego-involvement and strong beliefs (Abelson & Prentice, 1989; Sherif & Cantril, 1947). Beliefs often instantiate certain suprapersonal values. Distancing oneself from those makes the individual feel that he or she has abandoned part of him- or herself. During the holocaust and the Rwanda genocide, some people undertook highly risky action, such as hiding persecuted individuals, giving as their motivation: "I just could not not do it. Had I declined what came my way, I could no longer have faced myself" (e.g., Block & Drucker, 1992: 49). Scientific truth and fidelity to one's scientific, philosophical or religious view, up to facing the pyre, can likewise come to represent strong concerns deriving their force from the emotional concern of retaining identity.

These various sources of sentiments may not be as different as it seems from the origin of sentiments in emotions. In all of the cases just discussed, one might say that the establishment of sentiments – the formation of solid and persisting beliefs – was mediated by emotion anticipations.

Emotion anticipations are the anticipations, foresights, and imaginings of actual emotions that might emerge under certain envisaged circumstances. Elsewhere, they are called "virtual emotions" (Frijda, in preparation), because they are often actually experienced and may turn into true emotions. Flashes of feeling, images of future emotional situations of derision and of the wailing and gnashing of teeth cross one's mind at moments of decision. We just made mention of thoughts like "I could no longer have faced myself" that make decisions flip the way of accepting a grave risk. They are the kinds of thoughts and feelings that cause us to protect our sense of self-esteem and "face," concerns that in some cultures are much more clearly recognized and articulated than in others.

Emotion anticipations have the structure of emotions. They consist of appraisals of the anticipated situations as well as anticipations of the ensuing affect and action readiness or, in other conditions, of imaginings of how someone else may appraise, feel, or become ready for. These anticipations are not conceptual. They are felt or imagined, rather than thought. It is likely that this involves low-level activation of some of the emotional response components that come to the fore more manifestly in actual emotions.

Such emotion anticipations control much of human life. They embody much of the mechanisms of emotion regulation. One prevents embarrassment, regret, shame, and guilt by avoiding behavior that might give rise to them. One also seeks out behavior that may produce positive emotions such as pride, social respect, and the happiness of being connected to one's group. Thus the distinction between sentiments stemming from emotional events and those with other origins is a fuzzy one.

Cultural differences in the emergence of sentiments

There may be cultural differences in the readiness with which sentiments arise. Two consecutive studies compared the emotional responses of Dutch people with those of two immigrant groups having a more collectivist orientation. In both studies the collectivist Surinamese and Turks showed many more sentiments than the individualist Dutch. This was true in positive situations such as achievement situations, as well as in negative situations such as an offense by an intimate other (Mesquita, in preparation).

Belief changes took different shapes, from lasting changes in self-esteem and confidence in the future for the positive situations to hate and loss of confidence in some other person in the negative ones.

These belief changes appeared to be consequential for the respondents' behavior. They are beliefs of importance, that is, true sentiments. One example comes from a Surinamese woman. Her friend had disclosed a secret she had confided to her to somebody else. The woman was reported to "want to have no dealings with someone like that." She clearly had come to believe in the despicable character of her former friend, which had clear consequences for the relationship between the two. Another example comes from a Turkish man who had a woman friend in whom he had a special interest. She married another man without telling the respondent in advance. The latter lost his faith in relationships in general, stating that "one must not take every relationship seriously." His belief in intimate relationships had changed and with it presumably his readiness to enter this type of relationship. These examples show that belief changes have an impact on the lives of the individuals who have them, as well as on their relationship with others.

Sentiments such as those reported here are fairly common in the Surinamese and Turkish groups. In the study that these examples were taken from, 71 per cent of both the Surinamese and the Turkish respondents, versus 17 per cent of the Dutch, reported sentiments when asked to recall "a situation in which an intimate other offended you." Although instances like those of the examples are conceivable in the Dutch group, they were much less frequent. Compared to the emotional accounts of respondents in the immigrant groups, the Dutch reports generally seem to lack certainty. Typical Dutch answers include that they did not understand what happened and that they were not sure how and if their friends or relatives meant what they did. Such thoughts are clearly less conducive to sentiments, since they lack the conviction of truth necessary for belief formation.

We assume that the differences in the readiness for sentiments between the Dutch and the immigrant groups in the Netherlands reflect a difference that one may expect to find between individualist and collectivist groups in general (Mesquita, under review). There are several reasons to expect collectivist groups to have a greater readiness for sentiments.

First, people from collectivist cultures are more interdependent. Therefore, the meaning of events is more likely to be shared than in individualist contexts, where the subjectivity of meaning is emphasized. This implies that in a collectivist context emotional appraisals are felt as socially shared beliefs, and thus as beliefs with supra-individual truth. The very fact that emotional appraisals are perceived as shared meanings already makes them more likely to last, and thus increases the chances that emotions transform into sentiments. Furthermore, in collectivist cultures shared meanings may represent an objective fact in addition to being a subjective assumption. Other people are more likely to share and confirm one's appraisal in a collectivist than in an individualist culture. This is indeed what we found for the collectivist cultures that we studied. In the collectivist groups other people were often reported to affirm the legitimacy of the individual's emotional beliefs.

There is a second reason that emotions in collectivist cultures may be more susceptible to being transformed into sentiments than in individualist cultures. People in collectivist cultures focus more on the social consequences of emotional situations – that is, on the implications for social position of the individual and his or her group. The awareness of lasting social consequences, such as impaired status, may call for a change in beliefs. Beliefs may be needed that neutralize the individual's status loss, for example by giving the other people involved a comparable loss of position. In the example of the Surinamese woman whose friend revealed her secret, the belief that her former friend was a despicable person may have been useful for dealing with the issue. The despicable nature of the friend makes for an acceptable explanation of the reason of her own compromised status, as well as balancing the positions of herself and her former friend by lowering that of her friend. In the largest of our studies, stepwise regression in fact suggested that impaired status or prestige accounted for 11 per cent of the belief changes in negative situations. Status or prestige seem to mediate some of the effects of culture, but only a small part of it. After entering culture in the regression, prestige or status still explained 8 per cent of the variance in belief changes. Culture by itself accounted for 9 per cent.

Cultural differences in the readiness for sentiments may thus be explained in terms of more general conditions underlying sentiment formation. One is the degree to which emotional appraisals are accredited supra-individual truth. Furthermore, across cultures, there may be differences in the rate of long-term social consequences of emotional events, either real or perceived. Sentiments are likely to be an answer to expected social consequences.

The sources of belief strength

How are emotions related to the resistance of beliefs to change and other aspects of belief strength? We can discern three major factors: concern relevance, emotional intensity, and the intervention of virtual emotions.

Concern relevance

The major causal factor is clear, both from the above analyses of emotions and sentiments, and from the existing literature on attitude strength (Krosnick & Petty, 1995). Most of the strength determinants discussed in the latter literature refer, in some way or other, to the relevance of beliefs to concerns. We encounter involvement, ego-involvement, and value-involvement, of which the latter in particular appears to be related to resistance (Johnson & Eagly, 1989, 1990); also importance (Krosnick, 1988), defined as what "people care very deeply about" or as "an individual's sense of the concern, caring, and significance he or she attaches to" an issue (Boninger *et al.*, 1995: 159, 160). Attitude strength is linked to the triad of self-interest, social identification, and value-relevance by Abelson (1995). We also encounter belief centrality, defined by the belief's links to the self (Krosnick, 1995), and vested interest, defined in terms of hedonic relevance (Crano, 1995). Other mentioned determinants involve concern relevance perhaps less clearly, but still derive their influence upon attitude strength from the relation to some concern. An example is commitment, "the pledging or binding of the individual to behavioral acts" (Kiesler, 1971: 30), presumably of influence because an individual is loath not to follow up what he or she as well as others expect him or her to do.

"Concern" is a broad notion. It is defined as "a disposition to desire occurrence or nonoccurrence of a given kind of situation" (Frijda, 1986: 335). It includes motives, major goals, personal sensitivities, attachments, and supra-personal values. It is the core concept in explaining emotions, in that emotions are held to arise when events are appraised or perceived as relevant to a concern, while at the same time there is uncertainty about protecting or satisfying one's concerns in a routine fashion (Frijda, 1986). As indicated earlier, there are concerns of different sorts: those pertaining to personal welfare, to the welfare of others, to hedonic satisfactions or the absence of aversive sensations, to values. It is useful to distinguish source concerns from surface concerns, the former having general states as their object (for example, bodily welfare, proximity to trusted other individuals, existence of beauty), and the latter a particular object (for example, not meeting spiders, proximity of a particular person), because the latter help to recognize more clearly the concerns behind emotions.

Emotional intensity

The theory of emotional intensity (Frijda, Ortony, Sonnemans, & Clore, 1992; Sonnemans & Frijda, 1994) gives clear clues to understanding belief strength. Belief strength can be considered an aspect of emotional intensity. Emotional intensity appears to be a function of a number of independent determinants. Strength or centrality of concerns is the major one; closely related is the number of concerns to which the eliciting event is relevant. In the study by Sonnemans and Frijda (1994) of self-reported emotion incidents, the summed products of rated concern relevance and the strength of each relevant concern correlated .47 with rated emotional intensity. The number of concerns deemed relevant alone, however, already correlated .42. Both the appraised need for dealing or coping with the event and the appraised likelihood that one can indeed deal or cope make their own contributions. The urgency of doing something about an event is one of the decisive determinants of acute emotions, defined by the occurrence of activation change and control precedence (Frijda, 1986). Perceived possibility to cope can be recognized among the factors influencing belief strength. Attribution of causal agency generally determines or enhances anger (Frijda, 1986); so does perceiving that anger affects one's antagonist; it is a factor that explains the increases of anger during fighting, and the belief polarization during discussions (Abelson, 1995; Tesser, Martin, & Mendolia, 1995). If it is clear that nothing can be done, emotional intensity often drops, making for a curvilinear or saw-toothed relationship between severity of threats and emotional intensity (Brehm, 1999). Regulation efforts weaken overt emotional intensity, including the extremity of beliefs, but at the same time they index the intensity of the emotion in the first place (Sonnemans & Frijda, 1994).

Emotion anticipations

But the emotional sources of belief strength are, as we tried to show, not restricted to actual emotions. The emotional power of concern relevance becomes evident, we think, not only in acute emotions, but also in emotion anticipations. Planning of behavior and actual behavior are probably more powerfully controlled through such anticipations or virtual emotions than through actual emotions defined by strong feelings, bodily arousal and in changes of action readiness with control precedence.

Emotion anticipations are probably what maintains or strengthens the beliefs that belong to sentiments, when these beliefs meet contradicting information. Not chasing out the Tutsis: the very idea makes the shivers run down your spine – the very idea of the old oppressive days returning, or the idea of losing wealth and social power. The same applies for the glimpses of what it would mean if God or Allah had not ordained the order of society, as this is the pattern of rules of behavior that guide daily life. The thoughts are probably not much less powerful when there are no shivers but only glimpses of an unacceptable future state, offensive to one's values. Abstract values such as notions of social order, identity, group belongingness, can marshal convictions by merely making them subjects for discussion, through the evoked emotion anticipations.

It probably is the anticipation of emotional situations and corresponding emotions that can give beliefs their enormous power when challenged. You perceive your world as collapsing, the organization of your life coming apart. In the attitude strength literature, much is made of the cognitive perspective that resistance to change is determined to a large extent by the degree to which beliefs are embedded in belief systems. Eagly and Chaiken (1993) called it the "domino theory." Changing one belief would require changing a whole system of beliefs. That is no doubt the case, but the explanation might not merely be people's desire for cognitive consistency. Major beliefs are linked to action. They guide everyday judgments and decisions and modes of interpersonal conduct. Considering others as superiors, as inferiors, or as equals, dictates how to behave, how to distribute your time, how to set priorities. Challenging the belief about other people's positions challenges the principles, which challenges everyday efforts and satisfactions. Generally speaking, challenging major beliefs challenges an individual's world view, which challenges sense of security. According to terror management theory (Pyszczynski, Greenberg, & Holt, 1985), the latter tends to evoke terror. Anticipating such basic terror evokes reactions to prevent that terror, among which is derogating the carrier of the challenging beliefs and increasing the strength of the challenged ones (Greenberg, Solomon, & Pyszczynski, 1997).

Emotional thinking

Still, how do emotions, sentiments, and emotion anticipations do it? How are beliefs maintained in the face of clearly incompatible evidence? How do people with a vested interest – believers, addicts, partisans, and people in love– manage it? The illustrations given show that this is not an esoteric question.

Emotions influence thinking in general, and not only beliefs. They do so by motivating thought as well as by influencing information selection. Emotions make you want certain things, and make you pay attention to some things, and not to everything that you could have attended to or thought of.

Emotion-steered thinking shows four features that may help explain its influence upon beliefs. The first is instrumentality. We entertain thoughts that might help to achieve our emotional goals, and because they might help. Emotional thinking tries to solve the problems posed by the emotional predicament. The second is motivational force. The more urgent our goals, the greater the inclination to do what may help to reach them, including thought. Emotional thinking is driven by emotional urge. The third is control of the scope of thought. Emotional thinking is loath to waste time and energy by attending to irrelevant detail or indulging in complex inferencing. The fourth feature is motivated bias. Emotional thinking is biased towards beliefs that support one's emotional aims, and towards retrieving or generating information that does.

Instrumentality

Cognitive activity in emotions fulfills a functional role. Like overt action, it is instrumental in achieving the aims of the action readiness that forms the core of most emotions (Frijda, 1986). Anger involves readiness for putting an end to an agent-caused interference, and activation of pertinent behavior. Fear involves self-protection and urge to avoid the threat. Guilt emotion includes desire for atonement, and so forth. Thinking during emotions is steered by those desires. It can be understood to represent a means for reaching those ends. It includes functional distribution of attention, and cognitive actions such as pondering what one might do or might want to do under the circumstances, as well as exploring the detailed nature of the emotional situation and one's possible actions.

The means of fear include attentional sensitization to signs of danger (Williams, Watts, MacLeod, & Mathews, 1997). The anger repertoire includes being set to identify a causal agent (Keltner, Ellsworth, & Edwards, 1993), and thus to identify a target, which may guide hostile action to remedy the situation, as in scapegoating, attribution of malevolence (Abelson, 1995), or smashing the kitchen cabinet on which you hurt your head. Depression brings about selective recall of sad events, and elaboration of thoughts of worthlessness (e.g., Teasdale, 1988), perhaps serving to adjust one's position to an environment with fewer resources after loss. Guilt emotion, by holding oneself responsible even if one isn't, provides an explanation of distress (both after having hurt someone and after loss), that in turn provides a peephole into what perhaps could be done to undo the distress (Frijda, 1986, 1993).

Many beliefs in emotion do not so much help to modify the emotional event, however, but one's sense of competence in the given relationship. For instance, they modify one's felt power relationship with the environment. Explaining an opponent's critical remarks by believing him envious is a way to escape from feeling inferior; it may be the reason why being insulted strengthens negative attitudes (Abelson, 1995). Smashing the kitchen cabinet does not reduce the pain but it does restore one's sense of being in control. Taking revenge reinstates felt power equality with the offender as well as one's trust in one's coping capacity (Frijda, 1994). In many social conflicts, thinking generates new arguments that solidify one's belief in one's position, and thereby help in gaining and keeping the upper hand (Abelson, 1995).

In other words, some beliefs just help to make you feel better. One explores alleyways towards that goal, and does so more readily than exploring those which lead towards feeling worse. Perhaps that is one of the reasons why people tend to take credit for one's successes, and blame failures upon others or circumstances (Weiner, 1985), as if often more optimistic about one's future and health than conditions warrant (Weinstein, 1980, 1982).

Emotions not only generate functional beliefs. They also make one accept existing beliefs, or strengthen beliefs, for similar functional reasons. War propaganda is believed because it sustains hope. Small signs of attention are taken as signs of affection because they open the gate to further approach. An ambiguous statement ("I really like you") is understood as an understatement ("she really likes me!") because it encourages action.

Beliefs created in the course of emotions may be functional in a somewhat wider context. Beliefs may be generated to fill out the picture of one's emotional situation, or changed to make the latter coherent or intelligible, or to get rid of dissonance (Harmon-Jones, this volume). Other beliefs are created to explain or justify one's emotion, towards others or for the benefit of one's self-esteem. An example is that of finding more and more fault with the antagonist during angry rumination.

Motivational force

During emotions, thought continues on the wings of action readiness. The instrumental thoughts are motivated by one's desire to get rid of discomfort, or to achieve pleasure and harmony. Even when they do not really help, one is unable or unwilling to leave things alone. Even if nothing useful can be thought of, one may feel one cannot allow oneself to stop trying. Exploring what has happened, what might happen or what could have happened sometimes has a kind of magical quality, for not being surprised by unthought implications or for keeping possible evil at bay. Sometimes, thinking brings direct emotional satisfactions. Thinking about a beloved or a lost person is a way of having him or her around, if only in thought. It explains the incessant thinking about the person in infatuation as well as in grief.

The motivational source of the beliefs does much to explain their resistance against change. Abandoning a belief may undermine one's readiness to act, and one may feel that one cannot afford that. It is difficult to continue fighting for a cause one does not believe in. The falling apart of communist rule in the Soviet Union was a result of the younger leadership having lost faith, according to Ignatieff (1995). At the opposite pole, beliefs may provide a reason to act, and not only a means; and they may provide the motivational force. "Hope lets one live" is a Dutch idiomatic expression that has truth value. When action lacks perspective, its organization may decay, and action readiness be replaced by dull apathy. How far this can go is known from concentration and POW camps (e.g., Strassman, Thaler, & Schein, 1956, on prisoners of war in Korea). Giving up a belief that sustains coping action – say, that feeds indignation or blaming – may weaken assault or resistance to assault. There are emotional snakes here, biting their own tails. If the other party is not as evil as I think, I might not have the resources to fight them, which I cannot afford, because they are so evil. As Elster (1999b) observes, sometimes testing a belief is so risky or costly that one cannot afford to do so.

Control of the scope of thought

Emotional arousal controls the direction of attention. It controls which information to attend and not to attend to (see also Clore and Gasper, this volume). It also controls whether and where to explore implications, or to test them, and how much information is felt to be needed before one can accept evidence. When entertaining hope, why spoil it by pondering possible difficulties? When afraid, why lose time by reflecting upon the true magnitude of danger? When succeeding in an emotionally important action such as machine-gunning all enemy sailors swimming in the sea around their sinking ship, why ponder the belief that it is an admissible means to win the battle? (Dower, 1986, reports that the commanding officer was given a medal for this action).

All this goes back in part to elementary mechanisms of the distribution of attention and resource allocation. Emotions generally tend to "restrict the range of cue utilization," as the theory of Easterbrook (1959) has it. Evidence can be found by comparing recall of emotional versus nonemotional incidents: core elements of emotional incidents are recalled better, but peripheral elements less well (Christianson & Loftus, 1992). In other words, one of the reasons that emotion-charged beliefs are resistant to change is that one is focused upon information that is directly relevant and that one lacks resources as well as motivation to explore implications that are further removed and require more effort to be explored.

Motivated bias

But biased information processing is not only due to such elementary mechanisms. It is also influenced by motivational factors, and in part results from emotional urge. Passion makes us jump to conclusions, says Elster (1999b), and this because we are eager to see a particular outcome, we hope to see it and grab the chance, we are all too willing to weigh the evidence in a way favorable to our pursuits, we are disinclined to explore trains of thought that lead elsewhere. James (1902/1982) argued for the role of "shifts in emotional focus" to explain the conviction in religious conversion. Information that concerns and that confirms the emotional value of an object or message is absorbed like a precious drink, and it is looked for and searched for. A Nazi reads *Mein Kampf,* and finds support for his views as well as his hatreds there, and an environmentalist buys Rachel Carson's *Silent Spring.* One of the most potent factors in resistance of beliefs to change may well be that a partisan is not only not open to alternative views, but also not interested in them. He does not really strive for an objective judgment. He builds a case; he may have an honest disinclination to try his best to be objective. Elster describes this as a seduction of not trying one's best and a true disability to pay attention to alternative courses of action or explanation (Elster, 1999b: 138). One may add a standing readiness for subjecting discordant information to critical scrutiny.

One may not be inclined to follow up implications in thought, and explicitly not attend to available information. Overt action may help in this. One may indulge in action to prevent thinking, including the thinking of thoughts that might challenge one's beliefs. One might engage in killing just to get into the frenzy that blocks everything else. Keane (1995) mentions this as a process that seems to have taken place in Rwanda. Choosing ways to block reflection has been mentioned in other literatures, including the literature on addiction (e.g., Heatherton & Baumeister, 1991, with regard to binge eating).

In all, one can follow Kunda (1990), who makes a strong case that effects of motivation on thought can be explained by bias in memory search and in the construction of beliefs from generated information. Such bias is usually (though not always) counterbalanced by efforts at objectivity. There is considerable evidence that people want to be able to justify their beliefs, and be convincing to others (Kunda, 1990). At times, this may lead to strengthening bias because the deeper memory search may still be biased and dig up more supporting than contradicting information.

The process of belief formation

The functional and motivational processes that influence the strength of beliefs can be understood from the structure of belief formation in general. "Belief," in this chapter, refers to a proposition considered to be true. Truth judgments are largely based upon probability, credibility, and plausibility estimates. Probability here refers to the likelihood that states of the world indeed obtain, indeed have the meaning they seem to have, and have the consequences one thinks or hears they might have. By credibility, we first of all think of how credible some information is, given the credibility of the information sources. When using "plausibility," we primarily think of the likelihood that some explanation applies, given one's expectations, mental schemas or mental "mechanisms" (Elster, 1999). Estimates of probability, credibility and plausibility are intuitive, based upon information, thought, and preference, and therefore sensitive to a variety of influences, among which are emotional ones.

A major factor that influences subjective probability for a proposition to be true is what we will call the indubitability of relevant information, its "apparent reality" (cf. the "law of apparent reality," as one of the conditions for emotion; Frijda, 1988). An event that is present to the senses cannot easily be doubted to exist. Imminence of an event – that is, clear signs that it is bound to happen soon – is likewise a cue for the reality of its impact. Nearness in space and time are determinants of emotional intensity, because they allow little room for ideas contradicting their reality (Spinoza, 1677/1989). Emotional meanings, too, are often beyond doubt to the individual. Emotional meaning is usually the outcome of an interaction between an object or event and the individual's concerns. It may be perceived as intrinsic to the object or event. This is so in particular when that meaning originated in an earlier emotional experience. A sound that had been linked to electric shock is frightening, pretty much as the electric shock itself (LeDoux, 1996); so is a house that looks like it may contain spiders, for the arachnaphobic. Indubitability sometimes extends to the causes of events. There exists perceived causality that quite easily extends to the attribution of intentions or inherent properties to the perceived cause. For a Serbian, America has clearly committed aggression because "its" planes were perceived to attack.

There is a curious inverse to the factor of presence to the senses and proximity in space and time: time discounting, which is extensively discussed by Elster (1999b). Events remote in time have little emotional impact. One can suppose that the emotional impact of future events declines with time, in a nonlinear (perhaps hyperbolic) fashion. It may be due to the uncertainties involved; things may happen between now and then, much as Spinoza pointed out. But future events and consequences of what happens now – smoking, unsafe sex – lack the trimmings for indubitability, unless represented with those trimmings as film and fiction may provide.

Beyond stimulus effects and immediately accessible associated information, one may expect truth judgments to depend upon the amount of supportive over contradicting information, and the value of that information as being supportive or contradicting. That value would seem to be highly dependent upon estimated plausibility and credibility, in addition to probability cues.

A belief is plausible when it agrees with mental models and mechanisms, and with expectations. These include the opinions current in the social environment, as well as the attribution rules that underlie the emotional instrumentality of beliefs. Misery must have a cause, and someone must be to blame for it, and so forth.

Plausibility and probability estimates show several forms of bias that in part may have direct emotional reasons, and in part are inherent in more general cognitive processes. Much of this is in line with the effects of what we discussed in connection with "indubitability." An example is confirmation bias. Confirming evidence generally receives more attention than disconfirming evidence, and it plays a more prominent role in reasoning in various domains (Snyder & Cantor, 1979; Wagenaar, 1988; Wason & Johnson-Laird, 1965). Gamblers interpret wins as confirmations of their strategy, and losses less strongly as disconfirming it, since many losing outcomes can be interpreted as "near wins" (Gilovich, 1983). People overestimate their desirable qualities, and their capacities for control over complex or dangerous conditions (Klein & Kunda, 1994; Kunda, 1987), perhaps for the same reasons as the "fundamental attribution error," that is, the inclination to attribute other people's actions to their inherent dispositions, and one's own actions to circumstance; an explanation may be that there is so much more information about one's own plans, presumed capacities etc., than about those of others. But affective biases may go many ways. It is often felt as "impossible," as "unjust," as impossible to conceive, that great misery is not someone's fault or could not be modified.

Credibility of a belief has been extensively discussed in the attitude literature as an important determinant of belief strength (Kelman, 1958; Petty & Wegener, 1998). Reports vary in credibility, and even facts that are perceived, as eye-witness reports attest. So, of course, may the credibility of the meanings attributed to events, such as the attested value of intelligence tests or the purported objectivity of a judge. Disbelieving is an important mechanism by which information that contradicts one's convictions can be discounted. Disbelieving is supported by considering the information sources as untrustworthy. Information provided by an enemy can be written off. There is indeed solid evidence that those people who voice dissenting world views are being derogated (Pyszczynski, Greenberg, & Holt, 1985; Greenberg, Solomon, & Pyszczynski, 1997). At the opposite pole, credibility of an information source may shortcut questioning the validity of information. Acceptance of religious truth spoken by prophets or the Godhead him- or herself was mentioned when discussing both religious and political beliefs. Source credibility thus is one of the easy entrance points for emotional influences upon beliefs, credibility is an essential aspect of all belief formation, and almost always is a matter of feeling rather than one of reasoning.

All estimates depend upon the amount of available supporting and contradicting information. The attitude strength literature has emphasized the role of embeddedness of a belief in a belief system, as a factor in resistance to change (e.g., Scott, 1968; Eagly & Chaiken, 1993). However, what counts, one would expect, is not the amount of available information but, rather, the amount that is accessible and that is actually being accessed. The importance of actual exploration appears from the effects of discussion-stimulated thought (Tesser, Martin, & Mendolia 1995) and thought elaboration (as in the Elaboration Likelihood Model of Petty and colleagues (Petty, Haugtvedt, & Smith, 1995)) upon belief strength. Subjective certainty and belief extremity are related to the amount of supportive information (Gross, Holtz, & Miller, 1995), as well as to source credibility. The networks of connected beliefs do not merely function as cognitive support of a belief's credibility. As indicated earlier, they also represent an emotional factor. One hundred Mexicans can't be wrong, in particular when one is Mexican oneself; and by leaving the warm bed of one's convictions one enters the cold, in particular when these convictions are socially shared (Greenberg, Solomon, & Pyszczynski, 1997).

Degree of exploration of available information (including thinking it through, by generating implications and counterarguments) is largely a motivational matter. Coming to a truth judgment follows a for instance in accordance with the "satisficing" principle (Simon, 1957). Don't look for the best, but for what is good enough, for satisfying whatever criteria for "truth," or for "sufficiently credible, probable and plausible" there are. This sort of notion was advanced for perceptual recognition by Neisser (1975) in his "analysis-by-synthesis" model. Exploration of information continues until a stable cognitive state has been reached.

Concern relevance of information, or a belief under scrutiny, may be expected to influence the settings of the satisficing criteria, and those of credibility, probability, and plausibility. For instance, depth of exploration has been shown to depend upon one's desire to be as accurate as possible in one's judgments (Kunda, 1990). The influence of truly emotional concerns will be different. Exploration may be curtailed, or be extended to as far or as deep as one can go, or be biased, going in certain directions rather than others, depending upon circumstances. Kruglanski (e.g., Kruglanski & Freund, 1983) found evidence for what he called the "freezing" of inferencing, presumably when a satisfying judgment was arrived at. In other conditions, one may want to be as sure as one can of a given state of affairs. Extent of cognitive exploration is indeed correlated with emotional involvement (Thomsen, Borgida, & Lavine, 1995; although in their study it is unclear whether involvement motivates exploration or the amount of available cognitions).

Biased exploration has been well documented in the literature;

Kunda (1990) reviewed the evidence. Goals render goal-relevant information more salient. Presumably, they prime search models for information in the environment as well as in memory, since "there is considerable evidence that people access different beliefs and rules on different occasions" (Kunda, 1990: 483). Emotions have the same effects. Anxiety makes fearful stimuli stand out (Williams *et al.*, 1997; Eysenck, this volume). Goals and affective states also control the strategies of information acquisition and processing, as appears in studies of the cognitive effects of positive versus negative moods (Fiedler, this volume; Forgas, this volume).

Then there is differential weighting of the accessed information. It may in part depend upon cognitive strategies (Kahneman, Slovic, & Tversky, 1982; Nisbett & Ross, 1980). The availability heuristic, for instance (Kahneman, Slovic & Tversky, 1982), may be responsible for the influence of source credibility upon judgments of argument credibility. You don't seek further when your information comes from a reliable source. And arguments that are consonant with one's attitudes are likely to receive less probing scrutiny than discordant ones, unless the risks of being wrong are salient.

One may assume that satisficing settings depends upon the estimated costs of pursuing and of freezing exploration. Continuing to think takes time and energy; hence the effects of haste upon the depth of memory search, found by Kruglanski & Freund (1983). The costs include straightforwardly emotional ones: why spoil one's pleasure by wondering how justified it is? The time-perspective issue mentioned above will play a role here. Pleasure and cues that one may be right are here and now; possible doubts have often to be fetched from further away. Certain beliefs allow one to keep emotional gains or to maintain illusions. "She does not dare admit that she loves me" belongs to that class; so does "I know I am hooked, there is nothing I can do about it." And there may be strong motives to forget about one's intents and come to believe what one thought. Self-serving cognitions are fairly readily understood from this angle.

Conclusions

Our analysis argues that emotions influence beliefs, by creating beliefs and by strengthening beliefs, in particular in making them resistant to change. These influences are in part the direct result of acute emotions, in part from emotion anticipations, and in part from standing dispositional emotions or "sentiments." Sentiments have diverse origins. Some are the outcomes of previous emotions; others are taken from the social environment.

At the center of these emotional influences on beliefs is concern relevance. Concern relevance is the core notion in explaining emotions, as it is of understanding sentiments. Sentiments are defined as attitudes in which the attitude object has concern relevance.

Emotions and sentiments exert these influences upon beliefs because forming temporary beliefs simply is an aspect of emotions. Temporary beliefs turn into standing beliefs under various conditions, among which are cultural propensities as well as social support for doing so. Extensive belief formation, in addition, has a functional role in shaping and supporting what emotions motivate the individual to do.

Emotions strengthen beliefs (or produce strong beliefs) by influencing parameters common to any belief formation. They influence the credibility of information and inferences, and the estimated likelihood that information is true, via affective biases in thinking, and by modulating the range of implications that is followed up in thought and in information utilization in general.

Notes

[1] We are grateful to Tony Manstead and Bob Zajonc for detailed criticism of an earlier version, and to Kathleen Higgins for pointing to the relevance of the work of William James on religious belief formation.

[2] National Public Radio, USA, March 30, 1999.

[3] Throughout this paper, we use "guilt emotion" to refer to emotions involving a sense of guilt. We prefer it to "guilt," as this is a factual or juridical concept, and to "guilt feeling" because of the latter's connotation of the feeling being unjustified.

References

Abelson, R. P. (1986). Beliefs are like possessions. *Journal for the Theory of Social Behavior, 16,* 223–250.

Abelson, R. P. (1988). Conviction. *American Psychologist, 43,* 267–275.

Abelson, R. P. (1995). Attitude extremity. In J. A. Krosnick & R. E. Petty (Eds.), *Attitude strength: Antecedents and consequences* (pp. 25–41). Mahwah, NJ: Erlbaum.

Abelson, R. P., & Prentice, D. A. (1989). Beliefs as possessions: A functional perspective. In A. R. Pratkanis, S. J. Breckler, & A. G. Greenwald (Eds.), *Attitude structure and function* (pp. 361–381). Hillsdale, NJ: Erlbaum.

Arnold, M. B. (1960). *Emotion and Personality.* Vols. I and II. New York: Columbia University Press.

Bain, A. (1859). *Emotions and the will.* London: Longmans, Green & Co.

Baumeister, R. F., & Leary, R. M. (1995). The need to belong: Desire for interpersonal attachment as a fundamental human motivation. *Psychological Bulletin, 117,* 497–529.

Beck, A. T. (1976). *Cognitive therapy and the emotional disorders.* New York: International Universities Press.

Block, G., & Drucker, M. (1992). *Rescuers: Portraits of moral courage in the holocaust.* New York: TV Books.

Boninger, D. S., Krosnick, J. A., & Berent, M. K. (1995). Origins of attitude importance: Self-interest, social identification, and value relevance. *Journal of Personality and Social Psychology, 68*, 61–80.

Bregstein, P. (1995) *Terug naar Litouwen [Back to Lithuania]*. Amsterdam: Van Gennept.

Brehm, J. (1999). The intensity of emotion. *Personality and Social Psychology Review, 3*, 2–22.

Coyne, J. C. & Gotlib, I. H. (1983). The role of cognition in depression: A critical appraisal. *Psychological Bulletin, 94*, 472–505.

Crano, W. D. (1995). Attitude strength and vested interest. In J. A. Krosnick & R. E. Petty (Eds.), *Attitude strength: Antecedents and consequences* (pp. 131–158). Mahwah, NJ: Erlbaum.

Christianson, S.-A. & Loftus, E. (1992). *The handbook of emotion and memory: Research and Theory.* Hillsdale, NJ: Erlbaum.

Dower, J. W. (1986). *War without mercy: Race and power in the Pacific war.* New York: Pantheon Books.

Eagly, A. H., & Chaiken, S. (1993). *The psychology of attitudes.* New York: Harcourt Brace Jovanovitch.

Eagly, A. H., & Chaiken, S. (1995). Attitude strength, attitude structure, and resistance to change. In J. A. Krosnick & R. E. Petty (Eds.), *Attitude strength: Antecedents and consequences* (pp. 413–432). Mahwah, NJ: Erlbaum.

Easterbrook, J. A. (1959). The effects of emotion on cue utilization and the organization of behavior. *Psychological Review, 66*, 183–201.

Elster, J. (1999a). *Alchemies of the mind.* Cambridge: Cambridge University Press.

Elster, J. (1999b). *Strong feelings: Emotion, addiction, and human behavior.* Cambridge, MA: MIT Press.

Fisk, R. (1991). *Pity the nation: Lebanon at war.* Oxford: Oxford University Press.

Fiske, S. T. (1982). Schema-triggered affect: Applications to social perception. In M. S. Clark & S. T. Fiske (Eds.), *Affect and cognition: the 17th Annual Carnegie Symposium on Cognition* (pp. 55–78). Hillsdale, NJ: Erlbaum.

Frijda, N. H. (1986). *The emotions.* Cambridge: Cambridge University Press.

Frijda, N. H. (1988). The laws of emotion. *American Psychologist, 43*, 349–358.

Frijda, N. H. (1993). The place of appraisal in emotion. *Cognition and Emotion, 7*, 357–388.

Frijda, N. H. (1994). The Lex Talionis: On vengeance. In S. H. M. Van Goozen, N. E. Van de Poll, & J. A. Sergeant (Eds.), *Emotions: Essays on emotion theory* (pp. 263–290). Hillsdale, NJ: Erlbaum.

Frijda, N. H. (in preparation). The nature and experience of emotions. In A. W. Kaszniak and B. Laukes (Eds.), *Emotions, qualia, and consciousness.*

Frijda, N. H., Mesquita, B., Sonnemans, J., & Van Goozen, S. (1991). The duration of affective phenomena, or emotions, sentiments and passions. In K. Strongman (Ed.), *International Review of Emotion and Motivation* (pp. 187–225). New York: Wiley.

Frijda, N. H., Ortony, A., Sonnemans, J., & Clore, G. (1992). The complexity of intensity. In M. Clark (Ed.), *Emotion: Review of personality and social psychology* (Vol. 13, pp. 60–89). Beverly Hills, CA: Sage.

Gilovich, T. (1983). Biased evaluation and persistence in gambling. *Journal of Personality and Social Psychology, 44*, 1110–1126.

Girard, R. (1982). *Le bouc émissaire.* [The scapegoat]. Paris: Grasset.

Glenny, M. (1992). *The fall of Yugoslavia: The third Balkan war.* Harmondworth: Penguin Books.

Goldhagen, D. J. (1996). *Hitler's willing executioners.* New York: Knopf.

Greenberg, J., Solomon, S., & Pyszczynski, T. (1997). Terror management theory of self-esteem and cultural world-views: Empirical assessments and conceptual refinements. In M. P. Zanna (Ed.), *Advances in experimental social psychology* (Vol. 29, pp. 61–139). San Diego, CA: Academic Press.

Gross, S. R., Holtz, R., & Miller, N. (1995). Attitude certainty. In J. A. Krosnick & R. E. Petty (Eds.), *Attitude strength: Antecedents and consequences* (pp. 125–246). Mahwah, NJ: Erlbaum.

Hall, G. S. (1899). A study of anger. *American Journal of Psychology, 10,* 516–591.

Heatherton, T. F., & Baumeister, R. F. (1991). Binge eating as escape from self-awareness. *Psychological Bulletin, 110,* 87–108.

Hume, D. (1740). *A treatise of human nature.* Harmondsworth: Penguin Books, 1984.

Ignatieff, M. (1995). De macht der poezie [The power of poetry]. *Nexus, 15,* 3–25.

James, W. (1902/1982). *The varieties of religious experience.* Harmondsworth: Penguin Books.

Johnson, B. T., & Eagly, A. H. (1989). The effects of involvement on persuasion: A meta-analysis. *Psychological Bulletin, 106,* 290–314.

Johnson, B. T., & Eagly, A. H. (1990). Involvement and persuasion: Types, traditions, and evidence. *Psychological Bulletin, 107,* 375–384.

Jones, E. E., & Harris, V. A. (1967). The attribution of attitudes. *Journal of Experimental Social Psychology, 3,* 1–24.

Judd, C. M., & Brauer, M. (1995). Repetition and evaluative extremity. In J. A. Krosnick & R. E. Petty (Eds.), *Attitude strength: Antecedents and consequences* (pp. 43–72). Mahwah, NJ: Erlbaum.

Kahneman, D., Slovic, P., & Tversky, A. (1982). *Judgment under uncertainty: Heuristics and biases.* Cambridge: Cambridge University Press.

Keane, F. (1995). *Season of blood: A Rwandan journey.* Harmondsworth: Penguin.

Kelman, H. C. (1958). Compliance, identification, and internalization: Three processes of attitude change. *Journal of Conflict Resolution, 2,* 51–60.

Keltner, D., Ellsworth, P. C., & Edwards, K. (1993). Beyond simple pessimism: Effects of sadness and anger on social perception. *Journal of Personality and Social Psychology, 64,* 740–752.

Kiesler, C. A. (1971). *The psychology of commitment: Experiments linking behavior to belief.* New York: Academic Press.

Klein, W. M., & Kunda, Z. (1994). Exaggerated self-assessments and the preference for controllable risks. *Organizational Behavior and Human Decision Processes, 59,* 410–427.

Krosnick, J. A., & Petty, R. E. (1995). Attitude strength: An overview. In J. A. Krosnick & R. E. Petty (Eds.), *Attitude strength: Antecedents and consequences.* (pp.1–24). Mahwah, NJ: Erlbaum.

Krosnick, J. A. (1988). Attitude importance and attitude change. *Journal of Experimental Social Psychology, 24,* 240–255.

Kruglanski, A. W., & Freund, T. (1983). The freezing and unfreezing of lay-inferences: Effects on impressional primacy, ethnic stereotyping, and numerical anchoring. *Journal of Experimental Social Psychology, 19,* 448–468.

Kunda, Z. (1987). Motivation and inference: Self-serving generation and evaluation of evidence. *Journal of Personality and Social Psychology, 53,* 636–647.

Kunda, Z. (1990). The case for motivated reasoning. *Psychological Bulletin, 108,* 480–498.

Lazarus, R. S. (1991). *Emotion and adaptation.* New York: Oxford University Press.

LeDoux, J. (1996). *The emotional brain.* New York: Simon & Schuster.

Lewis, M. (1996). Self-organizing cognitive appraisals. *Cognition and Emotion, 10,* 1–26.

Merkelbach, H. L. G. J. (1989). Preparedness and classical conditioning of fear: A critical inquiry. Maastricht: University of Limburg, Ph. D. Thesis.

Mesquita, B. (under review). Emotions in individualist and collectivist contexts. *Journal of Personality and Social Psychology.*

Mesquita, B. (in preparation). *Cultural variations in emotions: A comparative study of Dutch, Surinamese and Turkish people in the Netherlands.* Oxford: Oxford University Press.

Miller, W. I. (1993). *Humiliation.* Ithaca, NY: Cornell University Press.

Neisser, U. (1975). *Cognition and reality: Principles and implications of cognitive psychology.* San Francisco: W. H. Freeman.

Nisbett, R. E. & Ross, L. (1980). *Human inference: Strategies and shortcomings of social judgment.* Englewood-Cliffs, NJ: Prentice-Hall.

Nolen-Hoeksema, S. (1987). Sex differences in uniopolar depression: Evidence and theory. *Psychological Bulletin, 101,* 259–282.

Nolen-Hoeksema, S., Morrow, J., & Fredrickson, B. L. (1993). Response styles and the duration of episodes of depressed mood. *Journal of Abnormal Psychology, 102,* 20–28.

Nolen-Hoeksema, S., Parker, L. E., & Larson, J. (1994). Ruminative coping with depressed mood following loss. *Journal of Personality and Social Psychology, 67,* 92–104.

Petty, R. E., Haugtvedt, C. P., & Smith, S. M. (1995). Elaboration as a determinant of attitude strength: Creating attitudes that are persistent, resistant, and preditive of behavior. In J. A. Krosnick & R. E. Petty (Eds.), *Attitude strength: Antecedents and consequences* (pp. 93–130). Mahwah, NJ: Erlbaum.

Petty, R. E., & Wegener, D. T. (1998). Attitude change: Multiple roles for persuasion variables. In D. T. Gilbert, S. T. Fiske & G. Lindzey (Eds.), *The handbook of social psychology,* 4th ed., pp. 323–390. Oxford: Oxford University Press.

Prunier, G. (1995). *The Rwanda crisis: History of a genocide.* London: Hurst.

Pyszczynski, T., & Greenberg, J. (1987). Toward an integration of cognitive and motivational perspectives on social inference: A biased-hypothesis-testing model. In L. Berkowitz (Ed.), *Advances in experimental social psychology* (Vol. 20, pp. 297–340). New York: Academic Press.

Pyszczynski, T., Greenberg, J., & Holt, K. (1985). Maintaining consistency between self-serving beliefs and available data: A bias in information evaluation. *Personality and Social Psychology Bulletin, 11,* 179–190.

Rimé, B. (1995). Mental rumination, social sharing, and the recovery from emotional exposure. In J. W. Pennebaker (Ed.), *Emotion, disclosure, and health* (pp. 271–291). Washington, DC: American Psychological Association.

Rozin, P. & Fallon, A. E. (1987). A perspective on disgust. *Psychological Review, 94,* 23–41.

Schama, S. (1989). *Citizens: A chronicle of the French Revolution.* New York: Albert Knopf.

Scott, W. A. (1968). Attitude measurement. In G. Lindzey & E. Aronson (Eds.), *Handbook of social psychology,* 2nd ed. (Vol. 2, pp. 204–273). Reading, MA: Addison Wesley.

Shand, A. F. (1922). The relations of complex and sentiment. III. *Journal of Psychology, 13,* 123–129.

Sherif, M., & Cantril, H. (1947). *The psychology of ego-involvements: Social attitudes and identifications.* New York: Wiley.

Simon, H. A. (1957). *Models of man: Social and rational.* New York: Wiley.

Simons, R. C. (1997). *Boo! Culture, experience, and the startle reflex.* Oxford: Oxford University Press.

Snyder, M., & Cantor, N. (1979). Testing hypotheses about other people: The use of historical knowledge. *Journal of Experimental Social Psychology, 15,* 330–342.

Sonnemans, J., & Frijda, N. H. (1994). The structure of subjective emotional intensity. *Cognition and Emotion, 8,* 329–350.

Spinoza, B. (1677). *Ethica.* Amsterdam: Rienwersz 1979. English trans. G. H. R. Parkinson. London: Everyman's Library, 1989.

Strassman, H. D., Thaler, M. B., & Schein, E. H. (1956). A prisoner of war syndrome: Apathy as a reaction to severe stress. *American Journal of Psychiatry, 112,* 998–1003.

Teasdale, J. (1988). Cognitive vulnerability to persistent depression. *Cognition and Emotion, 2,* 247–274.

Tesser, A., Martin, L., & Mendolia, M. (1995). The impact of thought on attitude extremity and attitude-behavior consistency. In J. A. Krosnick & R. E. Petty (Eds.), *Attitude strength: Antecedents and consequences* (pp. 73–92). Mahwah, NJ: Erlbaum.

Thomsen, C. J., Borgida, E., & Lavine, H. (1995). The causes and consequences of personal involvement. In J. A. Krosnick & R. E. Petty (Eds.), *Attitude strength: Antecedents and consequences* (pp. 149–190). Mahwah, NJ: Erlbaum.

Wagenaar, W. A. (1988). *Paradoxes of gambling behavior.* Hove: Erlbaum.

Wason, P. C., & Johnson-Laird, P. N. (1965). *Psychology of reasoning: Structure and content.* London: Batsford.

Weiner, B. (1985). An attributional theory of achievement motivation and emotion. *Psychological Review 92,* 548–573.

Weinstein, N. D. (1980). Unrealistic optimism about future life events. *Journal of Personality and Social Psychology, 39,* 806–820.

Weinstein, N. D. (1982). Unrealistic optimism about susceptibility about health problems. *Journal of Behavioral Medicine, 5,* 441–460.

Williams, J. M. G., Watts, F. N., MacLeod, C., & Mathews, A. (1997). *Cognitive psychology and emotional disorders,* 2nd ed. Chichester: Wiley.

4

The sentiments and beliefs of distributed cognition[1]

Keith Oatley

> When people are feeling friendly and placable, they think one sort of thing; when they are feeling angry they think either something totally different or the same thing with a different intensity.
>
> Aristotle, *Rhetoric*, 1377b, l. 31

Introduction

The question of the effects of emotions on beliefs and agency is also the question of the functions of emotions: what are they for, these intimate aspects of our mental lives? In this chapter I discuss the social emotions and the social goals they serve. Particularly, I consider long-term emotional states, together with the effects they have on our beliefs about what is most important to us, our relationships with others.

Cognitive theories of emotion generally, including the theory with which I have been associated (Oatley & Johnson-Laird, 1987; 1996), have been relatively good in their discussions of emotions as short-term events lasting from a few seconds to a few days, which happen to individuals, and which change the priority of goals. Moods, too, have been on the research agenda, especially as they affect social judgment (Forgas, 1995).

Such theories have been less good on emotional states as mediators of relationships between people, and as long-term dispositions. I start this chapter by describing these in turn, and then continue with a set of theoretical and empirical studies to explore their implications.

Socio-emotional goals

In terms of evolution, attachment made mammalian life possible. Though we usually define mammals as animals that bear live young, and feed them with milk, one could also say that behaviorally they are the animals that in infancy are vulnerable and depend on parents for safety. (Birds grow up in a comparable way, but I shall not consider them here.) Attachment by the infant, and its complement of maternal caring, provide the prototype of cooperative relating, and it is tempting to see cooperative behavior in the adulthood of many mammals as being based on it.

Bowlby's work on attachment (e.g. 1971) was the first in modern times to offer a serious function for an emotional system. Attachment is based on fear (anxiety) towards the various dangers that may befall a vulnerable offspring. Secure attachment means that the offspring feels safe, and has a base from which to start acting in the world.

Anxiety based attachment is, however, not the only cooperative mode. According to Lovejoy's (1981) hypothesis of male provisioning, a distinctive new phase of evolution occurred with the emergence of human beings. In this phase there occurred substantial developments of the emotional state called interpersonal warmth, or affection.

With increased brain size our hominid ancestors had to be more immature at birth than our ape cousins for the head to pass through the birth canal. This in turn involved a longer period of infant dependence. These changes coincided with the emergence of upright walking. Because of the changing shape of feet, there was diminished ability of the infant to cling, apelike, to the mother as she moved about. Upright walking, however, allowed the possibility of carrying food and other things to a campsite. The bag, not the stone tool, may have been the first important piece of human technology. Gender specific division of labor meant that women took primary care of infants during their infancy, and traveled less from campsites. At the same time the male made an economic contribution to a specific female and her offspring, perhaps as meat and other products of scavenging became available from wider traveling and bringing materials to campsites.

Lovejoy argued that all these adaptations emerged at the same time, five- to seven-million years ago. Although evolutionary biologists now argue that these adaptations may have occurred more gradually than Lovejoy proposed, so that the first upright walking primates were apelike, the hypothesis of a set of related adaptations remains important. Although extramarital relations are not uncommon, and although many societies allow males with large resources to have several wives, the practice of monogamy, with each human male making an economic contribution to the rearing of children whom he can recognize as his own is so common that it amounts to a universal (Van den Berghe, 1979).

Emotionally what this requires is a long-term commitment to a relationship begun with the emotions of sexual meeting, but continued with the sustained emotional state of warmth, or affection, which allows the extended cooperation of male and female in the shared enterprise of cooperative living and child rearing.

Warmth starts, however, not in sexual relationships, but in parental–infant relationships, alongside attachment. As proposed by Mac-Donald (1992), attachment and warmth are based on separate systems; attachment on the fear system and warmth on the system of happiness. Fox and Davidson (1987) have shown something of this separation: on the approach of their mother with open arms, infants showed joy and activation of the left side of the cortex. With the distress of separation from the mother, or with the approach of a stranger, the infants showed fear and activation of the right side of the cortex. As MacDonald points out, whereas attachment is universal among primates, only in some species is warmth seen. And, whereas attachment does indeed provide a prototype of cooperation, it is warmth that makes possible the sociality of the higher primates, especially ourselves.

It is this system of warmth and affection which I propose is the basis for most human cooperation. In order to set up a consistent nomenclature, let us say that the social goal that is served by warmth is affiliation. Correspondingly, the goal of attachment is protection.

The third social goal is dominance, which sociologists often describe as power (Kemper, 1990). As with attachment and warmth, we can see dominance clearly in our evolutionary history. Most primates, including ourselves, live in hierarchies of social dominance. In many primate species there is an alpha animal, typically a male, who, by fighting and alliances, has won the position at the head of the hierarchy. Animals of similar status, who meet after being apart for a while, are likely to fight or at least to threaten each other, to determine whether they should move in the hierarchy. And so it is with us. Our emotional inheritance of this system is anger and our propensity for assertion and aggression, together with our propensity for making deferential gestures when we signal that we are not a status threat.

These three goals – affiliation, protection, dominance – are all entirely social. Kemper has described dominance and affiliation as the two primary coordinates of social action, but for reasons given above, it seems better to add the third coordinate of protection. Social emotions, happiness, anger, fear, and so on, then occur as we move within the space of these coordinates. If our social goal is affiliation, we feel happy, and express the emotion, which structures the relationship into one of cooperation. If we want to challenge another, we feel angry and perhaps make threats, casting down the gauntlet of social conflict. Correspondingly if we lose status, we feel fear and shame. And if we lose an attachment partner we feel frightened and sad.

There is evidence that we are aware from childhood of both the social goals and consequences of different kinds of emotional state.

Jenkins and Ball (2000) studied the responses of children between six and twelve years old to vignettes in which emotions of dominance and affiliation were expressed by story characters. Children knew that anger was associated with an expressor feeling dominant in inter-action (getting what he or she wanted), and that anger often occurred in response. It was differentiated from sadness and fear, which were rarely differentiated from one another. Children also knew that ex-pressing sadness and fear did not make the expressor feel dominant; they knew also that these elicited more prosocial responses from recipients including comfort, proximity, and goal reinstatement. In a study of adults, Grazzani-Gavazzi and Oatley (1999) have made a comparable distinction between emotions of independence (which are assertive and include anger) and emotions of interdependence (which are affiliative and include being sorry for an action or omission).

Sentiments: longer-term emotional states

Just as cognitive theories have not focused much on the social goals on which many emotions are based, so they have not been good at the longer-term emotions. Nussbaum (1993), indeed, has criticized current cognitive theories for their neglect of longer-term emotional states, and proposed an Aristotelian theory of emotions as judgments of value, in which she gives these enduring dispositions a more proper place. Frijda, Mesquita, Sonnemans, and van Goozen (1991), in a paper on the duration of emotions, has called long-term emotions "sentiments," and I shall use this term here. I take sentiments to be enduring emotional dispositions, mainly towards other people. So it is possible to recognize sentiments of affection, despondency, antipathy, anxious wariness, and so forth.

In his chapter in this volume, Frijda argues that emotions are capable of generating beliefs, of maintaining them, and of affecting our reception of the beliefs of others. In my chapter I accept Frijda's proposals, and direct the discussion towards distributed cognition. Putting the subject of this chapter more formally, I argue that the functions and effects of the sentiments are to structure our relation-ships with other people, and with certain objects, while affecting what we believe about them, and what plans we make.

Studying distributed cognition means adopting a paradigm in which, rather than attending mainly to the individual mind, we attempt to understand people primarily in their interactions. We can start with just two people, interacting with each other and with some object, and pursuing social goals. Here, as I shall argue, some of the functional benefits of long-term emotional states become clearer, as do the relation of emotions to social goals. In the next section I describe different forms of distributed cognition.

Distributed cognition and its sentimental bases

When cognition is distributed, the distribution can occur in the three main modes described by Hutchins (1998); see also Hutchins (1995) and Salomon (1997).

Social distribution

The first, most fundamental mode, is socially distributed cognition: that is to say cognition distributed among people. We human beings could indeed be characterized as members of that vertebrate species who accomplish together very many things that we could not do individually. Examples range from the holding of conversations to the building of cities. In this way, we surmount some of the limitations of individual resources and mental models (belief structures).

In addition, by distributing cognition amongst ourselves, we can overcome certain defects of individual cognition, such as the bias of individual minds to seek confirmation of current beliefs (Wason, 1960). In his now standard account, Popper (1962) shows that scientific progress depends not on confirmation of theories, but on seeking disconfirmation. But it is hard to do this alone. Our individual bias makes us resistant to disconfirming evidence. Hutchins (1995) has devised a connectionist simulation, which shows that this problem only gets worse with larger brains and more knowledge: as the system knows more, potentially disconfirming evidence becomes less significant.

In the social world compelling examples of such bias come from the Inquisition and from witch hunts of former times: one knowledgeable person of high status, backed by a powerful administration almost inevitably finds an accused person guilty. We no longer believe that justice can be approached by one person being both prosecutor and judge. We need a system not of progressively strengthening belief, but of generating alternative views and weighing their likelihood. To counter this human mental defect of confirmation bias, systems of distributed cognition for the administration of justice have emerged in the West in which there are distinct roles: prosecutor, defense, and judge or jury to decide the outcome. In the seventeenth century, Hooke (1665) argued that legal decision making, in its reliance on the externalized representation of writing, and social judgments, was also a good model for science. Recently, Kevin Dunbar (1993) has shown that modern scientific reasoning depends very much on distributed cognition: investigators hold up their discoveries to critique and alternative explanations by others with different backgrounds, and different stakes in what is being discussed.

Many, perhaps most, human activities involve socially distributed cognition, from the first interactions of child-rearing, to interactions in families and organizations. In terms of the emotional implications, both confirmation bias, as people joyfully receive confirmation of what they are doing, and the emotions of triumph and anger and fear that arise in the dramas of courtroom and scientific conference, attest to the role of emotions of socially distributed cognition. In the long term, however, by far the most important social goal involved is affiliation. The sentiment on which all socially distributed cognition depends, which enables cooperation, is warmth: a friendly affection for the people on whom we can depend. In terms of beliefs, we trust those people to whom we feel this warmth and affection, and tend to accept what these people say and do.

Externalization

A second, equally human mode of distributing cognition is the movement of certain difficult-to-perform tasks from the mind into the world and, with the help of technology, their transformation into something relatively easy to accomplish. This can be called distribution by externalization. Writing is an example (I mentioned Hooke's proposal of its role in science in discussing the first mode). With the technologies and associated skills of writing and reading, we can externalize what we think by writing on paper. Not only has the written word now come to be understood as representation, altering the way we experience language (Olson, 1994), but it allows us to read, edit, transform, and rewrite what we have written to make it better. So writing becomes a form of thinking, transformed and augmented by the technology of writing. Tolstoy, for instance, wrote and rewrote *War and Peace* many times. There was socially distributed cognition here too – his wife would copy his difficult-to-read handwriting each day. There are fifteen extant versions of the opening scene of the novel (Feuer, 1996).

All technologies involve externalized cognition, indeed one can say that every technology consists of some artifact plus a skill for using it: pen-and-paper plus literacy, automobiles plus the perceptual-motor and social skills of driving, cities plus the skills of negotiating them, and so forth.

As to sentimental implications, I think there are two. One is the human joy of making things, with hand or brain. To experience enjoyment is to be thoroughly engaged in what we are doing. Without the human ability to engage in making, there would be no writing or any other technology. The sentiment may best be called enthusiasm. It is the sense of go, of encouragement to continue in an activity, or to continue at all. Its associated belief is hope. The second was proposed by Winnicott (1971). He argued that the whole world of human culture, including our technologies, grows in the space that opens between our infant selves and our caregivers, usually our mothers. To start with there is an almost complete merging of infant and mother, but then as separation begins, in this space there occur what Winnicott calls "transitional phenomena," which include the blanket or other thing that is the child's first cultural possession. It represents the mother, or rather the relationship with the mother. It has soothing properties, but it is external, and separate. Then this space begins to be filled with language, and later with other objects of culture, partly discovered, partly created, but always having the property of connectedness with the other, and hence being always imbued with some quality of love. All three social goals are involved in such externalizations: affiliation and attachment in the more cooperative modes, and dominance in competitive modes.

Temporal distribution

The third mode of distributed cognition, also equally human, is distribution over time. Learning in order to act differently in the future is one form of this mode, although it is usually considered under the aegis of individual cognition. But this mode becomes especially significant when what has been discovered is passed on culturally from generation to generation, or from teacher to learner. As D'Andrade (1981) argues, much of what we do is accomplished by means of culturally transmitted programs, or procedures of action. He illustrates the idea of such procedures with some passages from a children's book by Delia Ephron (1977), called *How to Eat Like a Child*. Rather than reiterating these passages, however, here is another example in similar vein, from Rust Hills (1993), from a book for adults: *How to Do Things Right*. This is on how to eat an ice-cream cone:

> First revolve the cone through the full 360 degrees, turning the cone by moving the thumb away from you and the forefinger towards you, so the cone moves counterclockwise. Snap at the loose gobs of ice cream as you do this. Then, with the cone still "wound," which will require the wrist to be bent at the full right angle towards you,

apply pressure with the mouth and tongue to accomplish overall realignment, straightening and settling the whole mess.

The humor of such passages is based on spelling out in detailed words what usually gets passed on implicitly. The ability to receive and pass on cultural procedures is a human universal, based perhaps on abilities such as imitation (Melzoff & Moore, 1977). But the issue goes deeper. As Donald (1991) argues, the ability of non-verbal mimesis has been an utterly essential, but not much remarked, step in human evolution. Notice what it involves: to do an action in a way that one sees someone else do it means having the ability that a former colleague, Guy Scott, called "remote software pickup." One observes only the output, the action. But cognitively one has to understand the goal and means. Then one must implement the lower-level programming steps that will generate the output action in such a way as to accomplish the goal. This ability is the very basis of all education, including education into technology. Thus, with a child, one can say: "Here, hold the pencil like this, see, and you can make a line on the paper." With the possible exception of some chimpanzees such as Kanzi who were brought up as human children, this is an ability far beyond non-human primates (Tomasello, Savage-Rumbaugh, & Kruger, 1993).

Cultural transmission is built on the social goals of affiliation and attachment. Their sentimental bases include the learner liking the person who is passing on the cultural procedure. They also include empathy, identification, wanting to be like that person. The associated beliefs are in the validity and worthwhileness of the procedure and the culture of which it is part.

The three modes together

The three modes of distributed cognition described above are closely interconnected. There is no culture without its associated skills and technologies, no technology without culture, and neither culture nor technology without society. Properly speaking, then, these modes are seldom separate; they are aspects of the partnerships among ourselves, other people, and our socially constructed world. In the end they all involve self-with-others.

Isen and her colleagues have shown that happiness not only has effects on the individual such as enhancing solo problem solving (Isen, Daubman, & Nowicki, 1987) but also, and more importantly, of encouraging social cooperation (Isen & Baron, 1991; Isen & Levin, 1972). In terms of this chapter, one can say this emotion structures relationships by prioritizing the goal of affiliation. The sentiments associated with the three modes of distributing cognition – affectionate warmth, enthusiasm, and empathetic identification with a person one likes – are all varieties of happiness. One might call them the positive sentiments.

Here is the fundamental hypothesis of this chapter: the three modes of distributed cognition are based as strongly on the positive sentiments as on the intellectual and procedural abilities of humankind. These sentiments, in turn, aim principally to accomplish the social goal of affiliation, or when cognition is distributed between self and the environment, the goal of enjoyable absorption in an activity.

Let me be clear. One view, which might be called the economists' view, is that social cooperation depends on exchanges that increase the net utility for each party. So the parties receive reinforcement from the increases they individually achieve. What I am arguing is the opposite. Exchanges occur because members of the human species often seek the social goal of affiliation, and so they happily cooperate with each other. Increases in utility are by-products.

Each sentiment has beliefs associated with it, which are absent without that sentiment. With warmth and affection there is trust, without it there is often distrust. With enthusiasm there is hope, without it there is ennui. With empathetic identification there is a belief in purpose, without it there is the emptiness of cultural alienation.

Functions and effects of sentiments based on four basic emotions

A number of writers have referred to the function of emotions in ways relevant to the topic of this chapter. Simon (1967) has argued that for cognitive beings who have multiple goals and who encounter unexpected outcomes there needs to be a system, which in us corresponds to the emotions, that can interrupt ongoing behavior and switch to a new plan. Tomkins (1970) has written of the function of emotion in terms of amplification of specific motivational systems, so that just one can control behavior at a particular time. Frijda (1986) has argued that an important function of emotions is to control the priority of goals. All these ideas are helpful, but just as compelling for the topic of this chapter is a new proposal by Aubé and Senteni (1996) that emotions are commitment operators.

Emotional states, and especially sentiments, thus control resources. In individual terms, an emotion or sentiment commits the person to a course of action and a certain set of beliefs. Interpersonally a positive sentiment commits resources to affiliative social goals with another person, and to trust and interdependence in that person.

One hypothesis that allows us to see how emotions have such effects is the hypothesis of basic emotions. It is a hypothesis that has sometimes been criticized, but which has not so far been replaced with anything better. At its center the hypothesis is not really that there is only some fixed number of emotions, but the idea that each basic emotion (however many there may be) has a function in individuals and in relationships.

In this chapter I shall not deal with the social emotions postulated by Oatley and Johnson-Laird (1996) as always having objects: the emotions of love and contempt. Instead I shall discuss the four emotions, associated moods, and sentiments, most commonly regarded as basic – happiness, sadness, anger, and fear – which can sometimes occur without objects. These each have a control function, to configure the mind and its resources for action in a particular kind of recurring contingency. Such modes offer an explanation of effects of emotions which is in many ways preferable to network models (Mathews, 1993). In these terms, happiness is the mode of committing oneself wholeheartedly to an activity when things are going well, also of the social goal of affiliation which – as I have argued above – is central to distributed cognition. Sadness is the mode of disengagement, giving up a commitment, when an important social goal is lost, also of eliciting sympathy and help from others. Anger is the mode of trying harder when frustrated, committing oneself especially to the social goal of dominance and for undertaking interpersonal conflict. Fear, or anxiety, is the mode of attention to danger and safety, also of the attachment goal of protection from it, also of committing attention to the needs of others and conforming to social customs. Each of these modes of processing is not perfectly adapted to everything that can happen, but it has heuristic properties, somewhat adapted to certain broad classes of recurring contingency: to successful progress towards a goal, to losses, to frustrations, to dangers. In each mode, social goals are prioritized, commitments are made, beliefs are affected, and cognitive resources are configured.

If it turned out that there were twenty basic emotion modes rather than (say) eight or nine, the hypothesis would be strengthened rather than damaged. If, however, there turned out to be an infinite number of emotions, then we would need quite different understandings of them than those being explored by cognitive researchers at present, because with an infinite set of emotional influences on action and belief, the effects would be indistinguishable from those of deliberative thinking. The hypothesis of basic emotions is that there are certain modes of processing, each associated with its own repertoire of actions, which prompt cognition into broad, functional categories of action and belief. I shall now examine the role of four of these modes in distributed cognition.

Happiness: the sentiment of warm affection and the belief of trust

As I have suggested above, among the long-term emotions, enjoyment is the mood of engaged commitment to what one is doing, with the goal of affiliation. The interpersonal sentiment based on happiness is warmth, a friendly affection towards the other that makes cooperation not only reliable but enjoyable.

In artificial intelligence, the first and in many ways still the most interesting program to model cooperation is that of Power (1979). In this program, Power sets up a structure for two agents, John and Mary, and sets up also the idea of tasks that neither one can accomplish alone. As you may see from Figure 4.1, John is Out. At the start of the program he has been given the goal to get In. The bolt is Down, locking the door. His belief is, therefore, that if he moves nothing happens. Mary is In and can operate the bolt, but she is blind. Here is a fragment of a transcript from a run of Power's program.

> 1a. John: Mary.
> 1b. Mary: Yes.
>
> 2a. John: I want to suggest a goal.
> 2b. Mary: Go ahead.
>
> 3a. John: Will you help me get in?
> 3b. Mary: By all means.
>
> 4a. John: Shall we make a plan?
> 4b.
>
> 5a. Mary: John.
> 5b. John: Yes.
>
> 6a. Mary: May I ask you something?
> 6b. John: Go ahead.
>
> 7a. Mary: Are you in?
> 7b. John: No.

John and Mary formulate and check sub-goals and plans, and they pass knowledge back and forth. Their first exchange is a summons and an acknowledgment, the second a suggestion and an assent, the third a request to cooperate on a shared goal and an agreement. Next John makes a further proposal, 4a, that they should make a plan to accomplish the shared goal. The sequence is interrupted by Mary, because, being blind, she does not know whether the goal of the proposed plan is already achieved. Like a good robot she wants to

Figure 4.1 Diagram of the simple world of Power's (1979) model of cooperation

check the state of the world to see if the goal has been attained, and this is what she is doing from 5 to 7.

The conversational plan-making and enactment proceed until John joins Mary in the part of the world called In. The agents construct a plan tree and enact it. The difference between this shared plan and an individual plan is that sub-goals and actions, as well as the plan construction process, are distributed between the agents. The key issue, therefore, is inter-reliance. Each agent has to rely on the other, just as in an individual plan one has to rely on oneself to accomplish what one has planned.

Power finesses the issue of social goals, of why people might want to cooperate anyway; he arranges that Mary will cooperate if she has nothing else to do, but as we all know this is only half the truth. In general Mary will cooperate, and commit resources to the activity, if she has nothing else to do, and if she has a friendly sentiment towards John. Power also finesses a related issue: that except in such instances as buying something in a shop in a town where one does not live, we human beings do not typically take part in once-only cooperative activities. Cooperation with any planning partner typically has both a history and an expected future. Each task that is accomplished allows us to build a model of that partner – whether he or she is willing or reluctant on that kind of task, competent or less skilled, fun to be with, and so forth.

Robin Dunbar (1996) has proposed that the size of the primate brain is related to the number of individuals known personally, or in terms of this discussion, to the number of individuals of whom one has distinctive mental models. Dunbar concludes that human social networks can include up to about 150 people who are known in this individual way, as compared with about fifty for chimpanzees. He also proposes that conversation is the human equivalent of mutual grooming, and has found that some 70 per cent of it is about the social lives of ourselves and our acquaintances. The people for whom we have individual models are friends and enemies, the trusted and the untrustworthy. What is known as gossip, the informal recitation and analysis of action and character, is about forming models of others with whom we have interacted in the past and with whom we may interact in the future.

In the experiments of Sherif (1956) on intergroup attitudes and behavior, when eleven-year-old boys at summer camp had been assigned to two groups, emotional commitment and solidarity arose strongly within each group. (Incidentally the boys formed dominance hierarchies as clear as those of any group of chimpanzees.) But when Sherif arranged that the two groups had to compete for a scarce resource, enmity between the groups became alarmingly fierce. For each boy, his models of individuals in the other group, even those who were previously friends, turned to disparagement. Arranging meetings, joint meals, and so forth, had no effect on the enmity, or made it worse. The only way Sherif found to dissolve the competitive intergroup enmity was to arrange joint tasks that required the boys from both groups to work with each other to accomplish a socially distributed task that was important to everyone. It required cooperation. For instance, Sherif arranged that the water supply into the camp was severed and the boys had to cooperate to find where the pipeline had broken. Also he arranged that the truck that brought supplies into the camp broke down, so that all the boys had to cooperate to haul and push it to get it started.

The sentiments of building a mental model of another person with whom one has a history and a future of successful cooperation, are warmth and affection. The corresponding belief is trust. Its converse is distrust, suspicion, and disparagement (such as occurred when Sherif set up competition between groups) which, as we all know, have the effect of biasing our interpretations of what another person does to be seen in a negative light.

Moreover, just as a new lover interprets every occasion of lateness by the other, and every missed opportunity to make a phone call, as a failure of the commitment and interest proper to an important relationship, so other kinds of meeting, although less salient, have similar potentialities. Every encounter, and every joint task, is an opportunity to accomplish something, usually in relation to some external object, which may range from a conversation to the joint contribution to some product. It is also the opportunity for amendments to be made to our models of each other in the relationship. I discuss these issues further below under the heading of anger.

Fortunately, as one might think, for our species, the bias seems to be set towards affiliation, towards experiencing relationships with others as having emotional importance, of therefore giving these relationships priority in our doings, and allowing latitude to others in their lapses.

Sadness: the sentiment of despondency and the belief of hopelessness

Loss of a friend or loved one is, obviously, the converse of the attainment of an affectionate trusting relationship. It occurs when an affiliative or attachment relationship is irretrievably lost. It becomes difficult to relinquish an affiliative or attachment goal, in part because relationships which form on these bases are unique. In a real sense they are irreplaceable. What is nevertheless required with a serious loss is backtracking and much cognitive work. During this time, one is sad, nothing is enjoyable (nor does one want it to be). Sentiments turn to despondency, and enthusiasm ebbs. Beliefs turn to hopelessness.

By far the most important studies of the emotions of loss have been carried out by Brown and his colleagues (Brown & Harris, 1978; Brown, Harris, & Hepworth, 1994). This work shows that the onset of depression (the most common psychiatric disorder in Western industrialized societies) is usually caused not by something going wrong in people's minds but by something going wrong in their lives. Its causes are such events as bereavements, marital separations, job losses without prospect of re-employment, or such chronic conditions as poverty, or living with an abusive spouse from whom there seems no escape. These studies are based on epidemiological research, and I have discussed elsewhere their relationship to the issues of forming new affiliative plans, and new roles, following a social loss (Oatley & Bolton, 1985; Oatley & Jenkins, 1996).

In contrast to the epidemiological approach, here is a study using an experimental paradigm, in which the effects of sad states on beliefs were directly explored. A mood of sadness was induced, and its effects compared with those of inducing happiness, in a study of juror reasoning, which is a classic setting of socially distributed cognition.

In court trials, two adversarial presentations are offered which each take the form of narratives that touch on some pieces of an array of evidence, composed partly from the utterances of agents in the drama who are called witnesses. In his or her narrative, the prosecutor ascribes to the accused intent and method for a crime. The narrative of the defense counsel is an alternative story, in which this intent and method are denied. The jury is asked to choose between these stories on the basis of their plausibility.

Recent research has shown effects of mood on social judgment and the evaluation of arguments (Mackie & Worth, 1991; Schwarz & Bless, 1991). In this literature, happiness has been found to produce a bias towards short-cut reasoning (sometimes called heuristic reasoning), whereas sadness produces a bias towards analytical reasoning and more exhaustive search processes.

Seema Nundy and I (see Oatley, 1996) therefore arranged a task to simulate the reasoning of jurors in a murder trial. We argued that induced moods would affect participants' reasoning and beliefs, and hence the verdicts they reached. Following previous results, of Mackie, Schwarz, and others, we predicted that participants in whom a happy mood was induced would employ short-cut reasoning to reach their verdict, and participants in whom a sad mood was induced would be more systematic and analytic.

Forty-four student participants were randomly assigned either to a happy or a sad mood induction. For the happy induction they were shown a ten-minute selection of scenes from the amusing movie *Splash*. For the sad induction, they were shown a ten-minute selection from the movie *Sophie's Choice*. After a distracter task in which participants rated the film clip, they then completed mood manipulation checks, which were separate 0 to 10 scales for happiness, sadness, anger, fear, disgust, and "any other kind of emotion."

Participants then completed a juror reasoning task in which they were given a summary trial transcript based on real trial. The prosecution's case was that the accused woman had murdered her husband by shooting one night after a small party at the couple's house. The defense case was that the woman shot her husband in self-defense. Among the testimony which participants read was some from an expert witness who described battered woman syndrome and its effects. Participants also read the judge's instructions on the considerations for each possible verdict.

After participants had read the transcript it was removed, to ensure that their reasoning would be based (as in real trials) on memory. The judge's instructions were left with the participants, who were asked to offer a verdict, to explain how they came to it, and to rate how certain they were that their verdict was correct. Then they completed a series of nine-point scales, including one of rating how much they identified with the accused in her actions. They were also given post-task mood manipulation checks similar to the pre-task mood manipulation checks.

Table 4.1. *Numbers of participants in a study of juror reasoning by Nundy and Oatley showing different styles of reasoning (short-cut or analytic) following a mood manipulation (happy or sad)*

	Happy induction	Sad induction
Reasoning style		
Short-cut	5	17
Analytic	14	8
Totals	19	25

The explanations given by the participants of how they chose their verdicts were categorized as either short-cut or analytic. Short-cut responses were those in which participants were perfunctory in reaching a verdict, for instance they said they paid attention only to how they perceived the accused. Analytical responses were those in which the participants explained steps in their thinking, analyzed the situation, interpreted the judge's instructions, and used rather than merely repeated the facts of the case. All explanations were categorized by two independent raters, without reference to participants' moods. One rater was completely blind to the conditions of the study. There was 91 per cent agreement.

The mood manipulation check was satisfactory, in that the happy movie excerpt resulted in a mean of 4.9 on the happiness scale as compared with 1.0 on the sadness scale; whereas the sad movie clip produced a mean of 6.7 on the sadness scale, and 2.8 on the happy scale.

The main result of the study may be seen in Table 4.1. Contrary to our hypothesis, more participants who received the happy induction reasoned analytically, and more participants who received the sad induction reasoned using a short-cut. This difference was significant (Chi-square $(1, N = 44) = 7.5$, $p < 0.01$). There were no verdicts of murder in the first degree. People who reasoned analytically were more likely than those who reasoned by short-cut to give verdicts of murder in the second degree, rather than self-defense ($p < 0.05$).

As mentioned above, in most published experiments on effects of mood inductions (see for example, Forgas, this volume; Mackie & Worth, 1991; Schwarz & Bless, 1991) it has been found that people who received happy inductions were more likely to take short-cuts in reasoning about such matters as the advisability of legislation against pollutants that cause acid rain, while those who received sad inductions reasoned more analytically. Our finding of increased frequency of analytic reasoning by those who received the happy induction exactly contradicted our hypothesis and the conclusions of this previous research. How can we explain this?

First, we argue that the effects of emotional states on reasoning and beliefs are much more dependent on the content of the task than has previously been thought. The task of jury reasoning has not, so far as we know, been previously studied following mood inductions. It is possible that whereas many of the tasks given to participants in mood induction experiments might not have had much personal meaning to them. In our study, by contrast, the participants were highly involved.

Second, although showing excerpts from movies is the standard method in experiments on the effects of mood on judgment, and indeed *Splash* and *Sophie's Choice* have been specifically recommended respectively for happy and sad inductions, we assumed there would simply be just mood effects. We did not think beforehand of the analogies between the content of the sad film excerpt and the task of juror reasoning. In our excerpt of *Sophie's Choice*, we included the central scene in which Sophie is given the choice by a Nazi SS officer of saving just one of her two children. The excerpt was highly effective in inducing a mood, as judged by the mood manipulation check scale for sadness. I can also vouch personally that I found myself feeling sad for several hours after seeing the excerpt. But the mood was not content free. It included beliefs and reflections, such as consideration of the sadistic effects of an aggressive (male) world. It is likely that similar effects occurred for our participants, and heightened their identification with the female defendant in the juror reasoning task. On the identification scale that we asked participants to complete, we found that those who reasoned by means of a short-cut were more likely to have identified with the accused woman's actions (F = 11.9, df 1, p < 0.01).

With an emotional, identification-based, belief state, the reasoning task became simple. Only a short-cut was necessary to reach the verdict that the accused women had indeed, as the expert witness proposed, suffered from battered woman syndrome, which resulted in her shooting her husband in self-defense. The social goal for participants who were in this state was one of empathetic affiliation with the accused. It became unnecessary to go analytically through a legal argument.

If warmth and affection are the sentiments of cooperation then, as proposed above, sadness is the emotion of loss, with despondency as its corresponding sentiment, and hopelessness as its most extreme belief. But sadness has other effects. When one person loses an important goal, sad and empathetic responses from others become likely. Thus the potentiality arises for joining with others in human solidarity in the face of tragedy.

Anger: the sentiment of antipathy and the belief of distrust

By no means all of human life is cooperative; we often come into conflict with others. Such conflicts have two main modes associated with them. Between social groups the conflictual emotional mode is contempt. (Such effects were seen in the studies of Sherif, 1956, on inter-group conflict, discussed above; I shall, however, not discuss contempt further in this paper.) Within social groups of families, friends, and organizations, however, the predominant mode of such conflict is anger. It serves the social goal of dominance.

To show some of the effects of anger on beliefs when cognition has been socially distributed in Western society, here are some results from studies of joint errors by Oatley and Larocque (1995), in several samples. In these studies, each participant kept a structured diary to record an incident in which something went wrong in a socially distributed plan or arrangement made with another person. Among other matters, participants were asked to record in their diary their emotions and any thoughts and beliefs they had about the other person involved in the error, also the emotions they thought the other person had and the person's beliefs about them.

I have argued that the emotional quality that enables a joint plan to be made in the first place is affectionate trust, although sometimes it may be social fear of losing love, or one's job, if one were not to do what was asked. The emotion that occurs on the large majority of occasions when something does go wrong is anger – one experiences frustration and a diminishment of self, and one tends to believe the other to have been responsible for the plan's failure.

If we were to take a purely technical view of cooperation, such as that depicted between the two robots in Power's (1979) program, the only issue in joint planning is the distribution of knowledge and plan fragments between agents. From such a view, the following result would come as a surprise: when a joint error occurred, it was typically the relationship rather than repair of the error, which became salient. Here is an example: one participant's error was to be late in meeting her husband for a Bluejays' baseball game because she waited for her daughter to finish her homework, a condition that had to be fulfilled for the girl to see the game. The husband had the tickets and waited for his wife and daughter outside the baseball ground. When they arrived, he was angry at having been kept from seeing the game so far.

Table 4.2. *Numbers of participants in a study of joint plan errors, who did not, or did, believe that the other had an untrustworthy trait, cross-tabulated with whether they did not, or did, feel angry*

	No belief of negative trait in other	Belief of negative trait in other
Presence of anger		
Participant not angry	47	7
Participant angry	60	43
Totals	107	50

He then missed several more innings arguing with his wife, trying to convince her that it was her fault that she was late.

Among our participants, we found that when asked to rate the importance of the original plan that had been made, and also to rate the importance of the relationship with the other person involved, on 0 to 10 scales, the relationship had, on average, a substantially and significantly higher rating than the plan. In other words there is not one but two aspects to a cooperative plan: the plan itself and the relationship with the other person. The relationship, or the potential relationship and the trust involved, is not only primary to doing the task at all, but is in general more important than any specific joint action taken within its context.

Let us now look more closely at people's beliefs about their planning-partners when an error occurred. In one sample of 157 people who kept joint-error diaries, fifty reported beliefs about the other's personality, resulting from the error. They described the other as: unthoughtful, untrustworthy, unreliable, disrespectful, dishonest, irresponsible, inconsiderate, insensitive, incompetent, indecisive, careless, selfish, self-involved, stupid, lazy, superficial, scatterbrained, childish, an idiot, a hypocrite, a bitch, and so forth.

Anger had a large effect on these negative beliefs as may be seen in Table 4.2. When participants were not angry they were unlikely to hold negative beliefs about the other. Those who were angry became more likely to hold beliefs about negative traits of the other, Chi-square $(1, N = 157) = 13.52$, $p < 0.001$. (Whether one held derogatory beliefs also depended on such matters as the importance of the relationship.)

Also, when participants thought the other was angry with them, they frequently imagined that other person held negative beliefs about them: stupid, irresponsible, unreliable, neglectful, careless, incompetent, scatty, flaky, lazy, and so forth, Chi-square $(1, N = 157) = 6.6$, $p < 0.01$.

For both the beliefs about the other, and the assumed beliefs of the other concerning the self, the recurrent theme was lack of conscientiousness, that is to say that the other, or the self in the other's view, was not to be trusted in joint activities.

Anger is an emotion mode that is treated very differently in different cultures. In an Inuit society it is shunned and avoided (Briggs, 1970), while among the Yanomamö it is celebrated and encouraged (Chagnon, 1968). Although members of our research group have not been able to study cultures as diverse as these, we have used diaries to compare the emotional consequences of an error in a joint plan in two cultures that are somewhat different on the continuum of independence–interdependence of the self: Anglophone Canada and Italy (Grazzani-Gavazzi & Oatley, 1999). In both Canada and Italy, anger was by far the most frequent emotion to occur in response to a joint error, but it was somewhat more frequent in the more independent culture of Canada. By contrast, sorrow was far more frequent in the more interdependent culture of Italy. We can say that in Anglophone Canada the goals of dominance are slightly more salient, and in Italy the goals of affiliation are far more salient.

The experience of emotions in the context of joint activity frequently centers on the interactive partner and on the relationship with that person. Following an appraisal of a partner's role in a bungled plan, for example, often prompted by anger, people adjust their model of how the other person will behave in future interactions. When people ascribe particular personality traits to others, their global judgments function as heuristics which are incorporated as changes in mental models of the other.

Averill (1982) studied anger in Massachusetts by asking 160 people to keep structured diaries of an incident when they became angry, and eighty to keep diaries when they were targets of someone else's anger. The incident for those who were targets, therefore, was one in which anger was overtly expressed. Although those who were angry thought the incident was due to the target people doing something unjustified, the target people – like the participants in our joint-error studies – tended to say the event was justified or beyond their control.

The result of expressed anger, for Averill's participants, was that more than half the angry participants reappraised the incident. Among the target people, 76 per cent said the episode helped them recognize their own faults, and about half said the relationship with the angry person was strengthened. In other words, within the temporary role of person-expressing-anger, derogatory beliefs of the other can be revised. Modification of the mental models in both partners can take place in such a way that the relationship can continue, and even improve.

For the most part, anger allows people to renegotiate those aspects of the relations to which insufficient attention had been paid so that it caused the error – at least in the eyes of the angry person. Hence every joint error that causes anger has potential for revising the mental model of the other. As Averill showed, in the majority of cases in which interpersonal anger was expressed, both participants come to recognize some responsibility for what went on, and the mental model of self and other was altered to assimilate the changes. The terms of the relationship were revised, and given some new basis.

Putting Averill's conclusions together with the results of our joint error studies: the terms of a relationship becomes salient when a joint plan goes wrong, and it is experienced in terms of dominance-based assertion. Explicit anger can frequently lead to successful repair of the relationship, that is to say to a reinstatement of trust, on terms that will allow future joint plans to be made. In Grazzani-Gavazzi and Oatley's cross-cultural study, we found that sorrow over the incident was more likely in Italy than in Canada. There is readier belief in the self's responsibility for repairing the error in Italian society, where social relationships are, perhaps, more important than among autonomous-minded North Americans. Cooperative and supportive sentiments may make repairs of the relationships after errors occur more likely, with the sad emotion of sorrow bringing to the repair a greater empathy and identification with the other.

If warmth is the sentiment of cooperation in joint plans, then anger is the emotion of antipathy, with its associated beliefs in the untrustworthiness of the other. If as Power (1979) showed, joint planning is based on interreliance, then each episode of such planning is an occasion for assessing the degree of trust to be placed in this interreliance with any particular person.

Most episodes of anger are with people one knows and likes, and most are resolved. Properly the study of anger, therefore, should include both the elicitation of anger, its effects in the relationship with the person who is the object of the anger, and the repair to the relationship that does or does not occur. If angry incidents were merely aggression without reconciliation, neither our primate cousins nor we could live socially. As Visalberghi and Sonetti (1994) have found, a typical angry incident consists of a triggering event, anger, aggression, and reconciliation. So anger is not just about dominance. It is typically about reinstating the social goal of affiliation when it has been threatened by a disturbing incident. One of the extraordinary characteriztics of higher primates, including ourselves, is the ability to cohabit on affectionate terms among those with whom we have been angry, and to tolerate inequalities in the dominance hierarchy.

Longer-term sentiments of settled antipathy and their associated beliefs do occur, however. In a substantial minority of cases, where there has been a joint error and resulting anger, the mental model of the other acquires the emotionally toned belief, and continuing sentiment, of distrust. Thus, one participant in our study of joint-errors waited for a new colleague in one restaurant, while he sat for over an hour in a different location of the same chain of restaurants, waiting for her. Our participant said: "He stood me up." Despite the fact that he also had waited for her, and that it was he who phoned her to find what had happened, and despite her acknowledgment that he was no more at fault than she, she said that his failure would be at the back of her mind the next time she had dealings with him. Another participant, who talked about her irritation with a friend who was often late and was always annoyingly over-apologetic, said, with reference to the score of 6, on the 0 to 10 scale, that she gave to the importance of the relationship with this person: "This is why she is not a 10."

In English there are many adjectives by which we describe others to indicate sentiments of antipathy, "aggressive," "hostile," "defiant," "domineering," and a special term "paranoid" for people who are generally distrustful of others.

Anxiety: the sentiment of wariness and the belief in one's own autonomy

A line of research important to the interpersonal sentiment of interpersonal fear-anxiety is Bowlby's (1971) attachment theory, discussed briefly above. Bowlby's idea was that in infancy, the child constructs mental models of self-with-other based on the reliability of the other in relation to danger, and that these mental models guide emotional development, in what he called goal-corrected partnerships. I shall treat attachment anxiety as a sentiment in such relationships.

Ainsworth, Blehar, Waters, and Wall (1978) developed Bowlby's idea of attachment, and described three styles of attachment based on a test in a "strange situation" that was somewhat threatening to the child. In the test, the mother leaves her infant for a few minutes in a room that is strange to the child, a stranger enters and leaves, and subsequently the mother reunites with the child. Ainsworth *et al.* used infants' responses to describe three categories of attachment. Children classed as anxious-avoidant avoid the mother when she returns. Children classed as secure are distressed at parting but allow themselves to be comforted when the mother returns. Children classified as anxious-ambivalent approach their mother, often angrily, when she returns but do not allow themselves to be soothed. It is thought by attachment theorists that the anxious-avoidant style together with a preference for emotional autonomy develops when the caregiver is emotionally or physically unavailable. Secure attachment occurs when the caregiver is reliable, and feels safe to the child, so the infant develops a model of self-with-other based on trust. The ambivalent style develops when the caregiver is inconsistent or occasionally neglectful.

Main and her colleagues (George, Kaplan, & Main, 1985; Main, 1995) developed the Adult Attachment Interview, in which people give an account of their early attachment experiences, and also of their own current intimate relationships. Waters, Merrick, Albersheim, and Treboux (1995) followed up a group of people from age one, when their infant attachment styles were assessed using Ainsworth et al.'s strange situation test, to age twenty, when they were given Main's Adult Attachment Interview. They found considerable continuity: thirty-two of the fifty participants remained in the corresponding attachment category. Of twelve who were in the avoidant attachment category as infants, eight were classified as Avoidant (dismissing) adults. In terms of Main's categories these people perceived others as generally untrustworthy, the self as invulnerable and self-sufficient. They tended to regard relationships as threatening their sense of control. Of the twenty-nine people who as infants had been classified as securely attached, twenty were classified as Secure on the Adult Attachment Interview. They believed others to be trustworthy and dependable, felt the self as worthy and competent, and experienced their relationships as a continuous source of emotional nourishment. Of the nine people who as infants were classified as ambivalent, four in adulthood were classified on the Adult Attachment Interview as Preoccupied with Relationships. They viewed others as desirable but believed them to be largely unpredictable and difficult to understand. They tended to experience the self as vulnerable, fragile, and unlovable and found close relationships desirable but unattainable.

Mitra Gholamain and I (submitted) argued that people's adult attachment classification would predict how they responded to a short story (an externalized narrative of human action and emotions). We predicted that the sentiments installed in infants' mental models of self-in-relation (with their high continuity into adult attachment categories) would affect the interpretations that people made when reading fiction as adults. We recruited sixty-four participants who were regular readers of fiction. The story we chose was "Bardon Bus" by the celebrated short-story writer Alice Munro. In it, a woman recounts the loss of a romantic relationship.

We were not able to use Main's Adult Attachment Interview, but instead used Feeney, Noller, and Hanrahan's (1994) Attachment Style Questionnaire, which gives good correspondence to the categories of the interview by cluster analysis. The questionnaire is forty questions about adult attachment relationships. It has five scales: Confidence, Preoccupation with Relationships, Discomfort with Closeness, Need for Approval, and Relationships as Secondary. For the cluster analysis, we amalgamated the data from the sixty-four questionnaire responses from our participants with data from the same questionnaire from seventy-two participants from a similar population in a second study that also explored the connection between attachment and literary experience. We used McQueen's method; it delivered three cluster categories, which corresponded to Main's three attachment categories: Avoidant/Dismissing, Secure, Ambivalent/Preoccupied. Participants classified as Avoidant were high on Discomfort with Closeness, and Relationships as Secondary, and moderate in Confidence, Preoccupation with Relationships, and Need for Approval. We inferred that because the Avoidant participants showed moderate levels of Preoccupation with Relationships and Need for Approval, their attempts to maintain distance in personal relationships were partly anxiety-driven.

Participants classified as Secure were high in Confidence, and low on all other factors, that is to say they were confident in their relationships, felt comfortable with closeness, and viewed relationships as important without being very preoccupied with them.

Participants classified as Preoccupied were high on Preoccupation with Relationships and Need for Approval, moderate in Discomfort with Closeness, and low in Confidence and in Relationships as Secondary. They were very concerned about their relationships, but also tended to be uncomfortable with closeness, and to lack confidence in themselves and others. As Feeney *et al.* (1994: 143) noted for these people, "Since their attitudes toward relationships are complex and somewhat contradictory; (intimacy is desired but at the same time engenders discomfort), they are more likely to think and worry a lot about their close relationships."

We also performed a discriminant function analysis on these data, with cluster membership as the grouping variable and the five questionnaire scales as predictors. Feeney *et al.* (1994) said the superordinate dimensions underlying the Attachment Style Questionnaire were Anxiety, and Comfort with closeness. We found these two same dimensions, with Anxiety accounting for 73 per cent of the variance between the Secure and the other two groups. We can say that the Anxiety factor reflects an attachment-protection goal, and Comfort with closeness, an affiliative goal.

Table 4.3. *Frequencies of three categories of attachment style cross tabulated with three categories of reader-response*

	Attachment style		
	Avoidant	*Secure*	*Preoccupied*
Category of reader response			
Distanced	17	7	2
Autonomous	5	13	6
Kinetic	0	4	10
Totals	22	24	18

To measure reader's responses to the story, we asked participants to write a paragraph summarizing and giving their reaction to it. These responses were classified using a scheme of Bogdan (1992) which was taken from literary reader-response criticism. Bogdan originally used five categories of response, which we collapsed to three. People who gave a response that was mainly intellectual, in which, for instance, they wrote only about the style of the piece, were classified as Distanced. Participants who gave a response that combined emotion and analysis of the story were classified as Autonomous. Readers who gave a response that said merely what they liked or did not like about the story or its characters, or who related to story largely in an emotion-based way, were classified as Kinetic. All responses were categorized by two independent raters, without reference to participants' attachment categories. One rater was completely blind to the conditions of the study. There was 81 per cent agreement.

As you may see from Table 4.3, Avoidant participants gave predominantly Distanced reader-responses, Secure participants gave predominantly Autonomous responses, and Ambivalent participants gave predominantly Kinetic responses. The relationship between attachment style and reader-response categories was significant on a Fisher exact test, Chi-square (4, N=64) = 25.85, p < 0.0001.

Here for instance is an example of a distanced response, with characteristic avoidant tone and beliefs. This reader defends herself against the story, and does not allow herself to enter into it:

> The story to me seemed very unreal. The romantic chance meetings of lovers in exotic places; the whimsical offers of a ski trip in Vermont to vacations in Cuba all seem unbelievable. The way that people are described as being dressed (a little crushed velvet here, some deep red satin there) sounds ancient. Of course we all know that cotton/ polyester blend is certainly not conducive to romantic imagery! What irritated me about the story was the references to the rural and then

the urban; the linking up with lovers or friends who are anthropologists, clergymen, paroled prisoners, physiotherapists, botanical illustrators, etc. (no TTC bus drivers, hospital workers, or book binders) so pitched and elevated.

Here, by contrast, is a response that was classified as autonomous, which included intellectual analysis with emotional and personal issues:

> An extremely well-written, perceptive story. Thought-provoking; capturing the emotions of most of the characters – not necessarily Dennis but this is not a problem because he is a catalyst, it discusses opposing emotions and reactions equally. I very much like the "stream of consciousness" style in which it is written, allowing one to empathize easily with the writer (main character). It made me think about the different relationships between men and women and possibly the differences some men have in their attitude towards relationships all of which is somewhat different to my own experience.

And here is a kinetic response:

> I really enjoyed the story – even though it provoked painful memories and emotions, but overall I really enjoyed it – however, I felt that the ending was much too choppy or abrupt – the ending didn't flow with the rest of the story – left me hanging, wanting more, wanting characters to kiss, to hold each other – I felt sad, nostalgic, and empty at the end of the story remembering how I felt when I left my boyfriend. I'm left wanting to know more – what happens to the characters? Do they keep in touch? Do they love each other? I feel like I'm left hanging, and just like in real life, I didn't like this feeling – it is quite unsettling.

We concluded that one way to summarize the difference was that distanced responses were almost all intellect, and the kinetic almost all emotion; autonomous responses combined the two.

It may seem obvious that people would answer questionnaires about their own attachment experience and write about a literary story in ways that revealed a characteriztic underlying style based on their schemas of self-and-other, for instance distanced, or emotionally secure, or vulnerable to too-intense interpersonal emotions. We know, however, of no other empirical results relating a sentiment-based measure of personality to the styles of response that literary critics have defined. Furthermore the result confirms Holland's (1975) theory that when reading, people re-create in their responses to literature the structures of their own habitual defensive attitudes to the world. This was indicated here by participants' attachment styles, particularly in the way that anxiety affected their responses.

In this study, attachment anxiety in relationships, in which Waters *et al.* found continuity from assessment in the strange situation during infancy to the Adult Attachment Interview, was linked also to people's styles and beliefs in entering into a cultural narrative, a literary short story.

Social anxiety, or the sentiment of wariness, has several aspects. On one hand it can be socially valuable, as Lutz (1988) has shown, in promoting social harmony and conformity to social rules. It can set the tone for people to monitor each other's needs and emotions, making sure everyone is included in social activity. On the other hand, as in the Bowlby-Ainsworth-Main hypothesis of attachment, the social goal of security can militate against that of affiliation. It can distance people from intimate relationships, and even from emotions generally. Among the beliefs of avoidant people is a sense of the danger in close relationships, with the defensive alternative of a strong belief in the value of autonomy.

Conclusion

In this chapter I have taken distributed cognition (among people, between person and environment, and as transmitted by culture through time) as the focus. I have considered the social goals of affiliation, attachment-security, and dominance, in relation to long-term emotional states called sentiments. I have argued that although the traditional approach to cognition is to analyze how individual goals and knowledge are represented and used, we need also to understand social goals, and interpersonal sentiments, which profoundly affect beliefs such as whether another person is trustworthy enough to be involved with. Such beliefs make all the difference to shared tasks, to commitment to externalized cultural objects, and to enculturation.

Since the beginning of the cognitive revolution, it has been almost axiomatic that the task for cognitive science is to analyze knowledge structures. Nothing here contradicts this. I do suggest, however, that just as Winnicott has argued that without the space that grows in between infant and mother there would be no culture, without the sentiments of affection, despondency, antipathy, and wariness, there would be no knowledge structures.

Note

[1] I thank the members of my research group who collaborated in the research described here: Laurette Larocque, Seema Nundy, and Mitra Gholamain. I thank also the Social Sciences and Humanities Research Council of Canada for supporting this work.

References

Ainsworth, M. D. S., Blehar, M. C., Waters, E., & Wall, S. (1978). *Patterns of attachment: A psychological study of the strange situation.* Hillsdale, NJ: Erlbaum.

Aristotle (*c.* 330 BCE). *Rhetoric and Poetics* (Trans. W. R. Roberts). New York: Random House.

Aubé, M., & Senteni, A. (1996). Emotions as commitments operators: A foundation for control structure in multi-agents systems. In W. Van der Velde & J. W. Perram (Eds.), *Agents breaking away: Proceedings of the 7th European Workshop on MAAMAW, Lecture notes on artificial intelligence,* No. 1038, pp. 13–25. Berlin: Springer.

Averill, J. R. (1982). *Anger and aggression: An essay on emotion.* New York: Springer.

Bogdan, D. (1992). *Reeducating the imagination: Towards the poetics, politics, and pedagogy of literary engagement.* Toronto: Irwin.

Bowlby, J. (1971). *Attachment and loss, Volume 1. Attachment.* London: Hogarth Press (reprinted by Penguin, 1978).

Briggs, J. L. (1970). *Never in anger: Portrait of an Eskimo family.* Cambridge, MA: Harvard University Press.

Brown, G. W., & Harris, T. O. (1978). *Social origins of depression: A study of psychiatric disorder in women.* London: Tavistock.

Brown, G. W., Harris, T. O., & Hepworth, C. (1994). Loss, humiliation and entrapment among women developing depression: A patient and non-patient comparison. *Psychological Medicine, 25,* 7–21.

Chagnon, N. A. (1968). *Yanomamö: The fierce people.* New York: Holt Rinehart & Winston.

D'Andrade, R. G. (1981). The cultural part of cognition. *Cognitive Science, 5,* 179–195.

Donald, M. (1991). *Origins of the modern mind.* Cambridge, MA: Harvard University Press.

Dunbar, K. (1993). How scientists really reason: Scientific reasoning in real-world laboratories. In R. J. Sternberg & J. Davidson (Eds.), *Mechanisms of insight* (pp. 365–395). Cambridge, MA: MIT Press.

Dunbar, R. I. M. (1996). *Grooming, gossip and the evolution of language.* London: Faber & Faber.

Ephron, D. (1977). *How to eat like a child.* New York: Random House.

Feeney, J. A., Noller, P., & Hanrahan, M. (1994). Assessing adult attachment. In M. B. Sperling & W. H. Berman (Eds.), *Attachment in adults: Clinical and developmental perspectives.* New York: Guilford.

Feuer, K. B. (1996). *Tolstoy and the genesis of War and Peace.* Ithaca, NY: Cornell University Press.

Forgas, J. (1995). Mood and judgment: The affect infusion model (AIM). *Psychological Review, 117,* 39–66.

Fox, N., & Davidson, R. A. (1987). Electroencephalogram asymmetry in response to the approach of a stranger and maternal separation in 10-month-old infants. *Developmental Psychology, 23,* 233–240.

Frijda, N. H. (1986). *The emotions.* Cambridge: Cambridge University Press.

Frijda, N. H., Mesquita, B., Sonnemans, J., & van Goozen, S. (1991). The duration of affective phenomena or emotions, sentiments and passions. In

K. T. Strongman (Ed.), *International Review of Emotion*, Vol 1. Chichester: Wiley.

George, C., Kaplan, N., & Main, M. (1985). The Berkeley Adult Attachment Interview. *Unpublished protocol*. Department of Psychology, University of California, Berkeley.

Gholamain, M. & Oatley, K. (submitted for publication). Attachment dynamics, identification, and autobiographical memory in reader response.

Grazzani-Gavazzi, I., & Oatley, K. (1999). The experience of emotions of interdependence and independence following interpersonal errors in Italy and Anglophone Canada. *Cognition and Emotion, 13*, 49–63.

Hills, L. R. (1993). *How to do things right*. Boston: Godine.

Holland, N. N. (1975). *Five readers reading*. New Haven: Yale University Press.

Hooke, R. (1665). *Micrographia*. New York: Dover (current edition 1961).

Hutchins, E. (1995). *Cognition in the wild*. Cambridge, MA: MIT Press.

Hutchins, E. (1998). The scope of distributed cognition. Colloquium, Department of Psychology and Centre for Applied Cognitive Science, University of Toronto, 26 May.

Isen, A. M., & Baron, R. A. (1991). Positive affect as a factor in organizational behavior. In L. L. Cummings & B. M. Shaw (Eds.), *Research in organizational behavior* (Vol. 13, pp. 1–53). Greenwich, CT: JAI Press.

Isen, A. M., Daubman, K. A., & Nowicki, G. P. (1987). Positive affect facilitates creative problem solving. *Journal of Personality and Social Psychology, 52*, 1122–1131.

Isen, A. M., & Levin, P. F. (1972). The effect of feeling good on helping: Cookies and kindness. *Journal of Personality and Social Psychology, 21*, 384–388.

Jenkins, J. M., & Ball, S. (2000) Distinguishing between negative emotions: Children's understanding of the social regulatory aspects of emotion. *Cognition and Emotion 14*, 261–281.

Kemper, T. D (1990). Social relations and emotions: A structural approach. In T. D. Kemper (Ed.), *Research agendas in the sociology of emotions* (pp. 207–237). Albany, NY: SUNY Press.

Lovejoy, C. O. (1981). The origin of man. *Science, 211*, 341–350.

Lutz, C. A. (1988). *Unnatural emotions: Everyday sentiments on a Micronesian atoll and their challenge to Western theory*. Chicago: University of Chicago Press.

MacDonald, K. (1992). Warmth as a developmental construct: An evolutionary analysis. *Child Development, 63*, 753–773.

Mackie, D. M., & Worth, L. T. (1991). Feeling good, but not thinking straight: The impact of positive mood on persuasion. In J. P. Forgas (Ed.), *Emotion and social judgments* (pp. 201–219). Oxford: Pergamon.

Main, M. (1995). Recent studies in attachment: Overview with selected implications for clinical work. In S. Goldberg, R. Muir, & J. Kerr (Eds.), *Attachment theory: Social, developmental, and clinical perspectives* (pp. 407–474). Hillsdale, NJ: The Analytical Press.

Mathews, A. (1993). Biases in emotional processing. *The Psychologist, 6*, 493–499.

Melzoff, A. N., & Moore, M. K. (1977). Imitation of facial and manual gestures by human neonates. *Science, 198*, 75–78.

Nussbaum, M. (1993). *Upheavals of thought (manuscript draft developing the Gifford Lectures, University of Edinburgh, April–May)*.

Oatley, K. (1996). Emotions, rationality, and informal reasoning. In J. V. Oakhill & A. Garnham (Eds.), *Mental models in cognitive science* (pp. 175–196). Hove: Psychology Press.

Oatley, K., & Bolton, W. (1985). A social-cognitive theory of depression in reaction to life events. *Psychological Review, 92*, 372–388.

Oatley, K., & Jenkins, J. M. (1996). *Understanding emotions.* Oxford: Blackwell.

Oatley, K., & Johnson-Laird, P. N. (1987). Towards a cognitive theory of emotions. *Cognition and Emotion, 1*, 29–50.

Oatley, K., & Johnson-Laird, P. N. (1996). The communicative theory of emotions: Empirical tests, mental models, and implications for social interaction. In L. L. Martin & A. Tesser (Eds.), *Striving and feeling: Interactions among goals, affect, and self-regulation* (pp. 363–393). Mahwah, NJ: Erlbaum.

Oatley, K., & Larocque, L. (1995). Everyday concepts of emotions following every-other-day errors in joint plans. In J. Russell, J.-M. Fernandez-Dols, A. S. R. Manstead, & J. Wellenkamp (Eds.), *Everyday conceptions of Emotions: An introduction to the psychology, anthropology, and linguistics of emotion. NATO ASI Series D 81* (pp. 145–165). Dordrecht: Kluwer.

Olson, D. R. (1994). *The world on paper.* New York: Cambridge University Press.

Popper, K. R. (1962). *Conjectures and refutations.* New York: Basic Books.

Power, R. (1979). The organization of purposeful dialogues. *Linguistics, 17*, 107–152.

Salomon, G. (Ed.). (1997). *Distributed cognitions: Psychological and educational considerations.* New York: Cambridge University Press.

Schwarz, N., & Bless, H. (1991). Happy and mindless, but sad and smart? The impact of affective states on analytic reasoning. In J. Forgas (Ed.), *Emotion and social judgment* (pp. 55–71). Oxford: Pergamon.

Sherif, M. (1956). Experiments in group conflict. *Scientific American, 195 (November)*, 54–58.

Simon, H. A. (1967). Motivational and emotional controls of cognition. *Psychological Review, 74*, 29–39.

Tomasello, M., Savage-Rumbaugh, S., & Kruger, A. (1993). Imitative learning of actions on objects by children, chimpanzees, and enculturated chimpanzees. *Child Development, 64*, 1688–1705.

Tomkins, S. S. (1970). Affect as the primary motivational system. In M. B. Arnold (Ed.), *Feelings and emotions: The Loyola Symposium* (pp. 101–110). New York: Academic Press.

Van den Berghe, P. L. (1979). *Human family systems: An evolutionary view.* Amsterdam: Elsevier.

Visalberghi, E., & Sonetti, M. G. (1994). Lorenz's concept of aggression and recent primatological studies on aggressive and reconciliatory behaviors. *La Nuova Critica, Nuova serie, 23–24*, 57–67.

Wason, P. (1960). On the failure to eliminate hypotheses in a conceptual task. *Quarterly Journal of Experimental Psychology, 12*, 129–140.

Waters, E., Merrick, S. K., Albersheim, L. J., & Treboux, D. (1995). Attachment security from infancy to early adulthood: A 20–year longitudinal study of attachment security in infancy and early adulthood. In *Biennial Meeting of the Society for Research In Child Development*, Indianapolis, March 30–April 2.

Winnicott, D. W. (1971). *Playing and reality.* Harmondsworth: Penguin.

5

Feeling is believing? The role of processing strategies in mediating affective influences on beliefs[1]

Joseph P. Forgas

Introduction

Beliefs are stable, enduring cognitive representations that have a fundamental influence on the way people perceive, construct and interpret the social world. Recently, Ajzen defined beliefs as "people's information about themselves and about their social and non-social environment" (1995: 88–89). However, beliefs are also intensely personal, idiosyncratic creations. George Kelly (1955) argued over forty years ago that any meaningful understanding of social life must include a careful analysis and understanding of the personal belief systems, cognitive representations, or, in Kelly's terms, "personal constructs" that make the world intelligible and predictable for most of us. Unfortunately, social psychologists were relatively slow to follow Kelly's programatic call for the intensive study of the content and structure of individual construct systems. On the positive side however, recent social cognition research revealed much about the processes and mechanisms that are involved in the formation, maintenance and evolution of belief systems.

For Kelly, personal constructs were intensely personal, affect-laden ways of seeing the world. In contrast, much of social cognitive theorizing treated beliefs as essentially cold knowledge structures devoid of emotional loading. This chapter will argue that affective states are intimately involved in the creation, use and maintenance of all cognitive representations and beliefs about the world. It will be suggested that affect, including relatively mild and innocuous mood states that are with us all the time, can have a marked influence on our beliefs and judgments, as well as our social behaviors. This subtle link between affect and cognition, feeling and thinking has long been a source of fascination to artists, philosophers, and lay people, and has also been the subject of much psychological theorizing for almost a

108

century (Freud, 1915). However, it is only in the last twenty years or so that empirical research established that affective states have a widespread, automatic and largely unnoticed influence on both the content, and the process of cognition, processes that are heavily implicated in the creation and maintenance of beliefs (Fiedler, 1991; Forgas, 1992a, 1995a; Forgas & Moylan, 1987; Sedikides, 1995). For example, Fiedler and Bless (this volume) focus on the influence of moods on different information processing strategies such as assimilation and accommodation. In contrast, the present chapter emphasizes a reverse mechanism: we will propose that different information processing strategies, however induced, will play a key role in determining when, and how, affect will influence the content and valence of people's thoughts and beliefs.

Numerous mundane everyday experiences are capable of inducing affect. For example, watching a movie, taking a walk on a sunny day, listening to music, watching a football game, receiving a small gift, drinking a cup of coffee, succeeding or failing at a task, and getting (or not getting) a date on a Friday night can all generate subtle, lingering and frequently unconscious affective states. Such everyday moods often have an automatic mood-congruent influence on many cognitive tasks involving selective attention, learning, memory, associations and judgments – the same processes that are also heavily implicated in the construction and maintenance of beliefs (Bower, 1991; Fiedler, 1991). The cognitive consequences of moods are neither simple, nor straightforward, however. While numerous studies found a clear pattern of mood congruence in thoughts and judgments, many other experiments fail to find mood congruence, and even report an opposite, mood-incongruent effect on cognitions (see Forgas, 1995a, for a detailed review).

This chapter will suggest that affective influences on cognition and beliefs are best understood in terms of a multi-process theory that allows for the possibility that people can use different information processing strategies in response to different situational conditions. While mood congruence and affect infusion into beliefs occur when people adopt an open, constructive processing style, in other circumstances a more controlled, motivated processing strategy is used that leads to highly targeted information search patterns that are impervious to opportunistic affect-infusion effects (Forgas, 1995a; Berkowitz & Troccoli, 1990; Ciarrochi and Forgas, 1999a). This chapter will outline such a multi-process theory, the Affect Infusion Model (Forgas, 1992a, 1995a), before reviewing some of the most recent empirical evidence demonstrating the presence or absence of affective influences on cognition, beliefs and subsequent social behaviors.

Affect, mood and emotion

First, however, we must contend with one fundamental problem in understanding the links between affect, cognition and beliefs. This relates to the difficulty of defining and describing affective states. A number of unresolved conceptual problems plague this field. There is still little general agreement about how best to *define* terms such as affect, feelings, emotions or mood (Fiedler & Forgas, 1988; Forgas, 1992a, 1995a). We have argued elsewhere that *affect* may be used as a generic label to refer to both *moods* and *emotions*. *Moods* in turn could be described as "low-intensity, diffuse and relatively enduring affective states without a salient antecedent cause and therefore little cognitive content (e.g. feeling good or feeling bad)," whereas *emotions* "are more intense, short-lived and usually have a definite cause and clear cognitive content" (e.g. anger or fear) (Forgas, 1992a: 230). This distinction may be highly relevant to understanding the links between affect and beliefs. Considerable research now suggests that subtle, non-specific moods may often have a potentially more enduring and insidious influence on social cognition, beliefs and social behaviors than do distinct and intense emotions that are subject to explicit cognitive monitoring (Forgas, 1992a,b; Forgas, 1994, 1995a,b; 1998a,b,c; 1999a,b; Mayer, Gaschke, Braverman & Evans, 1992, Mayer, McCormick & Strong 1995; Sedikides, 1992). Much of the discussion that follows will focus on mood effects on beliefs and cognition.

Affect infusion: The process mediation of affective influences on beliefs and cognition

Although experiences of positive or negative affect accompany us throughout our daily lives, most of the time these mood states are not intense or salient enough to command conscious attention. Yet there is growing evidence suggesting that transient mood states do have a significant influence both on the content of cognition (what people think), as well as the process of cognition (how people think) (Bower, 1981; Fiedler & Bless, this volume; Forgas, 1995a; Schwarz & Clore, 1988). For the purposes of this discussion, *affect infusion* may be defined as a process whereby affectively loaded information exerts an influence on, and becomes incorporated into a person's cognitive processes, entering into their constructive deliberations and eventually coloring the outcome in a mood-congruent direction (Forgas, 1995a). Affect infusion occurs because processing social information typically requires high-level inferential cognitive processes. The classic work of Asch (1946), Heider (1958), and Kelly (1955) established that even the simplest kinds of beliefs or judgments are subject to such highly constructive biases.

Social information processors can only create a meaningful pattern or Gestalt of the confusing information available to them by the selective and constructive use of their pre-existing thoughts, memories and associations. Under certain conditions, affect can become part of the informational base used when interpreting information, producing a judgment or planning a behavior (Bower, 1981). There is now clear evidence that affect infusion into beliefs and cognition is most likely to occur in the course of such *constructive processing* that involves the substantial transformation rather than mere reproduction of existing cognitive representations (Fiedler, 1990). However, affect infusion is not an invariable phenomenon. Frequently, the affective state of a person appears to have no influence on the content of cognition, and may even have an inconsistent, mood-incongruent influence (Erber & Erber, 1994; Sedikides, 1994). How can we explain these apparently contradictory findings?

The Affect Infusion Model (AIM)

The Affect Infusion Model (AIM) (Forgas, 1995a) argues that the nature and extent of affect infusion into cognition depends fundamentally on what kind of cognitive strategy is adopted by a person in dealing with a particular task. The model identifies four distinct processing strategies. Two of these strategies (1) the *direct access* of pre-existing information, and (2) *motivated processing* in service of a pre-existing goal, involve highly predetermined and directed information search strategies that require little generative processing, limiting the scope of incidental affect-infusion effects. In contrast, when a cognitive task requires a degree of open, elaborate, constructive processing, people may adopt either (3) a *heuristic*, simplified or (4) a *substantive*, elaborate processing strategy to compute a response. These strategies involve some degree of constructive thinking and allow affect to influence outcomes either indirectly (through primed associations; Forgas & Bower, 1988) or directly (when affect is misattributed; Schwarz & Clore, 1988).

According to the AIM, processing choices should be determined by three categories of variables associated with the *task*, the *person* and the *situation*, respectively. A complete description of the AIM and the evidence supporting it is presented by Forgas (1995a), so it will not be reviewed in detail here. The major relevance of the AIM to our discussion is that it provides a framework within which instances of affect infusion into beliefs, as well as instances of an absence of affect infusion – based on motivated processing – can be explained.

The AIM can thus provide answers to a variety of intriguing questions about how affective states impact on beliefs and cognition, such as: How can we account for the apparent context sensitivity of many mood effects on beliefs? What sorts of information processing strategies are most likely to produce affect infusion into beliefs? What kinds of thoughts and beliefs are most and least likely to be open to affective distortions? How does the complexity or ambiguity of a cognitive task influence affect infusion? Is more prolonged, systematic processing more or less likely to produce affect infusion? In particular, this model can also explain some recent non-obvious results, indicating that more prolonged and extensive processing recruited by more complex and ambiguous tasks can paradoxically increase, rather than decrease the extent of affect-infusion into beliefs and cognition (Fiedler, 1991; Forgas, 1992a,b; 1994; 1995b; 1998a,b; Sedikides, 1995).

Distinguishing between these four processing strategies has considerable benefits for understanding the role of affect in the formation and maintenance of beliefs. In terms of the AIM, the *direct access* retrieval of pre-existing, stored beliefs is the simplest way of producing a social response. We all possess a rich repertoire of such pre-computed beliefs and ideas of various levels of abstractness and generality (Kelly, 1955). Direct access is a low affect-infusion strategy, as it requires little on-line constructive thinking, producing neither mood congruence nor incongruence. It is interesting that this simple and common strategy for accessing beliefs has received relatively little attention in theories of social cognition.

In contrast, *heuristic processing* occurs when people have no pre-computed beliefs, nor a strong motivation to guide them, and they seek to produce a response with the least amount of effort, using whatever shortcuts or simplification are readily available. This strategy is common when the task is simple or typical, of low personal relevance, or there is limited processing capacity, and the context does not call for greater elaboration. Social beliefs are often computed on the basis of such heuristic cues, based on stereotypes, irrelevant associations with environmental variables, or a misinterpretation of a prevailing affective state (e.g., Forgas & Moylan, 1987; Forgas & Fiedler, 1996). Heuristic processing can produce some affect infusion, for example when the "how do I feel about it?" heuristic is used to construct a belief (Clore, Schwarz & Conway, 1994).

According to the AIM, affect infusion into beliefs is most likely when a constructive, *substantive processing* strategy is employed. This involves selecting, learning and interpreting novel information, and relating this information to pre-existing knowledge structures. Substantive processing is more likely when the task is complex or atypical, there is adequate cognitive capacity, and there are no specific motivational goals to pre-determine the outcome. Most (but not all) cognitive theories in psychology implicitly assume that such exhaustive, elaborate and "dutiful" information processing is the norm. In contrast, the AIM suggests that substantive processing is frequently a default option, adopted only when less effortful cognitive strategies prove unequal to the task.

Affect infusion during substantive processing is best understood in terms of memory principles that can account for the role of affect in the selection, learning, interpretation and assimilation of novel information into a pre-existing knowledge base (Bower, 1981; 1991; Forgas & Bower, 1988). This occurs because the "activation of an emotion node also spreads activation throughout the memory structures to which it is connected" (Bower, 1981: 135). The more elaborate and substantive the processing strategy required, the more likely that affectively primed information will become accessible and be opportunistically incorporated into thinking, eventually infusing beliefs and representations (Fiedler, 1991; Forgas, 1992b; 1993; 1998a,b). In fact, more extensive processing tends to enhance affect infusion, a counterintuitive prediction that has been repeatedly confirmed in recent studies (Fiedler, 1991; Forgas, 1992b; 1994; 1998a; Sedikides, 1995).

In contrast, *motivated processing* typically occurs when thinking is guided by a specific goal, leading people to employ highly selective, motivated information search and integration strategies designed to produce a preferred outcome (for example, supporting an existing belief or construct, as suggested by Kelly, 1955). As motivated processing precludes genuinely open, constructive information search and selection strategies, the likelihood of affect infusion is reduced, and mood-incongruent outcomes are often produced. Motivated processing is also the prime technique for achieving mood control, as suggested by several recent studies (Clark & Isen, 1982; Erber & Erber, 1994; Forgas, 1990, 1991a; Forgas & Ciarrochi, 1999; Forgas & Fiedler, 1996; Wegner & Erber, 1993). Indeed, merely directing a person's attention to their affective state seems sufficient to trigger deliberate, motivated thinking (Berkowitz, Jaffee, Jo & Troccoli, in press; Berkowitz & Troccoli, 1990). Recent affect-cognition research identified several specific goals that can elicit motivated processing, such as mood-repair and mood-maintenance, self-evaluation maintenance, ego-enhancement, achievement motivation, affiliation and the like (Forgas, 1995a). Motivated processing as defined here involves more than just a motivation to be accurate (cf. Kunda, 1990): it involves a specific goal (such as mood-control) which dominates and guides information search strategies. Motivated processing is particularly likely when people become aware of the causes or consequences of their mood state (Berkowitz *et al.*, in press; Schwarz & Clore, 1988). We shall have more to say about this later.

Mechanisms of affect infusion

Affect infusion occurs because moods can either indirectly (through primed associations) or directly (through the direct use of affect as information) infuse thinking and beliefs. Affect-priming (Bower, 1981; Forgas & Bower, 1988) is more likely when substantive processing is adopted, while affect-as-information (Schwarz & Clore, 1988) should be limited to conditions when heuristic processing is used. The affect-as-information mechanism suggests that "individuals may . . . ask themselves: 'How do I feel about it?' and in doing so, they may mistake feelings due to a preexisting state" as informative about the current situation (Schwarz, 1990: 529). Supporting evidence comes from studies reporting mood congruence in certain evaluative judgments (Clore & Parrott, 1991). However, many of these results can be equally well explained by alternative, affect-priming models. Further, the affect-as-information model also lacks parsimony, as it deals with mood effects on cognitions and beliefs at the retrieval stage only. The kind of simple, heuristic processing implied by the affect-as-information approach is most likely when processing resources are limited, stored prior beliefs are not available, and the task is unfamiliar, non-specific, and of little personal relevance. Importantly, affect can only be used as information in constructing beliefs as long as people remain unaware of the true source of their mood (Schwarz and Clore, 1988).

In contrast to the affect-as-information view, the affect-priming mechanism suggests that affect can indirectly infuse cognitive processes by facilitating access to related memories and cognitive categories (Bower, 1981; Bower & Forgas, in press). According to this view, affective states have a specific node or unit in memory that is linked with propositions describing events from one's life during which that emotion was aroused. Activation of an emotion node spreads activation throughout the memory structures to which it is connected, increasing the chance that those memories will be retrieved and used (Bower, 1981). The priming model predicts mood-congruent biases in attention, encoding, learning (Bower, 1981; Forgas & Bower, 1987; Forgas, 1992b), memory retrieval (Bower, 1981; Forgas & Bower, 1988), and interpretation (Forgas & Bower, 1987). Despite initial problems with demonstrating mood-dependence in memory (Blaney, 1986), many studies using rich and elaborate encoding and retrieval cues have reliably demonstrated strong mood-priming effects on thinking, memory, judgments and beliefs (cf. Bower, 1981; Eich & Macauley, in press; Forgas, 1990, 1992b; Forgas & Bower, 1987, 1988; Salovey, O'Leary, Stretton, Fishkin & Drake, 1991). In particular, counter-intuitive evidence indicates that the more people need to engage in substantive processing to deal with more complex and demanding issues and beliefs, the stronger are the affect infusion and the mood-congruency effects obtained (e.g., Forgas, 1992b, 1993, 1995b; 1998a,b; Sedikides, 1995).

Basic predictions of the AIM

According to the AIM, the choice of processing strategy (and thus, subsequent affect infusion or the absence of it) should largely depend on three sets of factors: features of (1) the task (2) the person and (3) the situation (Forgas, 1995a). Task features include familiarity, typicality, and complexity; person features include specific motivation, cognitive capacity, motivation to be accurate, affective state, individual difference variables, and awareness of affective state; situational factors include features such as degree of critical scrutiny expected, accuracy expectations, etc. Several testable principles may be derived from this model. For example, cognitive tasks that are highly familiar should be processed using a direct access strategy precluding affect infusion (Srull, 1984). A strong prior motivation should also lead to directed and truncated information search strategies, and the absence of affect infusion into beliefs. Such a pattern was found in several recent experiments looking at mood effects on motivated interpersonal choices (Forgas, 1991a) and intergroup beliefs (Forgas & Fiedler, 1996). Motivated processing is also the primary mechanism to reverse mood congruence, when judges selectively process mood-incongruent information in an attempt to control and eliminate the deleterious effects of the prevailing mood state (Erber & Erber, 1994; Sedikides, 1994).

In the absence of task familiarity or specific motivation, atypical, unusual or complex tasks should generally recruit more substantive and elaborate processing, and typical or simple targets should recruit more simple, truncated processing. This pattern was supported in several recent studies, showing greater affect infusion due to the more substantive processing of complex or atypical targets (Forgas, 1992b; 1993; 1994; 1998a,b). The AIM also predicts that all things being equal, personally relevant tasks and beliefs are more likely to be processed using the motivated strategy, as found in some recent experiments (Forgas, 1989, 1991a). Finally, pragmatic situational demands (e.g., expected publicity or scrutiny, expectations of accuracy) also impact

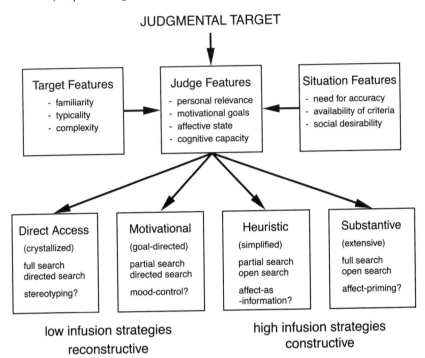

Figure 5.1 Outline of the multiprocess Affect Infusion Model (AIM): affect infusion in social cognition and beliefs depends on which of four alternative processing strategies is adopted in response to target, judge and situational features (after Forgas, 1995a)

on processing choices, triggering substantive rather than heuristic or direct access processing (Wegner & Erber, 1993). A schematic summary of the Affect Infusion Model is presented in Figure 5.1. As this figure shows, the choice of processing strategy is determined by a combination of input variables, which also include the prevailing affective state of the person.

Affect itself also has distinct processing consequences, as suggested by the AIM, and as also argued by Fiedler and Bless in their chapter here. Positive mood is likely to promote top-down, assimilative processing, while negative mood is more likely to produce a more systematic, externally focused, and accommodating processing style. However, unlike other theories, the AIM emphasizes that mood is just one influence among many determining information processing strategies. Features of the task, the situation and the person all have an impact on the processing strategies people adopt, and the subsequent likelihood of affect infusion. Indeed, several experiments found that task characteristics play a far greater role than moods in triggering a substantive, elaborate processing style. When the task is complex, ambiguous or otherwise problematic, an elaborate, substantive processing strategy will be adopted producing significant affect infusion *irrespective* of the person's mood state (Forgas, 1993, 1994, 1995b).

In the next section we will briefly survey some of the evidence illustrating affect infusion into beliefs, thoughts, judgments and cognitive representations in the course of substantive processing. Then, we will turn to discussing some research demonstrating the absence of affect infusion into beliefs in conditions likely to trigger motivated processing.

The evidence for affect infusion

Numerous studies have found that affect can infuse cognitive processes, and ultimately, thoughts and beliefs in circumstances that, according to the AIM, should trigger constructive, substantive processing strategies. In an early test of the affect-infusion hypothesis, we asked people induced to feel happy or sad (using a hypnotic mood-induction procedure) to view videotapes of their social interactions recorded on the previous day. Results showed that despite the availability of objective, videotaped evidence, their basic interpretations and beliefs about their behaviors were significantly distorted in a mood-consistent direction (Forgas, Bower & Krantz, 1984).

Subsequently, we found that moods can also impact on more complex, elaborate beliefs and judgments about problematic social episodes. People in a negative mood constructed more critical, self-deprecatory beliefs and interpretations of their own behaviors (such as succeeding or failing in an exam), while those in a positive mood constructed more lenient beliefs and explanations for identical outcomes (Forgas, Bower & Moylan, 1990). Remarkably, mood effects on beliefs can even influence evaluations of highly familiar, intimate interaction episodes, such as real-life conflicts in one's long-term relationships (Forgas, 1994). Other studies found a similar pattern of affect infusion into interviewers' beliefs about job applicants (Baron, 1987). Affect infusion may also distort highly important personal beliefs, such as peoples' perceptions of health and illness (Croyle & Uretzky, 1987; Salovey & Birnbaum, 1989). As implied by the AIM, "negative mood can affect subjective appraisals of health by increasing the accessibility of illness-related memories" (Croyle & Uretzky, 1987: 239).

Affect infusion into thoughts and beliefs has been demonstrated not only in the laboratory, but also in many real-life situations. In one of the largest unobtrusive field studies on this topic, involving almost a thousand subjects (Forgas & Moylan, 1987), we conducted a "street survey" and interviewed people about their beliefs concerning a number of topical issues as they were leaving movie theatres after seeing happy or sad films. On all questions, happy subjects (who just saw a happy film) reported having significantly more positive and lenient beliefs, and produced more optimistic judgments than did sad subjects. From such results, we may conclude that affect infusion into beliefs is quite a common phenomenon. However, what evidence is there that such affective coloring of beliefs is most likely to occur in the course of constructive, substantive processing?

Evidence for the process mediation of affect infusion into beliefs

The AIM makes the important and counter-intuitive prediction that longer and more substantive processing should increase affect infusion into beliefs. Several recent experiments tested this prediction. In these studies, happy or sad people were asked to deal with information that varied in typicality or complexity. For example, participants were asked to encode, and later recall and form beliefs and impressions about more or less typical other people (the "strange people" experiments; Forgas, 1992b), compute reactions to more or less well-matched couples (the "odd couples" experiments; Forgas, 1993, 1995b; Forgas & Moylan, 1991; Forgas, Levinger & Moylan., 1994), and to indicate their beliefs about more or less serious interpersonal conflicts in their current intimate relationships (the "sad and guilty" experiments; Forgas, 1994).

Atypical tasks increase affect infusion

The AIM suggests that atypical and unusual tasks should recruit a more open and substantive processing strategy and thus lead to greater mood-congruency effects. In one series of experiments, we asked people to read about, recall and form impressions about target persons who were described either as possessing highly consistent, prototypical characteristics, or were described as having a set of inconsistent, atypical features. Beliefs about salient person types such as "the radical feminist," "the loner" or "the typical housewife" are commonly shared in a subculture. Since prototypicality is a matter of degree, it seems that the greater the prototypicality (the more a target person "fits" a well-known person type), the more easily would information about such an individual be encoded, retrieved and elaborated. In contrast, information about atypical, unusual people is more difficult to interpret, and should require more extended and substantive processing leading to greater affect infusion.

In one study, people feeling happy, sad or neutral read about, and formed impressions of, people who were described either as highly prototypical (all features consistent with a common person prototype, e.g., "a radical feminist"), or highly atypical (half of the features were contrary to the prototype) (Forgas, 1992b: Exp. 1). Subsequent beliefs about these people showed a clear mood-congruent bias that was significantly greater when the targets were "strange," atypical people rather than prototypical. Mood also had a significantly greater influence on memory about atypical rather than typical targets (Forgas, 1992b: Exp. 2). Interestingly, atypical, inconsistent information was recalled better in a negative mood, and typical information was better remembered in a positive mood. It seems that the best recall performance occurred in circumstances when both mood, and target typicality called for similar styles of information processing (i.e., positive mood, and typical information both facilitate heuristic processing, and negative mood and atypical information are both likely to recruit more systematic processing). A further experiment also analyzed the length of time it took information about typical, and "strange" people to be processed (Forgas, 1992b: Exp. 3). Results showed that people took significantly longer to deal with strange, atypical compared to typical targets, and it was this more extended processing that was most open to affect infusion, as suggested by the AIM.

Frequently beliefs are constructed on the basis of visual information about people or groups. For example, we may observe couples who appear to be either well matched (typical) or poorly matched (atypical) in terms of physical attractiveness (Forgas, 1993, 1995b). We reasoned that observing a badly matched couple presents judges with more unusual, atypical information that requires more extensive processing, and should thus facilitate affect infusion in terms of the AIM. Well-matched couples in turn present a more typical and more easily processed information array, requiring less extensive elaboration, thus limiting affect infusion into beliefs about them. In these studies we presented images of more or less well-matched couples to subjects who were induced into a positive or a negative mood (for example, after watching happy or sad videotapes). We found that mood had a significantly greater influence on their beliefs about unusual, mis-matched couples that required more substantive processing. In a similar way, presenting images of a mixed-race (atypical) rather than a same-race (typical) dyad also produced more extensive, substantive processing, and greater affect infusion (Forgas & Moylan, 1991). In contrast, typical, unproblematic targets such as same-race couples

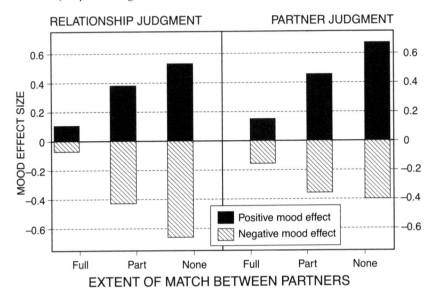

Figure 5.2 Mood effects on the perception of well-matched, partially matched and badly matched couples: the size of the mood effect is proportional to the degree of mismatch between the couples (after Forgas, 1995b).

received less substantive processing, and so produced weaker mood effects on subsequent beliefs.

Such findings may have interesting implications for the way moods influence our everyday beliefs about unusual people and groups. Beliefs about more atypical, unfamiliar people and groups may be more likely to be susceptible to affective biases than are impressions about typical, easy-to-process targets. In a final study using this paradigm, racial composition and physical attractiveness were simultaneously manipulated to create images of (a) fully matched (b) partially matched, or (c) fully mismatched couples. As expected, the extent of affect infusion into perceptions and beliefs was directly related to the degree of visible mismatch (Forgas, 1995b: Exp. 3; Fig. 5.2). Both recall, and processing latency data confirmed that greater mood effects were consistently linked to the more extensive and prolonged processing recruited by these "odd" couples (Forgas, 1995b: Exp. 4). A mediational analysis using regression procedures clearly supported the AIM, showing that processing strategy (as measured by encoding and judgmental latency) was a significant mediator of mood effects on memory and judgments. Overall, these experiments showed that (a) people take longer to encode, and process unusual, atypical information (b) they remember this information better, and (c) subsequent beliefs and judgments about these targets are significantly more mood congruent.

Affect infusion into beliefs about relationships

Do these mechanisms function in a similar way outside the laboratory, in more realistic, real-life cognitive tasks where people already possess detailed and personal beliefs about the target? A third series of experiments examined the influence of mood on how people compute beliefs about their real-life intimate relationships (Forgas, Levinger & Moylan, 1994), and their beliefs about the causes of more or less serious relationship conflicts (Forgas, 1994). In two experiments we found that good or bad mood had a significant mood-congruent influence on people's beliefs about their real-life intimate partners and close relationships. Surprisingly, these mood effects on relationship beliefs were just as powerful in well-established, long-term personal relationships as in short-term, superficial liaisons. At first this may appear surprising, since one might have expected weaker mood effects as the longevity and familiarity of a relationship increases. However, well-established relationships also provide partners with a particularly rich and heterogeneous range of memories and experiences. Mood can thus play a critical role in selectively priming mood-congruent details that partners remember and use as they try to compute an overall evaluation of their relationship (Forgas *et al.*, 1994).

It seems that mood may influence not only general beliefs about relationship quality, but also the way specific episodes and conflicts in a relationship are explained. In several studies, we asked happy or sad people to indicate their beliefs about the causes for recent happy and conflict events in their relationships (Forgas, 1994: Exp. 1). Consistent with the AIM, an overall pattern of affect infusion was detected in these beliefs, with more self-deprecatory ideas produced by sad than by happy subjects. In a further study people who had just seen happy, sad or neutral movies (cf. Forgas & Moylan, 1987) indicated their beliefs about the causes of simple vs. complex conflicts in their current intimate relationships (Forgas, 1994: Exp. 2). Sad mood produced significantly more pessimistic beliefs and explanations. Sad people identified more internal, stable and global causes for their conflicts than did happy subjects. Remarkably, these mood effects were greater on explanations for complex and serious conflicts compared to simple ones (Fig. 5.3). Again, it seems that the more extensive processing recruited by these more complex tasks (such as thinking about serious

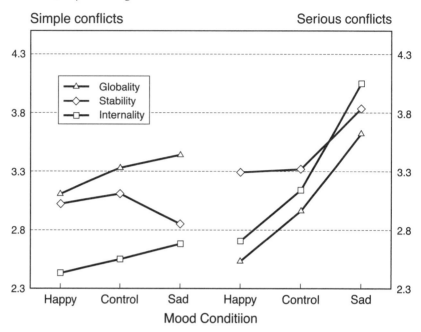

Figure 5.3 Mood effects on explanations and beliefs about simple and serious relationship conflicts: mood has a greater impact on judgments about serious, complex conflicts requiring longer, more substantive processing (after Forgas, 1994).

rather than simple conflicts) accentuated mood effects, even though judges were dealing with highly realistic and familiar information. The careful measurement of processing latencies (Forgas, 1994: Exp. 3) confirmed that even for these complex, real-life relationship beliefs, greater mood effects were consistently associated with longer processing times, as predicted by AIM.

These results help us understand mood effects on the dynamics of everyday belief formation. Dealing with information about other people, about relationships or conflict episodes are examples of complex, inferential cognitive tasks people must routinely undertake to make sense of their social world (Heider, 1958; Kelly, 1955). These experiments suggest that the longer and more constructively a person needs to think to compute a belief, the more likely that affect infusion will significantly influence the outcome. Complex, atypical or problematic beliefs that require more extensive, substantive processing are thus more likely to be influenced by affect infusion than would be the case for simple unproblematic beliefs.

Affect infusion and beliefs about the self

Beliefs about the self may be similarly mood dependent. In his review of mood effects on self-perception, Sedikides came to the general conclusion that "self-valence is affected by mood in a congruent manner" (1992: 301). Considerable clinical work also suggests that mood-induced biases in self-beliefs can be an integral part of mood disorders. According to the AIM, however, affective influences on self-beliefs should be most marked when people need to construct new evaluations, and cannot rely on direct access or motivated processing to arrive at one. The process-sensitivity of affect infusion into self-perception was recently confirmed in several experiments by Sedikides (1995). In these studies happy, sad or neutral mood was induced before subjects were asked to complete a series of self-descriptions. The processing latencies for computing trait self-descriptions were also recorded. Consistent with the AIM, Sedikides (1995) reports that mood effects were significantly greater on self-beliefs that are peripheral, and require more constructive and open processing for a response to be computed. In contrast, central self-descriptions – beliefs about the self that are highly elaborated, important and held with great certainty – were less influenced by mood, as people are more likely to use low-infusion strategies such as direct access or motivated processing when dealing with such information. All "four experiments converged on the notion that peripheral self-conceptions are modified in a mood-congruent fashion, whereas central self-conceptions are unaffected by mood" concludes Sedikides (1995: 39). Further, consistent with the AIM, "high on-line elaboration magnified the mood-congruency bias . . . [suggesting that] affect-priming is the vehicle that carries the effects of mood on peripheral self-conceptions" (p. 769). The results may not always hold true for depressed individuals, who tend to show mood congruence even in central self-conceptions, possibly because of their more vulnerable, uncertain and fluid central self-beliefs. From our perspective, the most important contribution of these experiments is that they were all "consistent with the AIM . . . [that] predicted the absence of mood effects in reference to central self-conceptions, but the presence of a mood-congruency bias in reference to peripheral self-conceptions" (Sedikides, 1995: 765).

Affect infusion and intergroup beliefs

Beliefs about social groups may be similarly influenced by affect infusion. Group membership can be the source of very powerful and emotionally involving experiences, and affect has long been suspected to play a role in intergroup attitudes, prejudice and stereotyping. Interestingly, the role of affect in intergroup beliefs has received relatively little attention. Several studies point to the role of affect-priming mechanisms in biasing intergroup perceptions under conditions that promote substantive processing. One study asked Canadian subjects feeling happy or sad after listening to music to indicate their beliefs, attitudes and affective associations about such groups as French Canadians and Pakistanis. There was a clear mood-congruent pattern, confirming that mood played a critical "role in the favorability of intergroup attitudes, stereotypes and emotional associates" (Haddock, Zanna & Esses, 1994: 198). Processing evidence suggested that substantive processing was a likely pre-requisite for these results. These authors found that "consistent with the affect-priming explanation . . . high [affect-intensity subjects] reported their images to be clearer . . . used significantly more words . . . [and made] more statements concerning their stereotypes and emotional associates" (p. 203).

Further evidence for the process mediation of mood effects on intergroup beliefs and judgments was obtained in some of our recent experiments (Forgas & Fiedler, 1996). These studies used the classic "minimal group paradigm." People in happy, sad or neutral moods made reward allocation decisions, and formed impressions about ingroup and outgroup members, defined only in terms of group category information. In terms of the AIM, we expected that both happy and sad moods may influence group beliefs and increase intergroup discrimination, albeit under different processing circumstances. When group membership is of little personal relevance (the traditional minimal group manipulation), positive mood should induce a faster and more heuristic judgmental style, leading to greater reliance on simple categorical information, and thus greater intergroup discrimination (for a related argument, see Fiedler and Bless, this volume). In the contrasting condition, group membership was made more personally relevant by telling subjects that they have been assigned to groups in terms of important personal characteriztics. It should now be *dysphoric* subjects who show greater intergroup bias, as they can rely on the positive distinctiveness of their ingroup as part of a self-enhancing, motivated mood-repair strategy (Clark & Isen, 1982; Forgas, 1991a, Forgas & Fiedler, 1996). As predicted, we found that positive mood resulted in faster, heuristic processing strategies, and greater ingroup favoritism when group relevance was low. In contrast, when the personal relevance of group membership was high, it was negative mood that enhanced discriminatory beliefs and ingroup favoritism as a result of more motivated processing strategies. Reac-

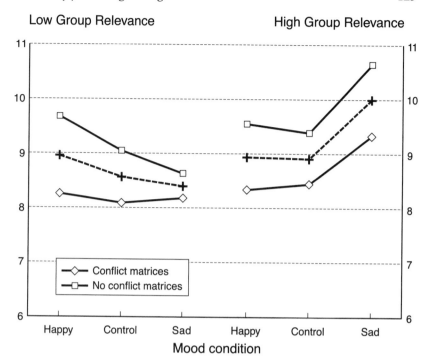

Figure 5.4 The effects of good and bad mood on intergroup beliefs and discrimination: happy mood increases ingroup favoritism when group relevance is low, but sad mood increases ingroup favoritism when group relevance is high (after Forgas & Fiedler, 1996).

tion time data and mediational analyses confirmed that these mood effects were indeed linked to different processing styles (Fig. 5.4).

To summarize, we have argued that low-level, fluctuating affective states and moods that are typically experienced by all of us in everyday life have a continuous, and often imperceptible cognitive influence on our beliefs and the way we think about, remember and evaluate complex social information. Such affect infusion seems most marked when a person needs to engage in constructive, substantive information processing to compute a belief based on complex, ambiguous or problematic information. Several experiments confirm that the longer and more constructively we need to think about a task, the more likely that affect infusion will occur. Thus, mood has a significantly greater effect on beliefs when the task is rare, unusual, atypical or complex. Affect infusion into thoughts and beliefs is just one side of the equation, however. In circumstances that produce controlled, motivated information processing strategies, beliefs and judgments should be more impervious to affect infusion, and indeed, are more likely to show a mood-incongruent bias.

The absence of affect infusion: Motivated processing strategies

Affect infusion represents just one, albeit frequently studied aspect of the delicate interrelationship between affect and cognition. While affect can and does impact on our cognitive processes and beliefs, often in ways that we don't realize, the opposite can also occur: targeted, motivated cognitive activity can eliminate and reverse affect infusion. *Motivated processing* is most likely to be employed when there are strong and specific motivational pressures for a particular cognitive outcome to be achieved. The defining feature of motivated processing is that it involves highly selective, guided, and targeted information search and integration strategies designed to achieve a pre-existing motivational objective. Motivated processing provides little opportunity for affectively primed information to be used, and is thus a low affect-infusion strategy. Indeed, motivated processing is the key strategy for achieving mood-incongruent outcomes (Forgas, Johnson & Ciarrochi, 1998).

It is important to note that motivated processing, as understood here, does not simply refer to a generic motivation to be careful and accurate. Indeed, an accuracy motive may simply produce more extensive and substantive processing, and paradoxically increase rather than reduce affect infusion, as we have seen before (e.g., Forgas, 1993, 1994, 1995b). Rather, motivated processing assumes the existence of a specific, pre-existing goal that dominates and directs information search and processing strategies. There are a number of factors that determine whether or not people will engage in motivated processing. For example, high personal relevance is more likely to trigger highly motivated and directed information search strategies that reduce the chances of incidental affect infusion (Forgas & Fiedler, 1996; Forgas, 1991a, 1995a). Becoming aware of the cause or consequence of a mood may in itself trigger motivated strategies designed to counteract mood congruent biases (Berkowitz *et al.*, in press; Ciarrochi & Forgas, 1999a). Several situational, task and personal variables can produce motivational processing, including high personal relevance, strong external pressures or expectations, the likelihood of external scrutiny or evaluation, and an internal need to balance or rectify aversive states. A more detailed discussion of these factors can be found in Forgas (1995a), and in Forgas, Johnson & Ciarrochi (1998). Despite growing interest in motivated processing, the precise cognitive characteriztics of this strategy have received insufficient attention, perhaps because most studies of social cognition use artificial and relatively uninvolving tasks. What is clear is that affect infusion tends to disappear under conditions that are conducive to motivated processing.

Group discussion and motivated processing

So far we have mainly focused on the effects of mood on beliefs constructed by isolated individuals. Yet many beliefs are based on interactions in groups, and group discussion is often assumed to be effective in eliminating the kind of affective biases that often distort individual judgments. We examined this assumption by comparing mood effects on individual as against group judgments (Forgas, 1990). In this study, the same people indicated their beliefs and formed judgments about various target groups (e.g., farmers, Catholics, doctors, Italians) first as individuals, and two weeks later, in a group. A happy, neutral or sad affective state was induced before each session. Individual beliefs showed the usual mood-congruent bias: the target groups were judged more positively in a happy mood, and more negatively in a sad mood, as implied by affect-priming models. However, group discussion had an interesting effect. Positive mood effects were further enhanced, but negative mood effects on beliefs about the target groups were significantly reduced. It seems that the combination of group discussion and negative mood indeed led to a more controlled, motivated processing strategy that reduced the influence of negative mood on beliefs. A motivated processing style is generally incompatible with affect infusion, as we have seen earlier, and as predicted by the AIM. These results show group discussion is likely to accentuate positive mood effects, but inhibit negative mood effects on beliefs and judgments, an issue that may have important practical implications for our understanding of belief formation in groups.

The interplay between substantive and motivated processing

In terms of the AIM, affect infusion is likely as long as an open, constructive processing strategy is used. More recent studies suggest however that such affect infusion may be self-limiting. In other words, mood-congruent thoughts and associations will only bias judgments and beliefs temporarily. Over time, people may automatically adjust their processing strategies and shift to motivated processing to limit the effects of affect infusion. Such a homeostatic mood-management process (Forgas *et al.*, 1998) implies that negative mood should initially lead to affect-infusion and mood-congruent recall until a threshold level of negativity is reached. At this point a spontaneous switch to more controlled, motivated processing may occur, leading to the targeted access of mood-incongruent, positive information. In a study supporting this hypothesis, Sedikides (1994) gave sad subjects a guided imagery mood induction. Subsequently, they were asked to generate open-ended self-descriptions, revealing their temporary beliefs about themselves. Initial responses showed a clear mood-congruent pattern. With the passage of time, however, self-descriptions in the negative mood group spontaneously changed, becoming markedly more positive. This result suggests that subjects came to adopt a motivated affect control strategy to "repair" their sad mood, but only after the initial negative mood effects due to affect infusion generated a sufficiently aversive state. More recently, we (Forgas & Ciarrochi, 1999) conducted a series of additional studies, testing the hypothesis that initial mood congruence and affect infusion into beliefs may be spontaneously reversed once a shift to a motivated, mood-incongruent affect control strategy occurs.

In study 1, subjects in a good or bad mood generated, as quickly as possible, trait adjectives (e.g., "gloomy," "intelligent"). We found that people in a negative mood tended to initially generate mood-congruent thoughts, but that over time, they switched to generating mood-incongruent (positive) adjectives in a pattern that is consistent with a conscious affect-control strategy. People in a positive mood, in contrast, first produced mood-congruent adjectives, then gradually reverted to more neutral adjectives. These findings suggest that negative, but not positive, mood prompts people to overcome unconscious affect infusion by intentionally accessing mood-incongruent information (Fig. 5.5).

In study 2, a more sensitive technique was used. Happy and sad subjects completed words given a starting letter (e.g., "t" might lead to "terrible" or "terrific"). A time-series regression analysis was used to assess changes in the valence of generated words (as rated by two independent raters) over time. As in study 1, affect infusion was the dominant pattern in the early stages of this generative cognitive task. Results again revealed that over time, happy subjects gradually changed from affect-congruent to neutral recall. However, sad subjects switched to motivated, incongruent recall actively producing positive rather than negative associations, as if seeking to control their aversive mood.

Individual differences between people, such as different levels of self-esteem may well mediate these effects, as people low in self-esteem are perhaps less able than others to engage in conscious affect control (Smith & Petty, 1995). In study 3, we asked happy or sad

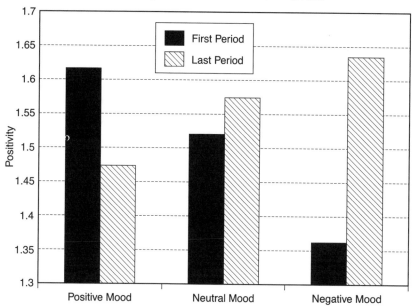

Figure 5.5 Evidence for motivated mood management over time: initially mood-congruent associations (indicating affect infusion) spontaneously become incongruent over time, as participants seek to control their affective states.

subjects to complete a series of sentences indicating their beliefs about themselves, beginning with "I am. . ." Results again indicated a clear "first congruent, then incongruent pattern" in the self-beliefs generated. This pattern was significantly stronger for high self-esteem subjects, who were able to rapidly eliminate an initially negative mood-congruent bias in their self-beliefs by switching to mood-incongruent, positive self-statements. For low SE people, negative, mood congruent beliefs continued to be produced during the entire time period, suggesting that they were less able to engage in motivated processing to control affect from infusing their cognitions. In summary, the results by Sedikides (1994) and Forgas and Ciarrochi (1999) suggest that there may exist a homeostatic mood-management system that spontaneously limits affect infusion into our thoughts, beliefs and judgments. Indeed, simply becoming aware of a mood can produce such a switch from affect infusion to motivated processing (Berkowitz & Troccoli, 1990; Clore & Parrott, 1991; Forgas, 1991a).

Evidence for motivated affect control is also provided by studies showing that people tend to over-compensate for their mood once they become aware of it. For example, Berkowitz *et al.* (in press) found that self-directed attention was sufficient to induce motivated processing, and to limit the infusion of affect into beliefs and judgments about another person. For those in the self-focused attention condition, the more negative they felt, the more positive became their judgments and beliefs. As Berkowitz *et al.* (in press) put it, it was as if aware subjects "leaned over backwards" to avoid letting their bad feelings affect their beliefs and judgments. However, being aware of one's mood is not always sufficient to produce a reversal of mood effects. Martin, Seta, and Crelia (1990) found that people must also have sufficient cognitive resources to engage in motivated processing. These authors found that subjects suffering from cognitive overload and distraction displayed the usual affect-infusion pattern. Only non-distracted subjects had the cognitive resources to actually correct for affect infusion. Sometimes, excessively positive mood states may also have deleterious effects, calling for motivated thinking to tone down euphoria (Parrott, 1993). In an interesting study illustrating motivated processing to control good mood, happy subjects who expected a demanding interaction with a stranger selectively read mood-incongruent, negative information, as if trying to tone down their prevailing affective state (Wegner & Erber, 1993).

Affective influences on processing style and belief construction

As noted earlier, in addition to producing mood congruence, affective states can also influence the processing strategies people employ when constructing a belief. Generally, positive moods facilitate top-down, schema-based processing and the assimilation of novel information into existing knowledge structures, while negative mood promotes bottom-up, stimulus-driven thinking and accommodation to situational demands. Thus, positive moods generally support reliance on existing belief systems, whereas negative states "question and weaken" beliefs (see Fiedler & Bless, this volume). The processing effects of mood may thus influence how observed information is attended to, and the subsequent construction of incorrect and even misleading beliefs. We found some evidence for such a tendency in two recent studies.

For example, we found that the kind of schematic, top-down processing typically recruited by positive moods tends to increase such common judgmental biases as the fundamental attribution error. In contrast, negative mood produced more vigilant, systematic attention to stimulus details and helped to reduce attribution errors and incorrect beliefs about the causes of behavior (Forgas, 1999a). In these experiments happy or sad subjects made inferences about the underlying attitudes of people who either freely chose, or were coerced into advocating either popular or unpopular opinions in an essay. Results showed that happy people were far more likely to commit the fundamental attribution error and mistakenly infer internal causation based on coerced unpopular arguments. In contrast, negative mood resulted in an elimination of the fundamental attribution error. These kinds of mood-induced attributional biases may have important practical implications in producing incorrect beliefs about people we observe.

Another experiment evaluated the effects of mood on beliefs, and memory about real observed episodes. Prior work by Loftus (1979) showed that eyewitness accounts of events are often distorted by later, incorrect information planted in the course of subsequent questioning. Based on past evidence for mood effects on processing strategies (Fiedler & Bless, this volume), we expected that people in a positive mood should be more likely to confuse original information with false details surreptitiously suggested to them after the event. We first exposed subjects to different events, such as a staged interruption during a lecture, or videotapes of positive (a wedding) or negative (a robbery) episodes. About a week later, subjects received a mood induction (viewed happy or sad films), and then answered some questions about the episodes they witnessed. The questions contained some intentionally misleading details about the episodes. For example, a question may ask "Did you see the woman in a brown jacket argue with the lecturer?" when she wore a black and not a brown jacket. Memory and beliefs about the episodes were later tested. We found that positive mood significantly increased memory distortions, and planted, false details were often recalled as correct. In contrast, negative mood improved eyewitness accuracy. These results add an important dimension to Fiedler and Bless's conclusion that positive moods support the use of existing beliefs, while negative moods weaken belief systems. When it comes to developing new beliefs based on external information, it appears that negative mood also improves attention to stimulus details and produces more accurate beliefs and representations. Positive mood on the other hand seems to reduce attention to situational details, and leads to an increase in judgmental errors and greater inaccuracy in eyewitness recollections and beliefs.

Individual differences in affect infusion

Individual differences may also play a critical role in mediating affect infusion into people's beliefs and ideas. As low self-esteem individuals may have fewer "affirmational resources" (Steele, Spencer & Lynch, 1993), they may also be less able to control mood effects on their beliefs. Smith and Petty (1995) found that high self-esteem subjects generated more mood-incongruent, positive ideas and memories when in a negative mood, while low self-esteem people succumbed to a more negative, mood-congruent pattern. Our recent experiments discussed above (Forgas & Ciarrochi, 1999) also showed that low self-esteem people were less able to switch to motivated mood-control strategies. It seems that there may be enduring individual differences between people in the extent to which they are inclined to trust their feelings, and allow moods to infuse their beliefs and judgments. In one recent series of studies, we induced good or bad mood in people who scored high or low on Costa and Macrae's (1985) Openness to Feelings scale (Ciarrochi & Forgas, 1999b). We then evaluated their beliefs about the subjective value of consumer items they possessed. Mood led to highly significant mood-congruent biases among people who scored high on Openness to Feelings (e.g., positive mood increased and negative mood decreased their beliefs about the value of consumer items). However, low Openness to Feelings people appeared to discount or discredit their "subjective" feelings, producing a mood-incongruent pattern. These findings suggest that Openness to Feelings scores can also significantly moderate mood effects on beliefs and judgments.

Trait anxiety is another individual difference variable likely to mediate affect infusion into cognition and beliefs. High trait-anxious people experience aversive moods more often, and in some circumstances, should be more likely to engage in motivated affect-control. In a recent study, Ciarrochi and Forgas (1999a) placed high and low trait-anxious subjects into an aversive or neutral mood and then assessed their beliefs about a racial out-group. Aversive mood led to unconscious affect infusion among low trait-anxious people, but produced an opposite, positive bias among high trait-anxious subjects. High trait-anxious people appeared to be more aware of their aversive moods and "bent over backwards" in an attempt to prevent it from infusing their beliefs. A host of other individual difference measures have also been implicated in mediating affect-infusion effects such as machiavellianism, social desirability and the like (Forgas, 1998a). In general, it appears that people who score high on personality measures that indicate enduring motivational tendencies (such as social desirability, machiavellianism, self-esteem, etc.; Forgas, 1998a) tend to be less subject to affect infusion than are low scorers who do not display such habitual motivated processing styles.

Affect infusion, beliefs and strategic social behaviors

Consistent with the AIM, several recent experiments confirm that manipulated affective states can influence not only on the beliefs people form, but also on the plans they make, and ultimately, their actual behavior in complex social situations (Forgas, 1998a,b,c; 1999a,b). In one series of experiments we explored the effects of mood on the way people formulate beliefs about a forthcoming encounter, and subsequently perform strategic behaviors such as produce a request. Requesting is an intrinsically ambiguous task, which must be formulated at the right degree of politeness so as to maximize compliance without risking giving offense. We expected that mood should significantly influence the beliefs about, and interpretations of, the request situation. Requesters in a good mood might form more optimistic beliefs and adopt a more confident, direct requesting strategy, consistent with the greater availability of positively valenced thoughts and associations (Forgas, 1998b,c, 1999a). Further, in terms of the AIM these mood effects should be greater when the request situation is more complex and demanding, and requires more substantive and elaborate processing. Consistent with these predictions, we found (Forgas, 1999b) that happy participants preferred more direct, impolite requests, while sad persons used indirect, polite request alternatives. In other studies we found that mood will also have a greater influence on more unusual, unconventional responses such as producing an impolite, direct request that requires more substantive processing (Forgas, in 1999b: Exp. 3). These findings confirm that mood effects on cognition, beliefs, and ultimately, behavior are indeed process-dependent, with affect infusion enhanced when more constructive and elaborate processing is required by a more difficult strategic task (Fiedler, 1991; Forgas, 1995a).

These effects were further confirmed in an unobtrusive experiment looking at naturally produced requests (Forgas,1998c: Exp. 2; Fig. 5.6). After receiving a mood induction (viewing films), participants were unexpectedly asked to get a file from a neighboring office "while the rest of the experiment is set up." Their words in requesting the file were recorded by a concealed tape recorder, and subsequently analyzed for politeness and other qualities. Results showed a significant mood effect on these natural, unobtrusively elicited responses. Sad mood produced more polite and more elaborate request forms while

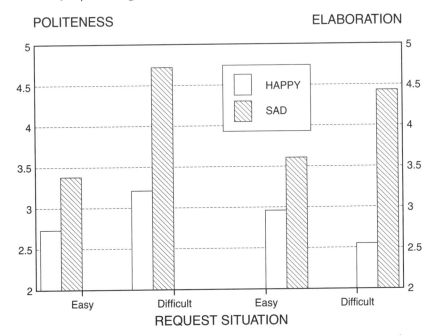

Figure 5.6 Mood effects on requests: positive mood increases, and negative mood decreases the degree of politeness and elaboration in strategic communications, and these effects are greater in more difficult rather than easy situations (after Forgas, in press, b).

happy people used more direct and less polite forms. Sad mood also led to a longer delay in making the request, consistent with the more cautious, defensive cognitive and behavioral strategies common in dysphoria. These results support the core prediction of the AIM that the greatest mood effects on cognition and behavior occur precisely when more elaborate, substantive processing is used.

These mood effects are not restricted to the *production* of requests, and should also influence the way people *respond* to problematic social situations. In another series of experiments (Forgas, 1998b) we looked at the role of temporary affective states in how people evaluate and react to more or less polite requests directed at them. Again, an unobtrusive strategy was used. Students entering a library found pictures or text placed on their desks designed to induce good or bad moods. A few minutes later, they received an unexpected polite or impolite request from a "stranger" for several sheets of paper needed to complete an essay. Results showed that people in an induced negative mood were more likely to form critical, negative beliefs about impolite requests and were less inclined to comply than were positive

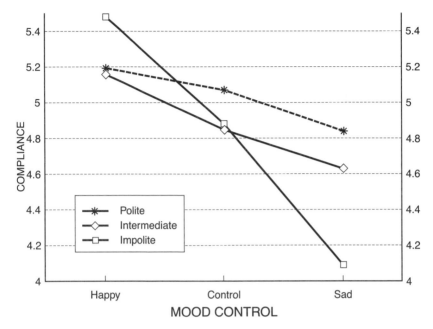

Figure 5.7 The influence of unobtrusively elicited affect on responding to naturalistic requests: Positive mood increases, and negative mood decreases compliance, and these mood effects are greatest in response to more impolite, unconventional requests that require more extensive processing (after Forgas, 1998b).

mood participants (Fig. 5.7). Further, these mood effects were significantly greater on the evaluation of impolite, unconventional requests that required more substantive processing, as confirmed by better recall of these messages later on. These experiments show that affect infusion into the planning and execution of strategic behaviors is significantly mediated by the kind of processing strategy people employ. The production of more complex, multi-action behavior sequences seem to be similarly affect sensitive, as we shall see in the next section.

Affect infusion into beliefs and behavior in complex encounters

It seems that even mild, temporary mood states can have a significant influence on the way people form beliefs and react to interpersonal situations. More complex interactions, such as negotiating encounters, show similar mood dependence (Forgas, 1998a). In these studies, positive, control or negative mood was induced before participants

INTERPERSONAL   INTERGROUP

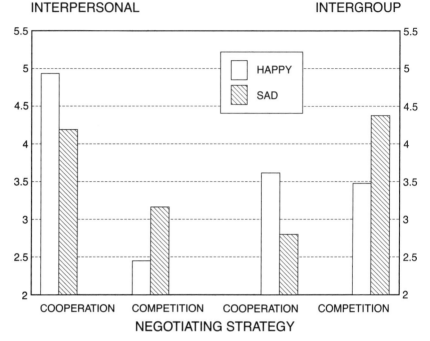

NEGOTIATING STRATEGY

Figure 5.8 Mood effects on beliefs about, and planned and actual behavior in bargaining situations: positive mood induces more positive expectations, and produces more cooperative and less competitive negotiating strategies both in interpersonal, and in intergroup negotiations.

engaged in an informal, interpersonal, and a formal, inter-group negotiating task. We were interested in how moods might influence people's beliefs about the situation, their goal-setting strategies and, ultimately, their behaviors. Positive mood subjects believed that the encounter will be potentially more cooperative, set themselves higher and more ambitious goals, formed more positive beliefs about the opposition, and formulated more cooperative and integrative action plans. Actual bargaining behaviors were in fact more cooperative in this group (Fig. 5.8). Surprisingly, these mood-induced differences in beliefs and behavior also produced more successful performances. Those in a good mood did significantly better in this bargaining task than did those induced to feel bad. These results provide clear evidence that even slight changes in mood due to an unrelated prior event can significantly influence the kind of interpersonal beliefs people construct, the kind of plans they formulate, and the way they actually behave in face-to-face encounters.

In terms of the AIM, these mood effects on beliefs and behavior can be explained as due to the operation of affect-priming mechanisms. Thinking about and planning a bargaining encounter is by definition a complex and indeterminate cognitive task requiring substantive processing. Positive mood should produce more optimistic beliefs and expectations and more cooperative expected and actual bargaining strategies as a result of the selective priming and greater use of positively valenced information. In contrast, negative mood should prime more pessimistic, negative beliefs and associations, leading to less ambitious goals and less cooperative and successful bargaining strategies.

Further experiments in this series showed, however, that these mood effects were reduced for individuals who scored high on individual differences measures such as machiavellianism and need for approval. In terms of the AIM, these individuals should have approached the bargaining task and formulated beliefs from a more predetermined, motivated perspective, that limited the degree of open, constructive processing they employed, and thus reduced the effects of affect infusion on their behaviors. These results suggests that individual differences may significantly mediate the extent to which affective states are likely to infuse thoughts, beliefs, goal-setting and strategic behaviors (Mayer & Salovey, 1988; Rusting, 1997).

Summary and conclusions

This chapter argued that the infusion of affect into cognitive processes and beliefs is highly process dependent, and predominantly occurs in the course of constructive, substantive processing that allows the incorporation of affectively primed thoughts and associations into the beliefs constructed. In contrast, more controlled, directed processing strategies such as motivated processing and direct-access processing tend to be impervious to affect-infusion effects. The Affect Infusion Model (AIM; Forgas, 1995a) highlights the role of different processing strategies in mediating affect infusion into beliefs and cognition. The first part of this chapter reviewed the considerable empirical evidence now available suggesting that even low-key, temporary moods can produce significant mood-congruent cognitive biases in beliefs and judgments. Happy persons are more likely to notice, encode, remember and use positively valenced information in constructing their beliefs and cognitive representations, while those in a negative mood are more likely to recall and focus on negatively valenced materials (Bower, 1981; Forgas, 1995a). Furthermore, considerable evidence suggests that these affect-infusion effects are most likely to occur in circumstances when people adopt an open, constructive processing strategy.

Several experiments also document the highly significant influence that moods can play in the way people construct and maintain beliefs about social situations, the kinds of goals and plans they formulate, and ultimately, the way they execute strategic social behaviors. The cognitive consequences of moods thus also extend to behavioral outcomes. Mood effects were demonstrated on the formulation of, and responses, to requests (Forgas, 1998b,c; 1999b), the planning and execution of strategic negotiations (Forgas, 1998a), and the monitoring and interpretation of complex interactive behaviors (Forgas, 1994; Forgas *et al.*, 1984, 1990).

However, affect infusion and mood congruence are by no means universal phenomena. In the second part of the chapter extensive evidence was reviewed indicating that in many circumstances, more conscious and motivated processing strategies may be adopted by people, leading to affect-incongruent cognitive outcomes. These mental strategies are usually characterized by a degree of targeted, directed thinking that is frequently triggered by a specific motivational goal. Increasing awareness of a person's affective state is often a sufficient condition for motivated thinking to be triggered. Most of the previous literature looked at affect infusion and affect control as distinct, dissociated cognitive strategies. In contrast, the Affect Infusion Model (Forgas, 1995a) suggests that these may be complementary processing strategies, selectively recruited in predictable – and testable – situational and psychological circumstances. Indeed, it may be that affect and infusion and affect control may operate in conjunction, representing complementary aspects of an automatic, homeostatic affect-management system. As negative affect produces negative thoughts and beliefs, once a threshold level of negativity is reached, a complementary affect-control strategy may be triggered, designed to reduce affective extremity to manageable levels. Several experiments illustrate the spontaneous recovery from aversive moods by people activating targeted, mood-incongruent thoughts, beliefs and behaviors (Berkowitz & Troccoli, 1990; Forgas & Ciarrochi, 1999; Sedikides, 1994). It now seems that a comprehensive theory of affect infusion also needs to take explicit account of the critical importance of motivated affect-regulation mechanisms.

Individual differences are also likely to play a significant role in affect infusion into beliefs, and the way different processing strategies are adopted by different people. There is some early evidence indicating that a habitual tendency to engage in motivated processing may be indicated by high scores on such characteristics as self-esteem or trait anxiety. It is also likely that the extent to which different people will tolerate affective fluctuations in their thoughts and beliefs may be somewhat idiosyncratic. One promising future line of research might address the role of individual variables in mediating affect sensitivity in cognition and beliefs (Rusting, 1997).

We started this discussion by suggesting that beliefs are highly personal, subjective and idiosyncratic creations (Heider, 1958; Kelly, 1955). It is hardly surprising then that fluctuations in daily mood can have such a delicate, subtle and ongoing influence on the kind of beliefs people formulate, access and use in charting their daily behaviors. We may conclude by observing that the critical link between affect and beliefs is the kind of information processing strategy people adopt to deal with a particular situation. Enduring differences in affectivity between people, or "temperament," are also an essential aspect of the affect/cognition interface (Mayer & Salovey, 1988; Rusting, 1997; Salovey & Mayer, 1990). A comprehensive theory of affect infusion would clearly benefit from greater attention to such individual difference variables. We hope that this chapter will help to generate further interest in this exciting and rapidly developing field.

Note

[1] Work on this chapter was supported by the Research Prize from the Alexander von Humboldt Foundation, Germany, and by a Special Investigator Award from the Australian Research Council. Please address all correspondence in connection with this chapter to Joseph P. Forgas, School of Psychology, University of New South Wales, Sydney 2052; email *JP.Forgas@unsw.edu.au*; internet: http://www.psy.unsw.edu.au/~joef/jforgas.htm.

References

Ajzen, I. (1995). Beliefs. In A. S. R. Manstead & M. Hewstone (Eds.) *The Blackwell encyclopaedia of social psychology* (pp. 88–89). Oxford: Blackwell.

Asch, S. E. (1946). Forming impressions of personality. *Journal of Abnormal and Social Psychology, 41*, 258–290.

Baron, R. (1987). Interviewers' moods and reactions to job applicants: The influence of affective states on applied social judgments. *Journal of Applied Social Psychology, 16*, 911–926.

Berkowitz, L., Jaffee, S. Jo, E. & Troccoli, T. (in press). On the correction of feeling-induced judgmental biases. In J. P. Forgas (Ed.), *Feeling and thinking: Affective influences on social cognition*. New York: Cambridge University Press.

Berkowitz, L., & Troccoli, B. T. (1990). Feelings, direction of attention, and expressed evaluations of others. *Cognition and Emotion, 4*, 305–325.

Blaney, P. H. (1986). Affect and memory: A review. *Psychological Bulletin, 99*, 229–246.

Bower, G. H. (1981). Mood and memory. *American Psychologist, 36*, 129–148.

Bower, G. H. (1991). Mood congruity of social judgments. In J. P. Forgas (Ed.), *Emotion and social judgments* (pp. 31–53). Elmsford, NY: Pergamon Press.

Bower, G. H., & Forgas, J. P. (in press). Affect, memory and social cognition. In E. Eich (Ed.), *Counterpoints: Cognition and emotion*. Oxford: Oxford University Press.

Ciarrochi, J. V., & Forgas, J. P. (1999a). On being tense yet tolerant: The paradoxical effects of aversive mood and trait anxiety on intergroup judgments. Manuscript under review.

Ciarrochi, J.V. & Forgas, J.P. (1999b) The pleasure of possessions: Mood effects on consumer judgments. Manuscript under review.

Clark, M. S., & Isen, A. M. (1982). Towards understanding the relationship between feeling states and social behavior. In A. H. Hastorf & A. M. Isen (Eds.), *Cognitive social psychology* (pp. 73–108). Amsterdam: Elsevier/North-Holland.

Clore, G. L., & Parrott, G. (1991). Moods and their vicissitudes: Thoughts and feelings as information. In J. P. Forgas (Ed.), *Emotion and social judgments* (pp. 109–123). Elmsford, NY: Pergamon Press.

Clore, G. L., Schwarz, N., & Conway, M. (1994). Affective causes and consequences of social information processing. In R. S. Wyer & T. K. Srull (Eds.), *Handbook of social cognition*. 2nd ed. (Vol. 1, pp. 323–419). Hillsdale, NJ: Erlbaum.

Costa, P. T., & McCrae, R. R. (1985). *The NEO Personality Inventory Manual*. Odesa, FA: Psychological Assessment Resources.

Croyle, R. T., & Uretsky, M. B. (1987). Effects of mood on self-appraisal of health status. *Health Psychology, 6*, 239–253.

Eich, E. E. & Macauley, D. (in press). Fundamental factors in mood dependent memory. In J. P. Forgas (Ed.), *Feeling and thinking: Affective influences on social cognition*. New York: Cambridge University Press.

Erber, R., & Erber, M. (1994). Beyond mood and social judgment: Mood incongruent recall and mood regulation. *European Journal of Social Psychology, 24*, 79–88.

Fiedler, K. (1990). Mood-dependent selectivity in social cognition. In W. Stroebe & M. Hewstone (Eds.), *European review of social psychology* (Vol. 1, pp. 1–32). New York: Wiley.

Fiedler, K. (1991). On the task, the measures and the mood in research on affect and social cognition. In J. P. Forgas (Ed.), *Emotion and social judgments* (pp. 83–104). Elmsford, NY: Pergamon Press.

Fiedler, K., & Forgas, J. P. (1988) (Eds.), *Affect, cognition, and social behavior: New evidence and integrative attempts* (pp. 44–62). Toronto: Hogrefe.

Forgas, J. P. (1989). Mood effects on decision-making strategies. *Australian Journal of Psychology, 41*, 192–214.

Forgas J. P. (1990). Affective influences on individual and group judgments. *European Journal of Social Psychology, 20*, 441–453.

Forgas, J. P. (1991a). Mood effects on partner choice: Role of affect in social decisions. *Journal of Personality and Social Psychology, 61*, 708–720.

Forgas, J. P. (Ed.). (1991b). *Emotion and social judgments*. Elmsford, NY: Pergamon Press.

Forgas, J. P. (1992a). Affect in social judgments and decisions: A multi-process model. In M. P. Zanna (Ed.), *Advances in experimental social psychology* (Vol. 25, pp. 227–275). San Diego, CA: Academic Press.

Forgas, J. P. (1992b). On bad mood and peculiar people: Affect and person typicality in impression formation. *Journal of Personality and Social Psychology, 62*, 863–875.

Forgas, J. P. (1993). On making sense of odd couple: Mood effects on the perception of mismatched relationships. *Personality and Social Psychology Bulletin, 19*, 59–71.

Forgas, J. P. (1994). Sad and guilty? Affective influences on the explanation of conflict episodes. *Journal of Personality and Social Psychology, 66*, 56–68.

Forgas, J. P. (1995a). Mood and judgment: The affect infusion model (AIM). *Psychological Bulletin, 117(1)*, 39–66.

Forgas, J. P. (1995b). Strange couples: Mood effects on judgments and memory about prototypical and atypical targets. *Personality and Social Psychology Bulletin, 21*, 747–765.

Forgas, J. P. (1998a). On feeling good and getting your way: Mood effects on negotiation strategies and outcomes. *Journal of Personality and Social Psychology, 74*, 565–577.

Forgas, J. P. (1998b). Asking nicely? Mood effects on responding to more or less polite requests. *Personality and Social Psychology Bulletin, 24*, 173–185.

Forgas, J. P. (1998c). Happy and mistaken? Mood effects on the fundamental attribution error. *Journal of Personality and Social Psychology, 75*, 318–331.

Forgas, J. P. (1999a). Feeling and speaking: Mood effects on verbal communication strategies. *Personality and Social Psychology Bulletin, 25, 75*, 850–863.

Forgas, J. P. (1999b). On feeling good and being rude: Affective influences on language use and request formulations. *Journal of Personality and Social Psychology, 76*, 928–939.

Forgas, J. P., & Bower, G. H. (1987). Mood effects on person-perception judgments. *Journal of Personality and Social Psychology, 53(1)*, 53–60.

Forgas, J. P. & Bower, G. H. (1988). Affect in social and personal judgments. In K. Fiedler & J. P. Forgas (Eds.), *Affect, cognition and social behavior*. Toronto: Hogrefe.

Forgas, J. P., Bower, G. H., & Krantz, S. (1984). The influence of mood on perceptions of social interactions. *Journal of Experimental Social Psychology, 20*, 497–413.

Forgas, J. P., Bower, G. H., & Moylan, S. J. (1990). Praise or blame? Affective influences in attributions for achievement. *Journal of Personality and Social Psychology, 59*, 809–818.

Forgas, J. P., & Ciarrochi, J. (1999). Mood congruent and incongruent thoughts over time: The role of self-esteem in mood management efficacy. Manuscript submitted for publication.

Forgas, J. P., & Fiedler, K. (1996). Us and them: Mood effects on intergroup discrimination. *Journal of Personality and Social Psychology, 70*, 36–52.

Forgas, J. P., Johnson, R., & Ciarrochi, J. (1998). Mood management: The role of processing strategies in affect control and affect infusion. In M. Kofta, G. Weary, & G. Sedek (Eds.), *Personal control in action: Cognitive and motivational mechanisms* (pp. 155–185). New York: Plenum Press.

Forgas, J. P., Levinger, G., & Moylan, S. J. (1994). Feeling good and feeling close: Affective influences on the perception of intimate relationships. *Personal Relationships, 1*, 165–184.

Forgas, J. P., & Moylan, S. J. (1987). After the movies: The effects of transient mood states on social judgments. *Personality and Social Psychology Bulletin, 13*, 478–489.

Forgas, J. P., & Moylan, S. (1991). Affective influences on stereotype judgments. *Cognition and Emotion, 5*, 379–397.

Freud, S. (1915). *The unconscious* (Vol. XIV). London: Hogarth Press.

Haddock, G., Zanna. M. P., & Esses, V. M. (1994). Mood and the expression of intergroup attitudes: The moderating role of affect intensity. *European Journal of Social Psychology, 24*, 189–206.

Heider, F. (1958). *The psychology of interpersonal relations.* New York: John Wiley.

Kelly, G. A. (1955). *The psychology of personal constructs.* New York: Norton.

Kunda, Z. (1990). The case for motivated reasoning. *Psychological Bulletin, 108*, 331–350.

Loftus, E. (1979). *Eyewitness testimony.* Cambridge, MA: MIT Press.

Martin, L., Seta, J., & Crelia, R. (1990). Assimilation and contrast as a function of people's willingness and ability to expend effort in forming an impression. *Journal of Personality and Social Psychology, 59*, 27–37.

Mayer, J. D., Gaschke, Y. N., Braverman, D. L., & Evans T. W. (1992). Mood congruent judgment is a general effect. *Journal of Personality and Social Psychology, 63*, 119–132.

Mayer, J., McCormick, L., & Strong, S. (1995). Mood-congruent memory and natural mood: New evidence. *Personality and Social Psychology Bulletin, 21*, 736–746.

Mayer, J. D., & Salovey, P. (1988). Personality moderates the interaction of mood on cognition. In K. Fiedler & J. P. Forgas (Eds.), *Affect, cognition, and social behavior* (pp. 87–99). Gottingen: Hogrefe.

Parrott, W. G. (1993). Beyond Hedonism: Motives for inhibiting good moods and for maintaining bad moods. In D. M. Wegner & J. W. Pennebaker (Eds.), *Handbook of mental control* (pp. 278–305). Englewood Cliffs, NJ: Prentice Hall.

Rusting, C. L. (1997). Interactive effects of personality and mood on judgment and recall. Manuscript submitted for publication.

Salovey, P., & Birnbaum, D. (1989). Influence of mood on health-related cognitions. *Journal of Personality and Social Psychology, 57*, 539–551.

Salovey, P., & Mayer, J. D. (1990). Emotional intelligence. *Imagination, Cognition, and Personality, 9*, 185–211.

Salovey, P., O'Leary, A., Stretton, M., Fishkin, S., & Drake, C. A. (1991). Influence of mood on judgments about health and illness. In J. P. Forgas (Ed.), *Emotion and social judgments* (pp. 241–262). Elmsford, NY: Pergamon Press.

Schwarz, N. (1990). Feelings as information: Informational and motivational functions of affective states. In E. T. Higgins & R. Sorrentino (Eds.), *Handbook of motivation and cognition: Foundations of social behavior* (Vol. 2, pp. 527–561). New York: Guilford Press.

Schwarz, N., & Clore, G. L. (1988). How do I feel about it? The informative function of affective states. In K. Fiedler & J. P. Forgas (Eds.), *Affect, cognition and social behavior.* (pp. 44–62). Toronto: Hogrefe.

Sedikides, C. (1992). Changes in the valence of self as a function of mood. *Review of Personality and Social Psychology, 14*, 271–311.

Sedikides, C. (1994). Incongruent effects of sad mood on self-conception valence: It's a matter of time. *European Journal of Social Psychology, 24*, 161–172.

Sedikides, C. (1995). Central and peripheral self-conceptions are differentially influenced by mood: Tests of the differential sensitivity hypothesis. *Journal of Personality and Social Psychology, 69(4)*, 759–777.

Smith, S. M., & Petty, R. E. (1995). Personality moderators of mood congruence effects on cognition: The role of self-esteem and negative mood regulation. *Journal of Personality and Social Psychology, 68*, 1092–1107.

Srull, T. K. (1984). The effects of subjective affective states on memory and judgment. In T. Kinnear (Ed.), *Advances in consumer research* (Vol. 11, pp. 530–533). Provo, UT: Association for Consumer Research.

Steele, C. M., Spencer, S. J., & Lynch, M. (1993). Self-image and dissonance: The role of affirmational resources. *Journal of Personality and Social Psychology, 64*, 885–896.

Wegner, D. M., & Erber, R. (1993). Social foundations of mental control. In D. M. Wegner & J. W. Pennebaker (Eds.), *Handbook of mental control* (pp. 36–56). Englewood Cliffs, NJ: Prentice Hall.

6

The formation of beliefs at the interface of affective and cognitive processes[1]

Klaus Fiedler and Herbert Bless

In all the huge and wide-spread literature on the psychology of cognition and emotion, there is almost no reference to research on beliefs. To be sure, countless articles have been concerned with affective influences on memory, thinking, social judgment (Clore, Schwarz & Conway, 1994; Forgas, 1995; Isen, 1984), and other "close relatives" of beliefs. However, hardly anybody has directly addressed that class of cognitive states that are usually referred to as beliefs. In the present chapter, we are going to argue that, in spite of this neglect, beliefs should be particularly sensitive to affective influences. Indeed, one might pretend that they are located at the very interface of emotion and cognition, characterized by all the conditions under which modern research predicts a strong impact of mood states on cognition.

So what are the defining features of beliefs and why are they supposed to be especially sensitive to emotional influence? Defining features are idiomatic in everyday language. One most common distinction is between *believing and knowing*. Believing presupposes not having perfect knowledge but taking some risk and adding some internally generated inference in adopting an idea, goal, or argument. A second distinction is between *believing and saying*. In everyday language, to believe means not only saying something publicly, not just paying lip-service for the sake of compliance or social desirability, but refers to an authentic, privately held attitude. In other words, the person who believes in an idea has been really convinced and not only yielded to public pressure. The third distinction is related but not equivalent. *Believing is not to distrust* a provider of new information, but to take the truth and validity of social communication for granted. Validity is attributed not only to the contents of a message but to social interaction partners as well. Fourth, and finally, the semantic surplus meaning of believing points to actively construed cognition under high involvement and cooperation, but is *not applicable to passively held or tolerated information.*

144

Assimilation versus accommodation

At a more general level, a common denominator underlying all these distinctive features can be found in Piaget's (1952) dialectic conception of two types of adaptive regulation, assimilation versus accommodation. To make active inferences under uncertainty, to rely on one's internalized knowledge, to be curious and not too cautious, and to actively elaborate on stimuli and structures – all these facets of believing are reminiscent of *assimilation* functions. The organism assimilates the external stimulus world to her own internal structures, rather than being driven or governed by external stimulus constraints. In other words, assimilation can be described as a top-down process by which the individual imposes her cognitive structures and schemata that have been successfully employed to new problems and affordances. This process reflects a good deal of adaptive self-confidence and trust in previously learned knowledge, values, and behavioral strategies. In contrast, the opposite process of *accommodation* is stimulus-driven and characterized by the organism's readiness to react reliably to external demands or threats. Thus, accommodation means sticking to the stimulus facts and updating one's internal structures as a function of external requirements.

Needless to say, successful adaptation in the physical and social world requires both assimilation and accommodation. However, different situations and different mental and emotional states call for different weightings of assimilation and accommodation. If we make a crude distinction between positive, appetitive situations and negative, aversive situations, it seems clear that an adaptive organism should have acquired learning sets that make assimilative processes more likely in appetitive situations, whereas accommodation is called for in aversive settings.

Supportive evidence for this assumption comes from decades of research in the behaviorist tradition, showing that appetitive learning is characterized by exploration behavior, curiosity, self-efficacy and other motives requiring assimilation. Conversely, aversive behavior is driven by cautious attention, extremely reliable and perfect avoidance learning, and sensitive accommodation. This basic distinction of approach and avoidance behavior is also central for modern approaches to social behavior regulation (Higgins, 1996; Higgins, Roney, Crowe & Hymes, 1994).

Our approach to affective-cognitive behavior regulation extends this adaptive heuristic to positive and negative situations, or cues, resulting from internal mood states. Even when the organism does not objectively face a serious aversive threat and even when the situation is not objectively very appetitive, an individual's subjective emotional state may signal a positive or negative situation and, like a conditioned reaction, move the process of behavior regulation in the direction of assimilation or accommodation. In accordance with the general notion above, this means that positive affective states should support assimilation tendencies whereas negative affective states should trigger accommodation processes.

These implications appear fairly straightforward and go but one step beyond the well-known differences between appetitive and aversive behavior. What is more important, these implications are in general agreement with empirical research on affect and cognition. Understanding the cognitive-behavioral consequences of positive and negative mood states in terms of assimilation and accommodation provides an integrated account of this research area, as documented in Forgas's chapter in this volume. Forgas's (1995) Affect Infusion Model (AIM) converges in many respects with the present account, pointing to further mood effects on social judgment and behavior to which the assimilation-accommodation distinction is applicable.

The remainder of this chapter is devoted to illustrating and substantiating this notion. We will first make our theoretical approach to affect and cognition more explicit and distinctive. Having demonstrated that the assimilation-accommodation construct can account for many "classical" findings, we will then present a series of experiments that we ourselves have conducted in testing crucial implications of our theorizing. As it will turn out, a majority of these studies could be reframed as referring to beliefs, conceived as cognitions that involve inference under uncertainty, genuine involvement, active elaboration, and cooperation. As beliefs belong to the domain of assimilation, rather than accommodation, the general conclusion will be that positive mood states serve to support the formation of beliefs at the interface of affect and cognition.

By the way, it may be no coincidence that the four features used to define beliefs in this introduction – inference making, being convinced, trusting, and active elaboration – correspond to four major research topics in the field of affect and cognition: social judgments (Schwarz & Clore, 1988), persuasion (Schwarz, Bless, & Bohner, 1991), pro-social behavior (Isen, 1987; Schaller & Cialdini, 1990), and cognitive styles (Fiedler, 1988; Isen 1987; Isen *et al.* 1982). We will return to these analogies in the following sections, along with particular empirical phenomena. However, let us first delineate our approach and its various testable implications.

Theoretical account

Our whole theorizing revolves around one basic assumption, namely, that positive mood states foster assimilation while negative mood states serve an accommodation function. However, this general statement is too vague to be tested immediately and thus needs some cognitive framework and operational definitions before distinct and original predictions can be derived.

Consider the task of judging someone's credibility. This is an almost ubiquitous social judgment task involved in many everyday encounters, such as accepting advice, lending money, purchasing a used car, hiring a co-worker, or comparing politicians in an election. As in any other cognitive process, there are two components in this judgment process that correspond (no surprise!) to accommodation and assimilation. First, there is the actual stimulus input about the target which provides the data, as it were, for the social judgment. The general term we use for this process component is *conservation*; conservation means keeping a record of whatever data input is perceived in the external world or retrieved from internal memory. Note that optimizing conservative performance means high stimulus fidelity, sticking to the facts, and minimizing information loss, reflecting pure accommodation.

However, any cognitive process involves a second component which is not stimulus-driven but governed by the top-down influence of pre-existing knowledge structures. We use the term *active generation* to express the generative, assimilative functions of this component, such as input transformation, inference making, productive thinking, or creativity. If no such active generation were involved, that is, if the input were merely conserved, we would hardly refer to a cognitive process. Thus, believing our impression of the politician is based on plain facts would be an illusion. We cannot avoid the contribution of prior knowledge and conscious or unconscious inferences even when we try. Even language comprehension (i.e., interpreting the politician's speech) involves active generation beyond mere conservation.

Having established the analytical distinction between two components that are involved in any cognitive process, we can reformulate our central theoretical assumption: *Positive emotional states facilitate active generation, whereas negative emotional states support the conservation of input data.* In other words, positive moods should encourage the application of prior knowledge structures (schemas, stereotypes, scripts) to infer new information beyond the available data. In contrast, negative mood states should induce a conservative set to adhere to the input data as carefully as possible.

The learning framework underlying this central assumption has been outlined above. We assume that the different learning sets that characterize appetitive and aversive settings have been acquired over a long history of ontogenetic and phylogenetic learning. Although the details of this evolution process are unknown, the very existence of such different learning sets is not in question. The only theoretical assumption we have to add is that emotional states – even very mild ones (Isen, 1984) and very subtle mood cues (Fiedler, 1991) – can serve as signals or conditional stimuli that induce the learning sets associated with truly appetitive and aversive situations.

The general notion that affective states inform the organism about adaptive behavior changes is not new but is crucial for leading approaches to emotion (see Frijda, 1986, 1988). For example, individuals' affective states have been conceptualized as "barometers of the ego" (Jacobsen, 1957), as a "source of information" (Nowlis & Nowlis, 1956), or as "monitors" (Pribram, 1970); indeed, Schwarz and Clore (1983, Schwarz, 1990) have explicitly linked the notion of "mood as information" to the information processing paradigm.

How can these abstract ideas be translated to concrete behavioral measures? With respect to our example, credibility judgment, the implications are fairly obvious. People in negative states should be more cautious, suspicious and careful than elated people in judging the truth. The emphasis they place on conservation should lead to a detailed observation process, longer hesitation before making a decision, a final decision that is highly predictable from the stimulus input, and a rather systematic diagnosis. Conversely, decisions made in a positive mood should be faster, more detached from stimulus constraints, and more prone to knowledge-based inferences (e.g., stereotypes based on the target's appearance); elated people might alternatively employ an unconventional concept of truth (e.g., one that is more tolerant of kidding, irony, fabulation, and other "soft" variants of deception).

The empirical literature on affect and social judgment provides rich support for the above sketch. There is wide agreement across numerous studies that negative affect induces a detailed and systematic processing style and increases the correspondence between the stimulus input and resulting judgments or decisions (for overviews see Clore et al., 1994; Fiedler, 1988; Forgas, 1995; Isen et al., 1982, 1987). In contrast, positive mood encourages spontaneous decisions detached from stimulus constraints, inferences beyond the information given, and creative and unconventional problem solving (see Isen, 1987; Forgas, this volume).

Thus, our assimilation-accommodation account is consistent with the different processing styles of people in positive and negative moods. Let us now turn to the other central research topic, mood congruency (Bower, 1981; Blaney, 1986). People in a good mood tend to recall more pleasant stimuli, whereas a sad mood gives a relative advantage to unpleasant stimuli. However, this congruency effect is not symmetrical; it is more pronounced in positive than in negative mood (Isen, 1984), presumably because motivated processes (mood repair) work against congruency in negative states.

This basic asymmetry mirrors the asymmetry of the two cognitive process components. While the conservative accommodation component is by definition stimulus-driven and therefore non-selective, any selective influence coming from internal affective states is due to the generative functions of the assimilation component. After all, the mood-congruency bias does not originate in the objective stimulus input itself but in the active cognitive processes applied to encoding and processing this input. Granting that positive mood supports this active process component, it follows that congruency effects are stronger in positive than in negative mood states.

The same associative rules that underlie the basic congruency effect imply that the activation of knowledge structures for the active elaboration stage should also tend to be mood congruent. Thus, in positive mood states, positively toned knowledge structures should be more likely to be activated than aversive structures, thereby embedding the stimulus input in numerous mood-congruent associations. This contribution to mood congruency should be much weaker in negative moods, simply because cognitive elaboration is less likely. In this way, the proposed model accounts for both the influence of emotional states on cognitive style and the typically asymmetric mood-congruency effect.

Empirical test of distinct theoretical implications

Several other recent approaches to affect and cognition (Forgas, this volume; Martin & Clore, 1999; Wegener, Petty, & Smith, 1995; Schwarz, 1990; Schwarz & Bless, 1991) converge with the present theory in many respects. There is wide agreement on the main empirical findings. However, some of these models' implications are radically different, offering quite different attributions for the same empirical phenomena. Thus, the processing style under positive mood that we have characterized as assimilation has been interpreted in terms of reduced cognitive effort (Schwarz, 1990), as peripheral (vs. central) processing (Wegener, Petty, & Smith, 1995), or as a consequence of reduced mental capacity during positive affective states (Mackie & Worth, 1989).

These conceptions not only differ in the wordings used to characterize creativity under positive mood as compared with careful processing under negative mood. They also differ in their basic assumptions about the nature of mood effects. The notion of assimilation implies that positive affective states elicit active cognitive processes. This assumption is in sharp contrast to the notion of reduced effort under positive mood or the assumption of superficial heuristic processes. To set the present approach apart from other theoretical positions, the following points should be kept in mind: (1) the congruency effect and the creative style that characterize people in positive mood states are not attributed to reduced capacity. (2) The effects of positive mood are not reduced to strategic effort reduction aimed at maintaining one's pleasant emotional state. (3) Positive mood effects on social judgment are not reduced to shallow response tendencies but originate in genuine memory processes. Finally (4) the notion of assimilation versus accommodation leads to several distinct predictions that could not be derived from any of the other approaches (see below). Let us now turn to an examination of empirical findings that speak to the predictions. While these findings have been obtained in different paradigms using different methods and procedures, they all provide convergent operations for measuring assimilation versus accommodation. Moreover, the set of reviewed findings will relate affective states to the defining features of beliefs (i.e., uncertainty, genuine involvement, cooperation, and active elaboration).

Empirical evidence

Affect, beliefs, and stereotypical expectations

According to the considerations outlined above, happy individuals should be more likely to rely on their general beliefs than sad individuals. We apply this general prediction to two different forms of beliefs, scripts (i.e., beliefs about the sequence and content of social events), and stereotypes (i.e., beliefs about social groups). In each case, we will first report evidence suggesting that (a) happy individuals are more likely than sad individuals to rely on general knowledge structures, and (b) that this is associated with active information processing rather than mere simplification or effort reduction.

Mood and scripts

In a series of studies, Bless and colleagues (Bless, Clore, Schwarz, Golisano, Rabe & Wölk, 1996) presented participants in different affective states with tape-recorded information about well-known activities (e.g., "going out for dinner"), for which they were likely to have a well-developed script (Abelson, 1981; Graesser, Gordon, & Sawyer, 1979). Some of this information was script-typical whereas other information was script-atypical. After a delay, participants received a surprise recognition test, assessing their memory for the daily activities information presented to them.

The analysis of participants' recognition performance revealed that happy participants were more likely than sad participants to recognize *typical* information as having been presented. However, they were also more likely to erroneously recognize typical behaviors that were not presented, resulting in a higher rate of intrusion errors (see Graesser *et al.*, 1979). Presumably, happy participants were more likely to rely on the script which allows individuals to infer script-typical behaviors, resulting in good recognition of typical behaviors that were actually presented as well as erroneous recognition of script-typical behaviors that were not presented. The mood effects on participants' recognition were restricted to typical information and were not obtained for *atypical* information that could not be derived from the script. Note that this differential pattern for typical and atypical information rules out an alternative explanation based on a mood-dependent tendency to give yes or no responses in general.

While participants were listening to the tape-recorded stories they were working on a *secondary task*. This secondary task was designed to assess participants' free resources (Macrae, Milne, & Bodenhausen, 1994; Navon & Gopher, 1979), and allowed us to tackle the question of whether or not happy participants' reliance on the script was caused by happy moods reducing processing resources. If happy individuals' reliance on general knowledge structures is due to motivational or capacity constraints, these constraints should influence performance on the secondary task. Thus, happy individuals should show poorer performance than sad individuals. What, however, if happy individuals rely on general knowledge structures for other reasons than reduced resources, as we suspect? In this case, their reliance on a script should simplify the processing of script-related information, thus making the primary task less taxing (cf. Macrae *et al.*, 1994). If so, happy people – who are assumed to rely on the script – should have more resources available to allocate to the secondary task. Accordingly, they should perform better on this task than sad individuals, in contrast to the predictions made by reduced processing assumptions.

The results confirm this prediction. Happy participants showed *better* performance on the secondary task than either sad or neutral mood participants. These findings suggest that happy participants' reliance on knowledge structures does not serve the function of laziness and reduced effort but enables them to allocate additional resources to the secondary task, resulting in improved performance.

Consistent with this interpretation, happy participants' advantage on the secondary task decreased with the amount of script-inconsistent information. Apparently, increasing the amount of atypical information decreased the resources that could be set free by relying on the script. Note, however, that mood states did not affect performance in a control condition in which the secondary task was the only task. This rules out a direct influence of mood on the secondary task.

In sum, these findings support the basic assumption that happy moods facilitate assimilation based on general knowledge structures. While this general conclusion is consistent with previous theorizing, the findings indicate that increased reliance on general knowledge structures is not *necessarily* accompanied by deficits in processing motivation or processing capacity.

Mood and stereotyping

Applying our general assumption to the impact of stereotyping on information processing, we should expect happy individuals to be more strongly influenced by stereotypes than sad individuals. A number of studies have explored the impact of moods on social stereotyping, and allow for a test of this prediction. For example, Bodenhausen, Kramer, and Süsser (1994; see also Bodenhausen, 1993) presented participants in different mood states with descriptions of an alleged student misconduct and asked participants to determine the target's guilt. Happy participants rated the offender as more guilty when he was identified as a member of a group that is stereotypically associated with the described offense than participants in a sad mood did. Similarly, Edwards and Weary (1993) reported converging evidence based on naturally depressed moods. Non-depressed participants were more likely to rely on category membership information than depressed participants, who were more strongly influenced by individuating information about the target. One might conjecture that happy individuals' increased reliance on stereotypes does not necessarily result from the assimilative processes we have outlined above, but could just as well stem from superficial processing (cf. Fiske & Neuberg, 1990). However, additional evidence pertaining to the impact of stereotype-inconsistent information renders the latter possibility rather unlikely. If happy mood indeed increases a superficial processing style (due either to limited capacity or to limited motivation), stereotypes should simply serve as peripheral cues that simplify the task. If so, specific information about the target is less likely to be elaborated. As a consequence, judgments should be independent of whether stereotype-consistent or stereotype-inconsistent individuating information is provided. Happy individuals may either not detect, or may simply ignore, the discrepant information. Hence, their judgments should only reflect category membership information, but not individuating information.

In contrast, different predictions result from the assumption that happy mood increases assimilative processes. In this case, individuals' encoding of new individuating information should be guided by the beliefs entailed in the activated stereotype. Inconsistent information is unlikely to go unnoticed – at least if sufficient processing resources are available. Dealing with stereotype-inconsistent information requires considerable cognitive resources (see Macrae, Hewstone, & Griffiths, 1993; Stangor & Duan, 1991; see also Fiske & Taylor, 1991; Srull & Wyer, 1989). Thus, observing a more pronounced impact of stereotype-inconsistent information under happy rather than sad mood conditions would argue against the assumption that being in a happy mood merely reduces processing capacity or processing motivation.

Bless, Schwarz, and Wieland (1996) tested these considerations by exploring the impact of moods under conditions where the individuating information is either consistent or inconsistent with the implications of the stereotype. Under conditions where the individuating information was *consistent* with the implications of the stereotype, the results replicated previous findings: happy participants provided stereotypical judgments, whereas sad participants did not. Most importantly, the findings for stereotype-*inconsistent* information suggest that happy participants' stereotypical beliefs led to deeper processing of discrepant information, rather than merely using them as a device to simplify their judgment (for more details, see Bless *et al.*, 1996).

Taken together, the evidence on both types of knowledge structures, scripts and stereotypes, suggests that happy, but not sad moods facilitate assimilative functions. Moreover, happy participants' enhanced performance on secondary tasks, and their particular attention to stereotype-inconsistent information, imply that their reliance on general knowledge is not due to processing deficits. Rather, it appears that happy individuals are actively using their prior beliefs for creative, assimilative functions.

Mood and persuasion revisited

As already mentioned, there is substantial evidence in the persuasion domain that happy individuals are less dependent on the quality of the provided arguments of a persuasive message than individuals in a neutral (Worth & Mackie, 1987) or sad (Bless, Bohner, Schwarz, & Strack, 1990; Bless, Mackie, & Schwarz, 1992) mood. Conversely, happy individuals were found to be more strongly influenced by a peripheral cue (Mackie & Worth, 1989), similar to happy individuals' reliance on stereotypes.

Within dual-process models of attitude change (Chaiken, 1980, 1987; Petty & Cacioppo, 1986), one might suggest that happy individuals were either not motivated or not capable of processing the content of the provided arguments. However, this interpretation deserves a closer look, with respect to both the underlying logic and the empirical evidence. First, it should be acknowledged that the assumption of dual-process models that reduced motivation or capacity decreases the sensitivity to message quality does not logically justify the reverse implication that low motivation or capacity can be inferred from lack of discrimination between strong and weak arguments. The latter finding may be caused by various other factors that trigger heuristic processing (cf. Bless & Schwarz, 1999).

Second, a closer look at the empirical evidence reveals some additional ambiguities. In the persuasion domain, it has been argued that happy participants do not elaborate on the content of the message and miss differences in message quality. Yet, the number of cognitive responses reported by happy and sad subjects is typically the same (e.g., Bless et al., 1990), although the valence of these responses – and the accompanying attitude judgments – reflect message quality for sad recipients, but not for happy recipients. However, the very same happy recipients have been found to differentiate between strong and weak messages (as much as neutral or sad mood participants) when asked to rate the quality of the message (e.g., Bless et al., 1990; Worth & Mackie, 1987). Hence, happy recipients processed message content in sufficient detail and did not lack the necessary capacity or cognitive resources. They simply did not require strong arguments in order to be persuaded. From the present perspective, we assume that recipients could base their *attitude judgments* either on their prior beliefs or on the presented arguments. Presumably, happy recipients relied more strongly on their prior beliefs while sad recipients relied more strongly on the presented arguments. Note that this differential focus does not necessarily imply more or less information processing. For evaluating the *strength of the presented arguments*, all participants had to rely on the provided information. As a consequence, any differences between happy and sad participants disappeared.

Third, in several studies (e.g., Bless et al., 1990) happy, neutral and sad mood participants did not differ in their ability to recall the content of a persuasive message, despite the usual differences in attitude judgments. Similarly in person perception, happy and sad participants' recall for individuating information did not differ, despite the enhanced reliance on stereotypes in positive mood (Bless *et al.*, 1996). If being happy decreases the amount of processing, however, we should expect a corresponding effect on recall. In any case, the lack of cogent evidence for happy moods decreasing the amount of systematic processing in persuasion provides a problem for dual-process models but not for the present theoretical approach.

Affect, priming, and dispositional inferences

The elementary paradigm of a category activation is priming. If it is the case that positive mood supports top-down processing based on activated knowledge structures, as we are proposing, then we should also expect stronger priming effects on social inference tasks under positive than negative mood. Note that the priming paradigm allows for deliberate manipulation of specific knowledge structures, whereas the knowledge employed in stereotyping and persuasion is not under experimental control. Supportive evidence for mood-dependent priming comes from Bless and Fiedler (1995) who presented their participants with a series of behaviors (verbs) and traits (adjectives) along with the task of confirming or disconfirming whether each attribute applies to a well-known person. The latency required for this decision was measured. When a semantically matched trait category (e.g., aggressive) had been judged (primed) a few trials before, the latency to make a decision about a subsequent corresponding behavior item (to attack) was reduced. As predicted, this facilitation effect was more pronounced in positive than negative mood (see upper part of Fig. 6.1).

However, importantly, this result is only obtained when the assimilative component governs the task (i.e, making an inference about a person). If the very same stimulus series is used (list of adjectives and verbs), but the assimilative task is turned into a purely accommodative, conservative task (deciding whether the current target word was among the last five stimuli), then the priming advantage of positive mood disappears. Instead, there is an advantage of the negative-mood condition, since the task relies on conservation of stimulus input and priming of semantically related categories can interfere with the task of differentiating present and absent stimuli (see lower part of Fig. 6.1).

Latency z transformed

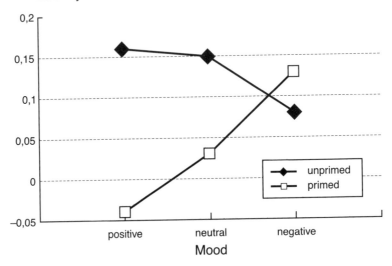

Latency z transformed

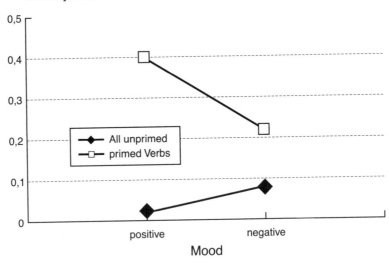

Figure 6.1 Positive mood reinforces priming effects on generative inference tasks (upper chart), whereas negative mood reinforces priming effects on conservative tasks (lower chart). Note that latencies may be lower in absolute terms for unprimed than for primed words, due to the use of different word categories.

Affect and memory for self-generated information

Most of the findings reviewed so far stem from social psychological experiments concerned with social judgment and stereotyping. The focus of these studies was clearly on mood-dependent cognitive styles. The central message was that cognitive processes under positive mood are not at all restricted by a lack of capacity or motivation but, on the contrary, are characterized by an increase of inferential and constructive activities.

In the present section, we shift the focus to mood-congruency effects obtained in experimental memory research. If the influence of positive mood reflects genuine assimilation effects rather than heuristic attempts to reduce cognitive effort, this should be evident in specific measures of memory performance. Indeed, some of the most distinctive predictions can be tested in memory tasks that call for varying degrees of cognitive elaboration. Our theory predicts superior performance in positive mood when the task calls for high inferential activities – contrary to the notion of reduced effort or capacity. One prominent paradigm in memory research that lends itself to a straightforward test of this prediction is the so-called generation effect (Dosher & Russo, 1976; Fiedler, Lachnit, Fay & Krug, 1992; Slamecka & Graf, 1978), referring to the memory advantage of self-generated as compared with experimenter-provided information. Participants are presented with complete stimuli (words, pictures) on some trials but they have to generate, or infer, the meaning of incomplete stimuli (words with missing letters, fragments of pictures) on other trials. Performance on a subsequent memory test is typically higher for self-generated than for experimenter-provided stimuli. Because the generation advantage is obviously due to elaborative encoding (Hirshman & Bjork, 1988), it relies on assimilative functions. The task is not confined to learning what the experimenter forces the participants to see for sure but extends to learning what they believe they see. A distinct prediction of our theory is that positive mood should reinforce the generation effect (i.e., increase the advantage of self-generated information). Moreover, because the knowledge structures activated in positive moods are also likely to be positive as well, this enhancement of the generation effect should interact with stimulus valence. Whereas positive mood should facilitate the generation of positive links, it should not facilitate, or even inhibit, the generation of negative links.

Note that these predictions provide a cogent test of the present theory, for several reasons. First, active generation trials are experienced as more difficult and effortful than the passive "read" trials.

Improved performance under positive mood is therefore incompatible with an interpretation in terms of effortless, shallow processing, or reduced capacity. Second, the generation effect paradigm allows for a within-subjects test; active generation trials call for assimilation whereas passive read trials call for accommodation to experimenter-provided stimuli. Such a within-subjects test rules out any interpretation in terms of cognitive capacity or motivational states. And third, the predicted interaction of mood and the generation effect is difficult to derive from other theories of affect and cognition.

Fiedler *et al.* (1992: Exp. 4) used a forty-eight-item list of evaluatively neutral stimulus words to be learned in paired-associate paradigm. Half of the target words were presented in complete format while the other half had to be generated from the semantically related paired associate and the first letter of the target word. Prior to the stimulus presentation, participants saw excerpts from two films that had been shown in pretesting to induce elated versus depressed mood states. Regardless of whether "generated" and "presented" trials appeared in blocks of six or alternated, a strong generation advantage was obtained. As predicted on theoretical grounds, this generation was markedly enhanced by positive as compared with negative mood (Fig. 6.2).

In another series of experiments using similar paired-associate learning (Fiedler, Nickel, Asbeck, & Pagel, 2000), the target stimuli were verbs with a clear positive or negative valence. Each stimulus verb was preceded by a semantically related word that served as a cue for generating the stimulus word from the initial letter. As predicted theoretically and as depicted in Figure 6.3, a mood × generation × valence interaction was obtained. Participants in positive mood recalled more positive stimuli that were self-generated, whereas the generation and recall of negative information was apparently hindered by positive mood states. Considered the other way around, the congruency effect in the experiment was largely confined to the self-generated subset of stimuli.

The same three-way interaction, reflecting enhanced mood congruency for self-generated information, was obtained in another experiment (Fiedler, 1991) using pictures as stimuli. The generative task was to construct picture stories from any subset of ten photographs presented on every trial. Stimulus pictures were either positive or negative in valence. After each participant had completed six picture stories, a surprise recall test was administered. In general, there was a huge recall advantage for those pictures that had been integrated in the self-generated stories, as compared with the remaining pictures, thus replicating the basic generation effect. There was also a general,

Recall Proportion

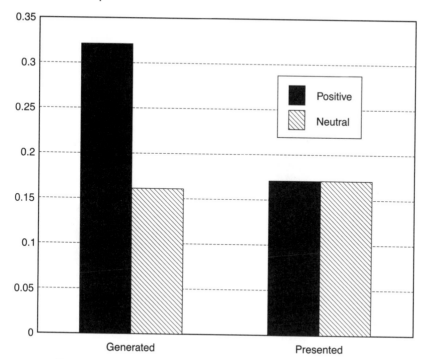

Figure 6.2 The influence of positive versus neutral mood on the generation effect.

asymmetric mood-congruency effect, especially for participants in positive mood. However, most importantly, the three-way interaction involving mood × valence × generation showed that mood congruency was almost totally due to actively elaborated information, and optimal performance was obtained for positive pictures actively elaborated in positive mood states.

Together, the memory findings reported in this section are hardly compatible with the view that positive mood reduces cognitive activities, capacity, and effort expenditure and induces a hedonic set that concentrates on the consumption of a pleasant state. Indeed, virtually no study has ever tested and confirmed the rather popular notion that positive mood reduces cognitive effort and induces laziness. What the present evidence strongly suggests, instead, is that positive mood supports assimilative functions involving high degrees of elaboration and active top-down processing. Positive mood benefits the active generation of powerful higher-order encoding structures that are

Mean Recall Proportion

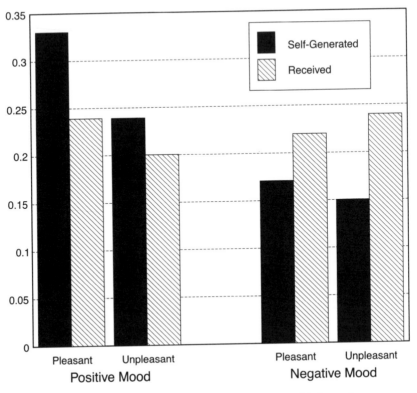

Figure 6.3 Mood congruency and self-generated information.

essential to memory performance. This characterization is consistent
with numerous other findings obtained by other researchers in
various paradigms, suggesting that positive mood increases creativity
(Isen, 1987) and flexibility (Conway, & Giannopoulos, 1993; Hertel &
Fiedler, 1994) and influences performance on unusual, demanding,
non-routine tasks (Forgas 1995). The often-noted heuristic style of
people in a good mood (Schwarz & Clore, 1988) may not reflect
reduced effort or capacity (Bless *et al.*, 1996) but rather result from
assimilative processes relying on internalized structures, analogies
and inference schemas.

Mood congruency as a genuine memory effect

The heuristic approach to affect and cognition (Schwarz & Clore, 1988)
raises the interesting but never properly investigated question of

whether the influence of affect on cognition is mediated by genuine memory effects, as opposed to shallow response tendencies. If social judgments or recall in good mood become more positive in valence than responses in negative mood, this may simply reflect an inclination (desire, motivation, heuristic inference) to present oneself in positive terms, rather than a genuine enhancement of congruent memory contents. The question is whether people are *unable* or simply *unwilling* to reproduce mood-incongruent information.

One methodological tool that could be applied to answer this question is signal detection analysis (Banks, 1970), which offers a rationale for separating genuine memory functions (sensitivity) from response tendencies (bias). This tool has hardly ever been applied in mood and memory research, because it requires a recognition task, which is rather insensitive to mood influences. Parenthetically, the fact that mood-congruency effects are mostly due to free recall and disappear on recognition tests provides further support for the assumption that only the active generation stage (which is prominent in free recall but largely eliminated in recognition) is influenced by selective mood effects.

In a recent investigation (Fiedler, Nickel, Mühlfriedel, & Unkelbach, 2000), we therefore developed a more constructive version of a recognition test which should invite more active inference-making and increase the assimilation component. Rather than merely presenting a recognition stimulus and leaving the judge to make a binary choice (old vs. new), the stimuli were first hidden behind a mask and appeared only gradually over several seconds as the pixels of the mask were removed in a random fashion. Moreover, to invite active inferences and perceptual hypotheses about the appearing stimuli, participants were given a semantically related cue word prior to each recognition trial (e.g., the word "death" before the stimulus "to murder" started to appear from behind the mask).

If our interpretation is correct that positive mood facilitates efficient coding, recoding, and other assimilative functions, and if our suspicion is correct that the missing assimilation component is responsible for the lack of mood congruency in recognition, then we should be able to demonstrate a congruency effect on this modified recognition test. Moreover, the signal detection model should demonstrate that mood states cause genuine memory effects and not just response tendencies.

Thirty positive or negative stimulus verbs were first presented orally. A subsequent memory test comprised the same thirty words, along with thirty semantically matched distracters (one for each stimulus, e.g., to murder and to kill) in order to rule out a purely

Mean Sensitivity d'

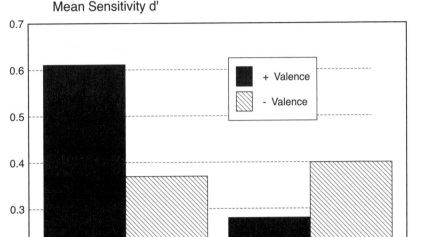

Figure 6.4 Recognition sensitivity (d') as a function of mood and stimulus valence.

familiarity based strategy. At the beginning of each recognition trial, a cue word (e.g., death as a cue for both murder and kill) appeared on the computer screen (i.e., the same cue for the stimulus and the foil in a matched pair). Happy versus sad film excerpts were used for mood induction prior to the recognition test.

Participants were instructed to press one of two response keys as soon as they recognized the gradually appearing word as old or new. This enabled the computation of hit rates (correct recognition of old stimuli) and false alarm rates (erroneous recognition of new foils), separately for positive and negative stimuli and relative to different time windows (i.e., based on responses in the first 40 per cent of total time range, 50 per cent, 60 per cent etc.).

Figure 6.4 shows the mean d' scores (i.e., the actual discrimination performance) for the initial 40 per cent of the recognition process, as a function of mood and stimulus valence. A mood-congruency effect is evident in higher d' values for positive stimuli when participants were in positive mood and a smaller advantage for negative stimuli for people in negative mood. A mood congruency on the ß measure (i.e., the response tendency to say Old on the recognition test) is also obtained, but the nature of this effect cannot be interpreted as a careless tendency to accept any mood-congruent stimulus as recognized. In fact, the response bias effect means that participants (especially those in good mood) are more cautious to confirm the recognition of mood-congruent than mood-incongruent stimuli.

It is interesting to note that these mood influences are almost totally confined to responses given in the initial time window (first 40 per cent) in which the recognition decision had to rely on active inferences and the top-down impact of perceptual hypotheses. In later stages, as more and more stimulus details became visible, that is, as the recognition task mutated from assimilation to accommodation, all mood effects disappeared.

Concluding remarks

There is by now rich empirical evidence that mood and feeling states can influence cognitive performance (mood-congruent memory and judgment) and processing style (creative vs. systematic). At the theoretical level, too, virtually all modern approaches to affect and cognition (cf. Martin & Clore, 1999) converge in emphasizing both a selective function (congruency) and an adaptive regulation function (cognitive style) of emotional states. Thus, the present approach in terms of the assimilation-accommodation distinction might appear to differ from other accounts (Erber & Wang Erber, 1999; Forgas, 1995, this volume; Schwarz, 1998) only at the rhetorical level.

Given this potential of confusion between multiple similar theories, we have made a deliberate attempt to establish convergent and divergent validity for the present theory. On the one hand, we have sought convergent evidence for the claim that positive states support assimilation whereas negative states support accommodation. We have operationalized the relative influence of knowledge-driven assimilation (as opposed to accommodation) functions in many heterogeneous ways: scripts and stereotypes are socially shared knowledge structures that serve to assimilate information about groups. The persuasion paradigm is concerned with the updating of knowledge in the light of new data in social communication. The priming paradigm allows for the experimental control of more specific knowledge categories. The generation effect paradigm applies to self-generated knowledge activation as opposed to experimenter-determined stimulus input. Finally, the modified, constructive recognition task we depicted in the previous section affords still another paradigm to encourage assimilation.

On the other hand, we were concerned not only with convergent validation but also with divergent validity. In doing so, we employed several paradigms that are not common in the affect and cognition literature – such as the generation, priming, dual-task, and recognition paradigms. The purpose here was to demonstrate mood effects on unusual variants of assimilative (vs. accommodative) tasks that could be hardly derived from other models. For example, the original prediction that positive mood enhances the so-called generation effect on memory lies simply outside the domain of theories which assume that positive mood reduces capacity (Mackie & Worth, 1989), that mood states serve informative functions (Schwarz, 1990, 1998), or that mood effects are sensitive to social constraints (Erber & Wang Erber, 1998). However, the effect could be predicted on theoretical grounds from the assumption that self-generated stimulus encoding involves more assimilation (based on internalized knowledge structures) than experimenter-provided stimulus encoding. A similar rationale applies to the interaction of mood with many superficially different but theoretically related knowledge influences, such as scripts, stereotypes, primed categories, or inferences during recognition.

In our attempt to demonstrate that mood-dependent assimilation and accommodation have genuine effects on memory and internal beliefs, not just superficial response tendencies or demand effects, we have employed experimental paradigms that allow for little voluntary control or reflected, tactical, demand-driven responding. Performance on secondary tasks, the generation effect, priming effects on response latencies, or recognition at threshold level are unobtrusive measures, hard to fake, and at a minimal level of consciousness. Thus, the apparently weak or vague notion of assimilation versus accommodation can be tied down to relatively "hard" paradigms that have a clear standing in cognitive psychology.

In closing, we return to the role of beliefs that provided our starting point. Beliefs – defined as inferences based on internalized knowledge, characterized by trust and genuine convictions, and driven by active processes in memory – can be conceived as almost pure agents of assimilation. Positive mood states, due to their assimilative power, increase the reliance on belief systems, especially positive beliefs. However, thanks to the accommodative function of negative affective states, beliefs systems can be updated in the light of new significant data, thus preventing the individual from loosing reality. We believe that this constitutes an important aspect of affective-cognitive behavior regulation.

Note

[1] The reported research was supported by grants from the Deutsche Forschungsgemeinschaft to H. Bless, N. Schwarz, & M. Wänke. Correspondence should be addressed to Klaus Fiedler, Psychologisches Institut, Universität Heidelberg, Hauptstrasse 47–51, D-69117 Heidelberg, Germany, email: kf@psi-sv2.psi.uni-heidelberg.de

References

Abelson, R. P. (1981). The psychological status of the script concept. *American Psychologist, 36,* 715–729.

Banks, W. P. (1970). Signal detection theory and human memory. *Psychological Bulletin, 74,* 81–99.

Blaney, P. H. (1986). Affect and memory: A review. *Psychological Bulletin, 99,* 229–246.

Bless, H., Bohner, G., Schwarz, N., & Strack, F. (1990). Mood and persuasion: A cognitive response analysis. *Personality and Social Psychology Bulletin, 16,* 331–345.

Bless, H., Clore, G., Schwarz, N., Golisano, V., Rabe, C., & Wölk, M. (1996). Mood and the use of scripts: Does happy mood make people really mindless? *Journal of Personality and Social Psychology, 71,* 665–679.

Bless, H., & Fiedler, K. (1995). Affective states and the influence of activated general knowledge structures. *Personality and Social Psychology Bulletin, 21,* 766–778.

Bless, H., Mackie, D. M., & Schwarz, N. (1992). Mood effects on encoding and judgmental processes in persuasion. *Journal of Personality and Social Psychology, 63,* 585–595.

Bless, H., & Schwarz, N. (1999). Sufficient and necessary conditions in dual process models: The case of mood and information processing. In S. Chaiken & Y. Trope (Eds.), *Dual Process Theories in Social Psychology* (423–440). New York: Guilford Press.

Bless, H., Schwarz, N., & Wieland, R. (1996). Mood and the impact of category membership and individuating information. *European Journal of Social Psychology, 26,* 935–959.

Bodenhausen, G. V. (1993). Emotions, arousal, and stereotypic judgments: A heuristic model of affect and stereotyping. In D. M. Mackie & D. L. Hamilton (Eds.), *Affect, cognition, and stereotyping* (pp. 13–37). San Diego, CA: Academic Press.

Bodenhausen, G. V., Kramer, G. P., & Süsser, K. (1994). Happiness and stereotypic thinking in social judgment. *Journal of Personality and Social Psychology, 66,* 621–632.

Bodenhausen, G. V., Sheppard, L. A., & Kramer, G. P. (1994). Negative affect and social judgment: The differential impact of anger and sadness. *European Journal of Social Psychology, 24,* 45–62.

Bower, G. H. (1981). Mood and memory. *American Psychologist, 36,* 129–148.

Bower, G. H., & Cohen, P. R. (1982). Emotional influences in memory and thinking: Data and theory. In M. S. Clark & S. T. Fiske (Eds.), *Affect and cognition* (pp. 291–332). Hillsdale, NJ: Erlbaum.

Bower, G. H., & Mayer, J. D. (1985). Failure to replicate mood congruent retrieval. *Bulletin of the Psychonomic Society, 23*, 39–42.

Clark, M. S., & Fiske, S. T. (Eds.), *Affect and cognition.* Hillsdale, NJ: Erlbaum.

Chaiken, S. (1980). Heuristic versus systematic information processing and the use of source versus message cues in persuasion. *Journal of Personality and Social Psychology, 39*, 752–766.

Chaiken, S. (1987). The heuristic model of persuasion. In M. P. Zanna, J. M. Olson, & C. P. Herman (Eds.), *Social influence: The Ontario Symposium* (Vol. 5, pp. 3–39). Hillsdale, NJ: Erlbaum.

Clark, M. S., Milberg, S., & Ross, J. (1983). Arousal cues arousal-related material in memory: Implications for understanding effects of mood on memory. *Journal of Verbal Learning and Verbal Behavior, 22*, 633–649.

Clore, G. L., Schwarz, N., & Conway, M. (1994). Cognitive causes and consequences of emotion. In R. S. Wyer & T. K. Srull (Eds.), *Handbook of social cognition*, 2nd ed. (pp. 323–417). Hillsdale, NJ: Erlbaum.

Conway, M., & Giannopoulos, C. (1993). Dysphoria and decision making: Limited information use for evaluations of multiattribute targets. *Journal of Personality and Social Psychology, 64*, 613–623.

Craik, F. I. M., & Tulving, E. (1975). Depth of processing and the retention of words in episodic memory. *Journal of Experimental Psychology: General, 104*, 268–294.

Dosher, B. A., & Russo, J. E. (1976). Memory for internally generated stimuli. *Journal of Experimental Psychology: Human Learning and Memory, 2*, 633–640.

Edwards, J. A., & Weary, G. (1993). Depression and the impression-formation continuum: Piecemeal processing despite the availability of category information. *Journal of Personality and Social Psychology, 64*, 636–645.

Ellis, H. C., & Ashbrook, P. W. (1988). Resource allocation model of the effects of depressed mood states on memory. In K. Fiedler & J. P. Forgas (Eds.), *Affect, cognition, and social behavior* (pp. 25–43). Toronto: Hogrefe.

Erber, R., & Wang Erber, M. (in press). Mood and processing: A view from a self-regulation perspective. In L. L. Martin & G. L. Clore (Eds.), *Mood and social cognition: Contrasting theories.* Mahwah, NJ: Erlbaum.

Fiedler, K. (1988). Emotional mood, cognitive style, and behavior regulation. In K. Fiedler & J. P. Forgas (Eds.), *Affect, cognition, and social behavior* (pp. 100–119). Toronto: Hogrefe.

Fiedler, K. (1990). Mood-dependent selectivity in social cognition. *European Review of Social Psychology, 1*, 1–32.

Fiedler, K. (1991). On the task, the measures, and the mood in research on affect and social cognition. In J. P. Forgas (Ed.), *Emotion and social judgments* (pp. 83–104). Cambridge: Cambridge University Press.

Fiedler, K. (in press). Affective states trigger processes of assimilation and accommodation. In L. L. Martin & G. L. Clore (Eds.), *Mood and social cognition: Contrasting theories.* Mahwah, NJ: Erlbaum.

Fiedler, K., Armbruster, T., Nickel, S., Walther, E., & Asbeck, J. (1996). Constructive biases in social judgment: Experiments on the self-verification of question contents. *Journal of Personality and Social Psychology 71*, 861–873.

Fiedler, K., Asbeck, J., & Nickel, S. (1991). Mood and constructive memory effects on social judgment. *Cognition and Emotion, 5*, 363–378.

Fiedler, K., & Forgas, J. P. (1988) (Eds.). *Affect, cognition, and social behavior*. Toronto: Hogrefe.

Fiedler, K., Lachnit, H., Fay, D., & Krug, C. (1992). Mobilization of cognitive resources and the generation effect. *Quarterly Journal of Experimental Psychology, 45A*, 149–171.

Fiedler, K., Nickel, S., & Asbeck, J. (1994). *Mood and the generation effect*. Unpublished research, University of Heidelberg.

Fiedler, K., Nickel, S., Asbeck, J., & Pagel. U. (2000). Mood and the generation effect. Submitted for publication.

Fiedler, K., Nickel, S., Mühlfriedel, T., & Unkelbach, C. (2000) Is mood congruency a matter of discrimination or response bias? Submitted for publication.

Fiedler, K., Pampe, H., & Scherf, U. (1986). Mood and memory for tightly organized social information. *European Journal of Social Psychology, 16*, 149–164.

Fiedler, K., & Stroehm, W. (1986). What kind of mood influences what kind of memory: The role of arousal and information structure. *Memory & Cognition, 14*, 181–188.

Fiske, S. T., & Neuberg, S. L. (1990). A continuum of impression formation from category-based to individuating processing: Influences of information and motivation on attention and interpretation. In M. P. Zanna (Ed.), *Advances in experimental social psychology* (Vol. 23, pp. 1–74). Orlando, FL: Academic Press.

Fiske, S. T., & Taylor, S. E. (1991). *Social Cognition*. New York: McGraw-Hill.

Forgas, J. P. (1992). Affect in social judgments and decisions: A multi-process model. In M. P. Zanna (Ed.), *Advances in experimental social psychology* (pp. 227–275). New York: Academic Press.

Forgas, J. P. (1995). Mood and judgment: The affect infusion model (AIM). *Psychological Bulletin, 117*, 39–66.

Forgas, J. P., & Bower, G. H. (1987). Mood effects on person perception judgments. *Journal of Personality and Social Psychology, 53*, 53–60.

Forgas, J. P., & Fiedler, K. (1996). Mood effects on intergroup discrimination: The role of affect in reward allocation decisions. *Journal of Personality and Social Psychology, 70*, 28–40.

Frijda, N. H. (1986). *The emotions*. New York: Cambridge University Press.

Frijda, N. H. (1988). The lays of emotion. *American Psychologist, 43*, 349–358.

Graesser, A. C., Gordon, S. E., & Sawyer, J. D. (1979). Memory for typical and atypical actions in scripted activities: Test of a script pointer + tag hypothesis. *Journal of Verbal Learning and Behavior, 18*, 319–332.

Hertel, G., & Fiedler, K. (1994). Affective and cognitive influences in a social dilemma game. *European Journal of Social Psychology, 24*, 131–145.

Hertel, P., & Hardin, T. S. (1990). Remembering with and without awareness in a depressed mood: Evidence of deficits in initiative. *Journal of Experimental Psychology: General, 119*, 45–59.

Higgins, E. T. (1996). Emotional experiences: The pains and pleasures of different regulatory systems. In R. D. Kavanaugh, & B. Zimmerberg (Eds.), *Emotion: Interdisciplinary perspectives* (pp. 203–241). Hillsdale, NJ: Erlbaum.

Higgins, E. T., Roney, C. J. R., Crowe, E., & Hymes, C. (1994). Ideal versus ought predilections for approach and avoidance: Different self-regulatory systems. *Journal of Personality and Social Psychology, 66,* 276–286.

Hirshman, E., & Bjork, R. A. (1988). The generation effect: Support for a two-factor theory. *Journal of Experimental Psychology: Learning, Memory and Cognition, 14,* 484–494.

Isen, A. M. (1984). Toward understanding the role of affect in cognition. In R. S. Wyer & T. K. Srull (Eds.), *Handbook of social cognition* (Vol. 3, pp. 179–236). Hillsdale, NJ: Erlbaum.

Isen, A. M. (1987). Positive affect, cognitive processes, and social behavior. In L. Berkowitz (Ed.), *Advances in experimental social psychology* (Vol. 20, pp. 203–253). San Diego, CA: Academic Press.

Isen, A. M., Johnson, M. M. S., Mertz, E., & Robinson, G. F. (1985). The influence of positive affect on the unusualness of word associations. *Journal of Personality and Social Psychology, 48,* 1413–1426.

Isen, A. M., & Means, B. (1983). The influence of positive affect on decision-making strategy. *Social Cognition, 2,* 18–31.

Isen, A. M., Means, B., Patrick, R., & Nowicki, G.P. (1982). Some factors influencing decision-making and risk taking. In M. S. Clark, & S. T. Fiske (Eds.), *Affect and cognition* (pp. 243–261). Hillsdale, NJ: Erlbaum.

Isen, A. M., & Nowicki, G. P. (1981). Positive affect and creative problem solving. Paper presented at the annual meeting of the Cognitive Science Society, Berkeley, California.

Isen, A. M., Shalker, T. E., Clark, M., & Karp, L. (1978). Positive affect, accessibility of material in memory, and behavior: A cognitive loop? *Journal of Personality and Social Psychology, 36,* 1–12.

Jacobsen, E. (1957). Normal and pathological moods: Their nature and function. In R. S. Eisler, A. F. Freud, H. Hartman, & E. Kris (Eds.), *The psychoanalytic study of the child* (pp. 73–113). New York: International University Press.

Mackie, D. M. & Worth, L. T. (1989). Cognitive deficits and the mediation of positive affect in persuasion. *Journal of Personality and Social Psychology, 57,* 27–40.

Macrae, C. N., Hewstone, M., & Griffith, R. J. (1993). Processing load and memory for stereotype-based information. *European Journal of Social Psychology, 23,* 77–87.

Macrae, C. N., Milne, A. B., & Bodenhausen, G. V. (1994). Stereotypes as energy-saving devices: A peek inside the toolbox. *Journal of Personality and Social Psychology, 66,* 37–47.

Martin, L. L., & Clore, G. L. (in press) (Eds.). *Mood and social cognition: Contrasting theories.* Mahwah, NJ: Erlbaum.

Martin, L. M., Ward, D. W., Achee, J. W., & Wyer, R. S. (1993). Mood as input: People have to interpret the motivational implications of their moods. *Journal of Personality and Social Psychology, 64,* 317–326.

Mayer, J. D., & Salovey, P. (1988). Personality moderates the interaction of mood and cognition. In K. Fiedler & J. P. Forgas (Eds.), *Affect, cognition, and social behavior* (pp. 87–99). Toronto: Hogrefe.

Morris, W. N. (1992). A functional analysis of the role of mood in affective systems. *Review of Personality and Social Psychology, 11,* 256–293. Beverly Hills, CA: Sage.

Murray, N., Sujan, H., Hirt, E. R., & Sujan, M. (1990). The influence of mood on categorization: A cognitive flexibility interpretation. *Journal of Personality and Social Psychology, 59*, 411–425.

Navon, D., & Gopher, D. (1979). On the economy of human processing system. *Psychological Review, 86*, 214–255.

Nowlis, V., & Nowlis, H. H. (1956). The description and analysis of mood. *Annals of the New York Academy of Sciences, 65*, 345–355.

Petty, R. E. & Cacioppo, J. T. (1986). The elaboration likelihood model of persuasion. In L. Berkowitz (Ed.), *Advances in experimental social psychology* (Vol. 19, pp. 124–203). New York: Academic Press.

Piaget, J. (1952). *The origins of intelligence in children.* New York: International University Press.

Pribram, K. H. (1970). Feelings as monitors. In M. Arnold (Ed.), *Feelings and emotions* (pp. 41–53). New York: Academic Press.

Rosnow, R. L., & Rosenthal, R. (1989). Definition and interpretation of interaction effects. *Psychological Bulletin, 105*, 143–146.

Schaller, M., & Cialdini, R. (1990). Happiness, sadness, and helping: A motivational integration. In E. T. Higgins & R. M. Sorrentino (Eds.), *Handbook of motivation and cognition* (Vol. 2, pp. 265–296). New York: Guilford.

Schwarz, N. (1990). Feelings as information: Informational and motivational functions of affective states. In E. T. Higgins & R. M. Sorrentino (Eds.), *Handbook of motivation and cognition: Foundations of social behavior* (Vol. 2, pp. 527–561). New York: Guilford.

Schwarz, N. (in press). Feelings as information: Implications for affective influences on information processing. In L. L. Martin & G. L. Clore (Eds.), *Mood and social cognition: Contrasting theories.* Mahwah, NJ: Erlbaum.

Schwarz, N., & Bless, H. (1991). Happy and mindless, but sad and smart ? The impact of affective states on analytic reasoning. In J. P. Forgas (Ed.), *Emotion and social judgments* (pp. 55–71). Oxford: Pergamon.

Schwarz, N., Bless, H., & Bohner, G. (1991). Mood and persuasion: Affective states influence the processing of persuasive communications. In M. Zanna (Ed.), *Advances in Experimental Social Psychology* (Vol. 24, pp. 161–197). New York: Academic Press.

Schwarz, N. & Clore, G. L. (1983). Mood, misattribution, and judgments of well-being: Informative and directive functions of affective states. *Journal of Personality and Social Psychology, 45*, 513–523.

Schwarz, N., & Clore, G. L. (1988). How do I feel about it? The informative function of affective states. In K. Fiedler & J. P. Forgas (Eds.), *Affect, cognition, and social behavior* (pp. 44–62). Toronto: Hogrefe.

Slamecka, N. J., & Graf, P. (1978). The generation effect: Delineation of a phenomenon. *Journal of Experimental Psychology: Learning, Memory and Cognition, 4*, 592–604.

Stangor, C., & Duan, C. (1991). Effects of multiple task demands upon memory for information about social groups. *Journal of Experimental Social Psychology, 27*, 357–378.

Srull, T. K., & Wyer, R. S. (1989). Person memory and judgment. *Psychological Review, 96*, 58–83.

Wegener, D. T., Petty, R. E., & Smith, S. M. (1995). Positive mood can increase or decrease message scrutiny: The hedonic contingency view of mood and message processing. *Journal of Personality and Social Psychology, 69,* 5–15.

Worth, L. T., & Mackie, D. M. (1987). Cognitive mediation of positive affect in persuasion. *Social Cognition, 5,* 76–94.

7

Anxiety, cognitive biases, and beliefs

Michael W. Eysenck

Introduction

This introductory section will indicate the scope of this chapter, which inevitably is less broad than a systematic examination of the general notion that emotions influence beliefs. Most of my research of relevance to this notion has involved only one emotion, which is anxiety. Accordingly, the central focus of this chapter will be on the interface between anxiety and cognition. What appears to be true of the relationship between anxiety and cognition may or may not be true of other emotions.

The main problem that is apparent when one considers some of the theoretical approaches to anxiety (or emotion generally) and cognition is that they are far more concerned with the impact of cognitive structures (e.g., beliefs; schemas) and cognitive processes (e.g., cognitive appraisal; cognitive biases) on emotion and on emotional experience than with the opposite direction of causality from emotion to cognitive processes and structures. More specifically, theorists such as Lazarus (1991), Beck and Clark (1988), and Eysenck (1992, 1997) have incorporated the notion that there are bi-directional effects between beliefs and cognitive processes on the one hand and emotion on the other hand, but their main research emphasis has been on the impact of beliefs and cognitive processes on emotion.

In spite of the difficulties posed by the above considerations, a systematic attempt will be made to relate theory and research to the issue of the impact of anxiety on beliefs. However, it should be emphasized at the start that there is a very long way to go before this issue is fully understood.

Lazarus's appraisal theory

The cognitive appraisal theory of emotion initially proposed by Lazarus in 1966 has been extremely influential. In its original form, it was assumed that the situations in which individuals find themselves are subject to three kinds of cognitive appraisal. Primary appraisal is the first form of appraisal. What happens at this stage is that the situation is interpreted as being positive, stressful, or irrelevant to well-being. Secondary appraisal follows. This involves the individual taking account of the resources he or she has available to cope with the current situation. If necessary, there is a further stage of re-appraisal, in which the primary and/or secondary appraisals are modified if necessary.

This appraisal theory was developed further by Smith and Lazarus (1993). They identified six appraisal components, of which two were related to primary appraisal and the other four of which related to secondary appraisal. The assessment of motivational relevance and motivational congruence are the two primary appraisal components, and accountability, problem-focused coping potential, emotion-focused coping potential, and future expectancy form the secondary appraisal components.

According to Smith and Lazarus (1993), the emotional state that is experienced depends on the precise patterning across the six appraisal components. So far as anxiety is concerned, it possesses the primary appraisal components of motivational relevance and motivational incongruence, combined with the secondary appraisal component of low or uncertain emotion-focused coping potential. Smith and Lazarus (1993) obtained support for appraisal theory by using various hypothetical scenarios to assess the emotional consequences of different patterns of appraisal.

Lazarus (1991) incorporated the appraisal process within a general theoretical framework. The outcome of the appraisal process has consequences for action tendencies, emotional experience, and physiological activity, and these consequences in turn influence the individual's coping strategies and behavior. The success or otherwise of these coping strategies then affect the individual's situational construal and this then affects his or her appraisal process. Thus, at least in principle, there are bi-directional effects of cognitive processes on emotional state and of emotional state on cognitive processes and structures.

Most of the research designed to test appraisal theory has focused on the prediction that manipulations of cognitive appraisal should influence participants' emotional experience and physiological activity. In one of the best-known studies, Speisman, Lazarus, Mordkoff, and Davison (1964) presented a film in which adolescent boys had their penises deeply cut. The key findings were that the psychological and physiological stress reactions produced by the film were significantly reduced when the accompanying soundtrack claimed that the film did not show a painful operation or encouraged the participants to look at the film from the perspective of an anthropologist viewing strange native customs. Similar findings have been reported in several other studies (see Eysenck, 1997, for a review).

Evaluation

Lazarus's appraisal theory has been extremely influential, but it suffers from various limitations. It is of disappointingly little value in addressing the issue of the impact of emotion on beliefs. There are two main reasons for this. First, little of the research generated by the theory has focused on the effects of emotional state on the cognitive appraisal process. Second, Lazarus's major concern has been with the cognitive appraisals produced in a specific situation at a specific time rather than on the long-term changes in cognitive structures (e.g., belief structures) produced by a series of emotional states.

There are other significant limitations and problems with Lazarus's theoretical approach. Some of these limitations were discussed by Parkinson and Manstead (1992). According to them, "Appraisal theory has taken the paradigm of emotional experience as an individual passive subject confronting a survival-threatening stimulus" (p. 146). This is unduly limited, because it takes little account of the fact that emotions generally occur in a social context, and it is rare for individuals to be in a totally unemotional state prior to encountering a threatening stimulus.

A final problem with Lazarus's approach is that it is generally very difficult to assess someone's cognitive appraisals, in part because these appraisals are not necessarily accessible to conscious awareness. According to Lazarus (1991: 169), "Appraisal implies nothing about rationality, deliberateness, or consciousness. A central postulate for dealing with this issue is to say that there is more than one way of knowing, and in the generation of an emotion these ways may be in conflict or may be contributed to simultaneously by two kinds of appraisal processes – one that operates automatically without awareness or volitional control, and one that is conscious, deliberate, and volitional."

Beck's schema theory

One of the most prominent approaches to anxiety that emphasizes the importance of beliefs is that of Beck (e.g., Beck & Emery, 1985; Beck & Clark, 1988). The central concept in his theory is that of schemas, which were defined by Beck and Clark (1988) as "functional structures

of relatively enduring representations of prior knowledge and experience" (p. 24). Many schemas can be regarded as consisting of complex
sets of beliefs. Schemas operate in a top-down fashion to influence all
stages of cognitive processing: "Cognitive structures [i.e., schemas]
guide the screening, encoding, organizing, storing and retrieving of
information. Stimuli consistent with existing schemas are elaborated
and encoded, while inconsistent or irrelevant information is ignored
or forgotten" (pp. 24–25).

How do schemas exert their influence on cognitive functioning? The
basic notion is that schemas play a role in directing processing
resources to any aspects of the external or internal environment which
are congruent with them. Thus, for example, individuals high in trait
anxiety have danger schemas which lead them to devote additional
processing resources to threat-related stimuli. The same is true for
anxious patients, whose anxiety-related schemas involve "perceived
physiological or psychological threat to one's personal domain as well
as an exaggerated sense of vulnerability" (p. 26).

The origins of threat-related schemas or beliefs are not made very
clear within schema theory. However, it follows from the theory that
there will be a vicious cycle for patients, in which the excessive
processing of threat-related information serves to confirm to them the
apparent correctness of their maladaptive schemas. Within this
vicious cycle, anxiety serves to strengthen the underlying schemas,
and the schemas serve to maintain or increase the level of anxiety.

Evaluation

Beck's schema theory is of limited value in the attempt to understand
the ways in which anxiety affects beliefs. The central concept of
"schema" is typically used in a rather imprecise fashion. Of greatest
concern, there is generally no independent evidence for the existence
of any specific schemas. As Eysenck (1997: 96) pointed out, "Behavioral evidence of a cognitive bias in anxious patients is used to infer
the presence of a schema, and then that schema is used to "explain"
the observed cognitive bias."

Eysenck's theoretical approach

Eysenck (1992, 1997) has developed a theoretical approach to anxiety
which represents in part a synthesis of various theories and programs
of empirical research. The starting point in considering the ways in
which anxiety might influence beliefs is to assume that individual
differences in anxiety depend to some extent on genetic factors. H. J.

Eysenck implausibly claimed that "genetic factors contribute something like two-thirds of the variance in major personality dimensions" (1982: 28). The true figure is much lower (see Eysenck, 1997, for a review). For example, consider the work of Pedersen, Plomin, McClearn, and Friberg (1988), who reported a study containing the largest numbers of monozygotic and dizygotic twins brought up apart of any personality study. They assessed neuroticism (which closely resembles trait anxiety) in 150 pairs of monozygotic twins brought up together, 95 monozygotic pairs brought up apart, 204 dizygotic pairs brought up together, and 220 pairs of dizygotic twins brought up apart. Some twin studies have been flawed because many of their twins brought up apart lived together for several years prior to separation. In the Pedersen *et al.* (1988) study, over 80 per cent of the twins brought up apart were separated by the age of five, and almost 50 per cent were separated at some point during the first year of life.

What did Pedersen *et al.* (1988) find? Monozygotic twins brought up together had a correlation of +.41 for neuroticism, monozygotic twins brought up apart had a correlation of +.28, and dizygotic twins brought up together and apart had correlations of +.24 and +.28, respectively. These findings indicated that approximately 31 per cent of individual differences in neuroticism are due to heredity. This is less than half the figure claimed by H. J. Eysenck (1982).

The next step theoretically is to assume that those who are predisposed genetically to experience high levels of anxiety are vulnerable to the development of various cognitive biases. The main cognitive biases are as follows: (1) selective attentional bias, which involves preferential attention to threat-related rather than neutral stimuli; (2) interpretive bias, which involves interpreting ambiguous stimuli and situations in a threatening fashion; and (3) memory bias, which involves a tendency to recall disproportionately more threat-related than neutral information. It is assumed that all of these biases depend interactively on trait anxiety and on state anxiety, and that those who are genetically predisposed tend to be relatively high on trait anxiety and above-averagely susceptible to state anxiety.

Evidence supporting some of the above assumptions will now be considered. Selective attentional bias was studied by MacLeod and Mathews (1988). They found that there was no evidence of selective attentional bias for examination-relevant threatening words in either high or low trait-anxious students several weeks prior to an important examination. However, high trait-anxious students showed clear evidence of attentional bias for the examination-related threatening words in the week before the examination itself. Thus, trait and state anxiety were both required in order to produce an attentional bias.

The same issue was also studied by Broadbent and Broadbent (1988). Their findings were consistent with those of MacLeod and Mathews (1988), in that they reported a significant interaction between trait and state anxiety. In this interaction, an attentional bias was only clearly present when trait and state anxiety were both high.

An interpretive bias has been reported in numerous studies (see Eysenck, 1997, for a review), only a few of which will be discussed here. Clear evidence was reported by Calvo and Eysenck (1995), in a study in which words had to be named as rapidly as possible after the presentation of ambiguous sentences. There were several conditions. However, the most important ones involved sentences in which a possible ego-threatening interpretation was confirmed or disconfirmed by the following sentence which contained the word that had to be named. The prediction that high-anxious individuals would show interpretive bias was supported by the finding that they (but not low-anxious individuals) had slower naming latencies to words disconfirming the threat than to those confirming it. Calvo and Eysenck (1995) obtained no evidence of an interpretive bias with ambiguous sentences containing a possible physical-threat interpretation. The implication is that high-anxious individuals primarily have an interpretive bias for social threat rather than for other kinds of threat.

The involvement of state anxiety or arousal in producing an interpretive bias was shown by MacLeod (1990), who discussed three of his own studies. Two of these studies made use of Eysenck's homophone task, in which sounds corresponding to both a threatening and a neutral word are presented auditorily, and the participants need to write down what they hear. Examples of the homophones used are pain/pane and die/dye. It was predicted that individuals high in trait anxiety would produce more threat-related spellings than those low in trait anxiety, and that this difference would be greater under high arousal. As expected, there was a significant interaction between trait anxiety and arousal in both studies. The pattern of this interaction was such that there was maximal evidence of an interpretive bias in high trait-anxious individuals under high arousal produced by means of physical exercise. In MacLeod's (1990) third study, ambiguous sentences were presented, with each one being followed by a word that was strongly associated with the threatening or the neutral interpretation of the sentence. This word had to be named as rapidly as possible. The clearest evidence for an interpretive bias was obtained in high trait-anxious individuals who were high in state anxiety.

An area of research which has been very slow to develop is concerned with the learning processes involved in producing interpretive bias. Evidence that a surprisingly short period of learning can lead to the development of interpretive bias was reported by Grey and Mathews (1997) in two experiments. In their first experiment, the participants were presented with homographs with threat-related and neutral meanings. Each homograph was followed by a related word fragment, and the participant's task was to identify the word. For half of the participants, the fragments came from words associated with the threatening meanings of the homographs, whereas they came from words associated with the non-threatening meanings for the re-mainder. The same task was used in the test phase. Word-fragment completion was significantly slower when the meaning of the homograph that needed to be accessed was the opposite of that needed during training, and this effect generalized to new homographs.

In their second experiment, Grey and Mathews (1997) used the same training task as was used in their first experiment. This was followed by a lexical decision task in which homographs were followed by letter strings. The key evidence for interpretive bias was that lexical decision times were faster for the trained meanings than for the untrained ones.

Studies of memory bias as a function of anxiety have produced apparently inconsistent findings (see Eysenck, 1997, for a review). However, there is a reasonable consensus that patients suffering from generalized anxiety disorder do not show a memory bias, whereas there are several studies on normals in which those high in trait anxiety exhibited a negative memory bias. For example, Breck and Smith (1983) asked their participants to decide whether various positive and negative trait adjectives were self-descriptive. There was a manipulation of state anxiety, with the participants (who were high or low in social anxiety) being informed that there would be a social interaction after the experiment. The participants who were high in social anxiety showed more evidence of a negative memory bias in the more stressful condition in which a social interaction was anticipated.

Some of the issues investigated by Breck and Smith (1983) were also considered by Bradley and Mogg (1994) and by Bradley, Mogg, Galbraith, and Perrett (1993). Similar findings were reported in both studies, with the extent of memory bias being determined interactively by neuroticism and by negative mood.

We have seen so far that attentional bias, interpretive bias, and memory bias are all strongest when the participants are high in both trait anxiety and state anxiety. In other words, high levels of state anxiety when combined with high trait anxiety lead individuals to attend excessively to threat-related environmental stimuli, to regard a high proportion of ambiguous stimuli (e.g., an unexpected sound in the middle of the night) as threatening, and a general tendency to retrieve threat-related information from long-term memory more readily than neutral information. What are the implications of these various biases for those high in trait and state anxiety? Most obviously, these three biases in conjunction should make high trait-anxious individuals feel that the world is a threatening place, and that they have been exposed to many threatening individuals and situations in the past. As a consequence, they should develop beliefs that the world is dangerous and that they are vulnerable. In other words, experienced anxiety can play a role in the development and expansion of the kinds of schemas and beliefs identified by Beck and Clark (1988) as being found in anxious individuals. It then becomes plausible to assume that there are bi-directional influences between anxiety and schemas: anxiety leads to the incremental development of danger and vulnerability schemas, and the development of these schemas increases the experience of anxiety via cognitive biases.

The discussion so far of Eysenck's theoretical approach has been based very much on Eysenck (1992) rather than Eysenck (1997). According to Eysenck (1997), one of the major limitations of Eysenck's (1992) theory was its assumption that emotional experience is determined primarily by cognitive appraisal of the situation. The weakness in this assumption is that it de-emphasizes the possibility that the experience of anxiety may depend on internal sources of information (e.g., perception of one's own physiological activity) as well as on external sources of information (p. 23).

The range of evidence indicating that the various cognitive biases can be found with internal stimuli is discussed in detail by Eysenck (1997). A few illustrative studies will be considered here. Derakshan and Eysenck (1997) obtained videotapes of participants exposed to a moderately stressful situation (e.g., presenting a short talk on psychology to a small group of fellow students). Several days thereafter, the participants and independent judges rated the videotapes for the amount of behavioral anxiety displayed. High trait-anxious individuals exhibited an interpretive bias for their own behavior, since they interpreted their own behavior as being significantly more anxious than it appeared to the judges.

Similar findings using a less adequate methodology had previously been reported by Beidel, Turner, and Dancu (1985). They compared self-reported and rated anxiety in three social situations. The high socially anxious participants had significantly greater self-reported than rated anxiety in the two most stressful conditions (talking to someone of the opposite sex; giving an unexpected talk), but they did not show an interpretive bias in the least stressful condition of talking to someone of the same sex. These findings suggest that an interpretive bias for one's own behavior depends interactively on social anxiety and on state anxiety. However, the evidence would have been more convincing if steps had been taken to ensure that the participants and the judges were utilizing the same information.

According to Eysenck's (1997) four-factor theory, cognitive biases can also apply to one's own physiological activity and to one's own cognitions. Veltman, van Zijderveld, and van Dyck (1994) considered the effects on state anxiety of administering an injection of adrenaline. High trait-anxious individuals reported a significantly larger increase than low trait-anxious individuals in state anxiety in response to the adrenaline. They also reported a greater number and intensity of symptoms.

Eysenck and Derakshan (1997) studied interpretive bias for one's own cognitions among students who were due to take important examinations a few weeks thereafter. Their predicted examination performance was compared against their actual performance in order to provide a measure of interpretive bias. The high-anxious participants predicted that their level of performance would be lower than it actually was, thus demonstrating an interpretive bias.

Some evidence that interpretive bias for examination performance may depend on state anxiety as well as on trait anxiety was reported by Butler and Mathews (1987). In their study, high trait-anxious students showed greater pessimism than low trait-anxious students about forthcoming examinations. In addition, their pessimism was greater one day rather than one month before the examinations.

The fact that high-anxious individuals possess cognitive biases of various kinds to various internal stimuli as well as to external threat-related stimuli has a number of implications. First, the existence of these cognitive biases makes it very clear why the beliefs and schemas of high-anxious individuals contain a wide range of threat-related information. Second, and more speculatively, it could be argued that cognitive biases for different sources of information relate to different sets of beliefs or schemas. More specifically, cognitive biases for external stimuli may be most strongly associated with danger schemas, whereas cognitive biases for internal stimuli may be most strongly associated with vulnerability schemas.

Repressors

The focus so far has been on those individuals who are high in trait anxiety. Historically, those scoring low on trait anxiety were regarded as a homogeneous group. However, the seminal work of Weinberger, Schwartz, and Davidson (1979), together with subsequent research (see Weinberger, 1990, for a review) has disconfirmed that view. Weinberger *et al.* (1979) divided those scoring low on trait anxiety into two groups: the low-anxious and repressors. The difference between the two groups was that the low-anxious obtained low scores on a measure of defensiveness, whereas the repressors obtained high defensiveness scores. There were clear differences between these groups in their physiological and behavioral responses in a moderately stressful situation. The repressors exhibited significantly more anxiety than the low-anxious on three physiological and three behavioral measures. Indeed, the repressors appeared even more anxious than the high-anxious participants on most of the measures. Similar findings have been reported in numerous other studies (see Eysenck, 1997, for a review).

Most of the research on repressors in stressful situations has indicated that they exhibit a clear discrepancy between low levels of self-reported anxiety and high levels of physiological and behavioral anxiety. One possible explanation of this discrepancy is that repressors deliberately distort their self-reports so as to pretend to others that they do not experience much anxiety. According to this view, there are close similarities between repressors and the high-anxious. As a consequence, the beliefs and schemas of repressors should presumably be like those of high-anxious individuals.

There is a considerable amount of research indicating that there are substantial differences between repressors and high-anxious individuals. For example, Eysenck and Derakshan (in press) asked close friends or relatives of repressors and high-anxious individuals to assess them for trait anxiety and defensiveness. The repressors were rated as substantially lower in trait anxiety than the high-anxious, but they were rated much higher in defensiveness. Thus, the patterns of behavior exhibited by the two groups are very different.

Derakshan and Eysenck (in press) addressed the issue of whether repressors' self-reported anxiety is deliberated distorted in a fairly direct way. They obtained initial self-report measures of trait anxiety and of defensiveness under standard conditions. Approximately two months later, they obtained the same measures a second time under bogus pipeline conditions. In essence, the bogus pipeline consists of physiological recording equipment which the participants are led to believe can detect whenever they distort the truth. There is much evidence, most of it from within social psychology, indicating that the bogus pipeline technique is effective (e.g., Millham & Kellogg, 1980). The key finding obtained by Derakshan and Eysenck (in press) was that repressors' level of trait anxiety increased non-significantly in the bogus pipeline condition. This finding is consistent with the notion that repressors genuinely experience relatively low levels of anxiety in spite of their frequently high levels of physiological and behavioral anxiety.

Eysenck (1997) assumed that repressors have schemas and beliefs relating to social vulnerability. These schemas and beliefs influence their physiological and behavioral reactions in stressful social situations, but typically have minimal effect on their experience of anxiety. Why is that the case? According to Eysenck (1997), repressors have opposite attentional biases and interpretive biases which they apply to their own behavior, physiology, and cognitions. Some relevant evidence was obtained by Derakshan and Eysenck (1997), in a videotape study which was discussed earlier. They found that repressors rated their own behavioral anxiety as being significantly lower than did independent judges, thus providing evidence for an opposite interpretive bias.

How have the social vulnerability beliefs and schemas developed? Some suggestive evidence was reported by Myers and Brewin (1994). They discovered from semi-structured interviews that repressors had experienced significantly more paternal indifference and apathy than high-anxious or low-anxious groups. Thus, the repressive coping style could have developed as a reaction to difficult and stressful family experiences.

Additional evidence that the adult repressive coping style may have its origins in anxious childhood experiences was reported by Dozier and Kobak (1992). They administered the Adult Attachment Interview, in which the participants were requested to remember occasions during childhood involving separation from their parents or the threat of it. Those participants whose answers seemed to indicate a repressive coping style had large increases in skin conductance associated with several questions, such as those concerned with separation from their parents or rejection by them.

Eysenck (1997) summarized the evidence on the origins of the repressive coping style as follows: "Young children who experience indifference and apathy from one or both parents develop an avoidant attachment style, combining apparent behavioral calmness with high physiological arousal. A related possibility (C. Brewin, pers. comm.) is that parental inconsistency plays a role in the development of an avoidant attachment style. An avoidant defensive coping style in children often develops into the adult defensive coping style characteriztic of repressors" (p. 88).

Conclusions

The theoretical approach adopted in this chapter has been based on the assumption that there are reciprocal relationships between anxiety and beliefs. When individuals are anxious, they exhibit increased use of cognitive biases which can lead to the expansion of existing danger and vulnerability schemas. In addition, the existence of danger and vulnerability schemas makes individuals more likely to experience anxiety. This theoretical approach is directly applicable to high-anxious individuals, but is less relevant to repressors.

There are three major unresolved problems in this area of research. First, the development of beliefs often occur over a period of months and years, and the techniques available to psychologists are not well suited to observing long-term changes. Second, the notion that anxiety can produce an expansion of negative beliefs, and negative beliefs can increase anxiety, seems to lead to the prediction that many people should become progressively more anxious over the years. In fact, however, levels of trait anxiety tend to decrease rather than increase during the years of adulthood (Eysenck, 1997). This decrease is in need of an explanation.

Third, it has proved remarkably difficult to obtain convincing evidence of the schemas and beliefs possessed by individuals. Most of the evidence is rather indirect in nature. It remains plausible to argue that many of the differences between high-anxious individuals and repressors depend on differences in the schematic information stored in long-term memory, but it is a matter of concern that it is difficult to point to clear-cut findings to support that argument.

References

Beck, A. T., & Clark, D. A. (1988). Anxiety and depression: An information-processing perspective. *Anxiety Research, 1*, 23–36.

Beck, A. T., & Emery, G. (1985). *Anxiety disorders and phobias: A cognitive perspective*. New York: Basic Books.

Beidel, D. C., Turner, S. M., & Dancu, C. V. (1985). Physiological, cognitive and behavioral aspects of social anxiety. *Behaviour Research and Therapy, 23*, 109–117.

Bradley, B. P., & Mogg, K. (1994). Mood and personality in recall of positive and negative information. *Behaviour Research and Therapy, 32*, 137–141.

Bradley, B. P., Mogg, K., Galbraith, M., & Perrett, A. (1993). Negative recall bias in neuroticism: State versus trait effects. *Behaviour Research and Therapy, 31*, 125–127.

Breck, B. E., & Smith, S. H. (1983). Selective recall of self-descriptive traits by socially anxious and nonanxious females. *Social Behavior and Personality, 11*, 71–76.

Broadbent, D. E., & Broadbent, M. (1988). Anxiety and attentional bias: State and trait. *Cognition and Emotion, 2*, 165–183.

Butler, G., & Mathews, A. (1987). Anticipatory anxiety and risk perception. *Cognitive Therapy and Research, 11*, 551–555.

Calvo, M., & Eysenck, M. W. (1995). Sesgo interpretativo en la ansiedad de evalucacion. *Ansiedad y Estres, 1*, 5–20.

Derakshan, N., & Eysenck, M. W. (1997). Interpretive biases for one's own behavior and physiology in high trait-anxious individuals and repressors. *Journal of Personality and Social Psychology, 73*, 816–825.

Derakshan, N., & Eysenck, M. W. (1998). Self-rated trait anxiety and defensiveness under standard and bogus pipeline conditions. *Cognition and Emotion, 12*.

Dozier, M., & Kobak, R. R. (1992). Psychophysiology in attachment interviews: Converging evidence for deactivating strategies. *Child Development, 63*, 1473–1480.

Eysenck, H. J. (1982). *Personality genetics and behavior.* New York: Praeger.

Eysenck, M. W. (1992). *Anxiety: The cognitive perspective.* Hove: Erlbaum.

Eysenck, M. W. (1997). *Anxiety and cognition: A unified theory.* Hove, UK: Psychology Press.

Eysenck, M. W., & Derakshan, N. (1997). Cognitive biases for future negative events as a function of trait anxiety and social desirability. *Personality and Individual Differences, 22*, 597–605.

Eysenck, M. W., & Derakshan, N. (1998). Self-rated and other-rated trait anxiety and defensiveness in high-anxious, low-anxious, defensive high-anxious, and repressor groups. *Anxiety, Stress, and Coping, 11*, .

Grey, S. J., & Mathews, A. M. (1997). *Interpretation of ambiguous words: The acquisition of bias towards threat in volunteers.* Poster presented at the London conference of the British Psychological Society, December.

Lazarus, R. S. (1966). *Psychological stress and the coping process.* New York: McGraw-Hill.

Lazarus, R. S. (1991). *Emotion and adaptation.* Oxford: Oxford University Press.

MacLeod, C. (1990). Mood disorders and cognition. In M. W. Eysenck (Ed.), *Cognitive psychology: An international review.* Chichester: Wiley.

MacLeod, C., & Mathews, A. (1988). Anxiety and the allocation of attention to threat. *Quarterly Journal of Experimental Psychology, 38A*, 659–670.

Millham, J., & Kellogg, R. W. (1980). Need for social appraisal: Impression management or self-deception? *Journal of Research in Personality, 14*, 445–457.

Myers, L. B., & Brewin, C. R. (1994). Recall of early experience and the repressive coping style. *Journal of Abnormal Psychology, 103*, 288–292.

Parkinson, B., & Manstead, A. S. R. (1992). Appraisal as a cause of emotion. In M. S. Clark (Ed.), *Review of personality and social psychology* (Vol. 13, pp. 122–149). New York: Sage.

Pedersen, N. L., Plomin, R., McClearn, G. E., & Friberg, L. (1988). Neuroticism, extraversion, and related traits in adult twins reared apart and reared together. *Journal of Personality and Social Psychology, 55*, 950–957.

Smith, C. A., & Lazarus, R. S. (1993). Appraisal components, core relational themes, and the emotions. *Cognition and Emotion, 7*, 233–269.

Speisman, J. C., Lazarus, R. S., Mordkoff, A., & Davison, L. (1964). Experimental reduction of stress based on ego-defence theory. *Journal of Abnormal and Social Psychology, 68*, 367–380.

Veltman, D. J., van Zijderveld, G. A., & van Dyck, R. (1994). Fear of fear, trait anxiety and aerobic fitness in relation to state anxiety during adrenaline provocation. *Anxiety, Stress, and Coping, 7,* 279–289.

Weinberger, D. A. (1990). The construct validity of the repressive coping style. In J. L. Singer (Ed.), *Repression and dissociation: Implications for personality theory, psychopathology, and health.* Chicago: University of Chicago Press.

Weinberger, D. A., Schwartz, G. E., & Davidson, J. R. (1979). Low-anxious, high-anxious, and repressive coping styles: Psychometric patterns and behavioral and physiological responses to stress. *Journal of Abnormal Psychology, 88,* 369–380.

8

A cognitive dissonance theory perspective on the role of emotion in the maintenance and change of beliefs and attitudes[1]

Eddie Harmon-Jones

. . . following the earthquake, the vast majority of the rumors that were widely circulated predicted even worse disasters to come in the very near future. Certainly the belief that horrible disasters were about to occur is not a very pleasant belief, and we may ask why rumors that were "anxiety provoking" arose and were so widely accepted. Finally a possible answer to this question occurred to us – an answer that held promise of having rather general application: perhaps these rumors predicting even worse disasters to come were not "anxiety provoking" at all but were rather "anxiety justifying." That is, as a result of the earthquake these people were already frightened, and the rumors served the function of giving them something to be frightened about. Perhaps these rumors provided people with information that fitted with the way they already felt.

(Festinger, 1957: vi–vii)

The above quotation, which appeared in the Foreword to *A Theory of Cognitive Dissonance*, describes how Leon Festinger and his colleagues arrived at the theory of cognitive dissonance, one of the most influential theories in psychology (Jones, 1985). According to the theory (Festinger, 1957), the presence of a cognitive inconsistency of sufficient magnitude will evoke a negative emotional state that will motivate cognitive work aimed at reducing the cognitive inconsistency. For the theory, a cognition is an element of knowledge. Cognitions can be beliefs, attitudes, values, and feelings about oneself, others, or the environment. Thus, the theory of cognitive dissonance is concerned with the cognitive antecedents of emotion, the intensity of emotional response, and the cognitive regulation of this emotional response.

The theory can be and has been applied to the study of the role of emotion in belief and attitude maintenance and change. In the present chapter, I will review the theory of cognitive dissonance, the major paradigms that have been used to test hypotheses derived from the theory, and research that has tested the theory's propositions re-garding the role of emotion in attitude and belief maintenance and change.

Overview of the theory of cognitive dissonance

The original statement of cognitive dissonance theory (Festinger, 1957) proposed that dissonant relations between cognitions have the poten-tial to create negative affect (dissonance) that motivates individuals to attempt to reduce or eliminate the discrepancies between cognitions. Festinger (1957) suggested that cognitions are dissonant with one another when they "do not fit together," or when they are inconsistent with each other or contradict one another. When proposing a formal definition of dissonant relations, he proposed that the existence of all other relevant cognitions should be disregarded and that the two cognitions alone should be considered. He then wrote, *"These two elements are in a dissonant relation if, considering these two alone, the obverse of one element would follow from the other.* To state it a bit more formally, *x* and *y* are dissonant if not-*x* follows from *y"* (p. 13). He proposed that dissonant relations "might exist because of what the person had learned or come to expect, because of what is considered appropriate or usual . . ." (p. 13). He also mentioned that motivations and desired consequences might be factors in determining whether two cognitions were in a dissonant relation. Much of what was written about consonant relations had to do with whether one cognition implied the other cognition. As Festinger (1957) discussed, whether cognitions psychologically imply one another may be determined by cultural mores, pressures to be logical, past experiences, behavioral commitments, because one cognition is part of a more general cogni-tion and so on.

The magnitude of dissonance aroused in regard to a particular cognition (a focal cognition) is a function of the number and psycholo-gical importance of cognitions dissonant and consonant with this cognition. Thus, dissonance will increase as the number and impor-tance of dissonant relative to consonant cognitions increases. The dissonance ratio has been proposed to formally specify the magnitude of dissonance. Accordingly, dissonant cognitions are multiplied by their importance and then divided by the sum of the dissonant and consonant cognitions, which are also multiplied by their importance (Festinger, 1957; Festinger & Carlsmith, 1959). This method of calcu-lating the magnitude of dissonance corresponds to Festinger's verbal definition of the method of calculating dissonance. However, a more complete method of calculating the magnitude of dissonance should include an additional variable that accounts for varying levels of importance of the focal cognition (Sakai, 1999).

The original theory posits that the routes of dissonance reduction would involve: subtracting dissonant cognitions, adding consonant cognitions, and decreasing the importance of dissonant cognitions. In addition to these modes of dissonance reduction, increasing the importance of consonant cognitions should be added because it logically follows from the ratio used to compute the magnitude of dissonance (dissonant cognitions / dissonant + consonant cognitions, with each weighted by its importance). Characterizing the modes of dissonance reduction in this manner reflects the abstract nature of the original theory of dissonance. These modes of dissonance reduction may manifest themselves in attitude, belief, value, or behavior maintenance or change. Dissonance reduction will be aimed at altering the cognition least resistant to change. The resistance to change of cognitions is an important concept that assists in predicting how cognitions will be affected as a result of dissonance.

In his writing on dissonance theory, Festinger (1957) referred to dissonance in two ways: (1) as the way in which cognitions are related; and (2) as the emotional state evoked by the existence of cognitions that are in a dissonant relationship. To clarify the presentation of these concepts in the present chapter, I will use the term "cognitive discrepancy" to refer to the dissonant relation between cognitions, and I will use the term "discrepancy reduction" to refer to the process of attempting to reduce this cognitive discrepancy. I will use the term "dissonance" to refer to the emotional state evoked by cognitive discrepancy, and I will use the term "dissonance reduction" as the reduction of this state.

Festinger proposed that cognitive discrepancy was inherently aversive. Other theorizts have proposed alternate motivations that underlie the motivating effects putatively due to cognitive discrepancy. Among these are the need to maintain and enhance self-esteem (J. Aronson, Cohen & Nail, 1999; Greenwald & Ronis, 1978; Leippe & Eisenstadt, 1999; Steele, 1988); the need for self-consistency (E. Aronson, 1968, 1999); the need to rationalize behavior (Beauvois & Joule, 1996, 1999); the need to avoid producing aversive consequences (Cooper, 1999; Cooper & Fazio, 1984; Mills, 1999); and the need for effective and unconflicted action (Beckmann & Irle, 1985; Harmon-Jones, 1999; Jones & Gerard, 1967). Much debate centers around determining the underlying motivation. However, most current versions of the theory accept the premise that negative emotion drives the discrepancy reduction.

Cognitive discrepancy may create negative affect because discrepancy among cognitions undermines the requirement for effective and unconflicted action (Beckmann & Irle, 1985; Harmon-Jones, 1999; Jones & Gerard, 1967). According to this view, dissonance is generally aroused when "two cognitions generate mutually incompatible behavior dispositions, such as approach and avoidance tendencies toward the same object . . ." (Jones & Gerard, 1967: 191). Research on the theory of dissonance has identified commitment as an important, if not necessary, condition for the arousal of dissonance (Beauvois & Joule, 1996; Brehm & Cohen, 1962; Festinger, 1964). For most dissonance theorizts, the notion of commitment implies that the person has engaged in a behavior for which s/he feels responsibility and that s/he has a definite understanding of the consequences of the behavior. However, persons can regard cognitions that may not involve a behavioral commitment as "true" and would experience dissonance if information were presented that was inconsistent with these cognitions. A good example of this type of cognition would be a person's knowledge of the law of gravity. Information that violates the law of gravity would probably arouse dissonance in most persons. Therefore, I submit that a commitment occurs when an individual regards a behavior, belief, attitude, or value as a meaningful truth. The psychological commitment to the cognition then guides information processing, which serves the ultimate function of producing and guiding behavior.

If dissonant information is encountered, negative emotion may result and cause the individual to engage in cognitive work to support the commitment. However, if dissonant information continues to mount, the negative emotion that results may motivate the individual to discontinue supporting the commitment and give in to the dissonant information. Whether the individual's cognitive work is aimed toward supporting the commitment or discontinuing the commitment would be determined by the resistance to change of each cognition. If the commitment is more resistant to change than the dissonant information, then cognitive work would be aimed at supporting the commitment. If, however, the dissonant information is more resistant to change than the commitment, then the cognitive work would be aimed at discontinuing the commitment. Resistance to change of cognitions is determined by the responsiveness of the cognitions to reality (e.g., the grass is green), the extent to which the cognitions are in relations of consonance to other cognitions, the difficulty of changing the cognition, and so on (Festinger, 1957). From the present view, resistance to change is ultimately determined by the degree to which individuals believe the information assists them in controlling and predicting outcomes and thus behaving effectively. Thus, when knowledge about the environment, about one's self, or about one's actions, beliefs, or attitudes are in a dissonant relation, the sense of being able to control and predict outcomes may be threatened and ultimately the need to act effectively would be undermined.

As an example, consider a situation where a hiker is lost deep in the woods. Based on her calculations, she is in the middle of the woods, has just enough time and resources to cover fifteen miles, and knows that an exit and thus safety is fifteen miles to the east or west. She perceives that she has two options: she can begin walking to the west or to the east. Each option has advantages (she is very familiar with the east route; she has heard that the west route requires less effort) and disadvantages (the east route will require crossing a river; the west route will require climbing a mountain). Once the hiker makes a decision to walk east, the disadvantages of walking east and the advantages of walking west become discrepant cognitions. If she continues to weigh the relative merits of the options, vacillating between them, beginning to walk one way and then turning around and walking the other, action will be impeded and she may never arrive to safety. She must reduce the discrepancy and follow through with the option she has chosen. Even if the route she chooses is not the best, she will be better off persisting in one course of action than in going halfway only to turn back.

From the current perspective, the *proximal* motivation to reduce cognitive discrepancy stems from the need to reduce negative emotion, while the *distal* motivation to reduce discrepancy stems from the requirement for effective action. When the maintenance of clear and certain knowledge and thus the potential for effective action is threatened, negative emotion results, which prompts attempts at the restoration of cognitions supportive of the action (i.e., discrepancy reduction). Thus, negative emotion works much like pain in that it provides the information and motivation that prompts the individual to action. The unpleasantness of the negative emotion forces a response, and thus prevents states of inaction. When the negative emotion is nonexistent, mild, or attributed to a source other than discrepancy, then efforts at discrepancy reduction will be minimal.

Thus, individuals find dissonance discomforting and try to reduce the discomfort because of the requirement for effective action. The present model characterizes the dissonance process as an adaptive or functional response. Characterizing the dissonance process as adaptive does not suggest that it is a rational process (based on logic). Most previous speculations on dissonance considered it an irrational and maladaptive process. Indeed, Elliot Aronson (1995), one of the most creative and influential dissonance researchers and theorists, summarized this perspective when he wrote, "I have referred to dissonance-reducing behavior as irrational. By this I mean it is often maladaptive, in that it can prevent people from learning important facts or from finding real solutions to their problems" (p. 185).

However, characterizing dissonance as a generally adaptive process may yield an increased understanding of the dissonance process. Of course, proposing that the dissonance process is adaptive does not mean that it will always be functional; it may become dysfunctional, just as chronic pain may serve no useful purpose. However, across the majority of situations, especially those requiring action, the dissonance process probably proves to be quite useful.

The action-based model builds on the original theory of dissonance. In accord with the original theory, it defines cognition rather broadly as "knowledge" about oneself, the social environment, or the physical environment, and it assumes that any of these cognitions can be involved in dissonance arousal and reduction. In contrast to other models of dissonance theory, such as self-consistency theory (E. Aronson, 1968, 1999), it does not assume that in order for dissonance to occur, the cognitions must be relevant to the self-concept. As has been discussed elsewhere (Brehm, 1992; Harmon-Jones, in press-a), dissonance processes are not exclusively the result of the self-concept. In one of the most dramatic demonstrations of this idea, Lawrence and Festinger (1962) demonstrated that white rats, who presumably lack a self-concept, show dissonance arousal and engage in dissonance reduction. Presumably any organism that has "knowledges" or mental representations about how the world operates would be able to experience dissonance and be motivated to reduce it.

Thus, the negative emotion of dissonance results from the appraisal (most likely, an unconscious appraisal) of the cognitive discrepancy as interfering with effective action. The emotion informs the individual that the event is relevant and may inform the individual of his/her perceived coping ability. In addition, the emotion informs the individual that action needs to be taken; in other words, the negative emotion aroused by a cognitive discrepancy motivates behavior aimed at resolving the discrepancy. This view of emotion fits with other general theories of emotion (e.g., Frijda, 1986, 1993).

Paradigms used to test the theory of cognitive dissonance

Induced compliance

Most research on the theory has been carried out using the induced compliance paradigm. In this paradigm, participants are induced to act contrary to an attitude or belief, and if they are provided with few consonant cognitions (few reasons or little justification) for doing so, they are hypothesized to experience dissonance and to be motivated to reduce it. The most often assessed manner in which persons presumably attempt to reduce dissonance is changing attitudes or beliefs to be more consistent with the behavior.

In this situation, the person is confronted with a choice to act contrary to an attitude or belief or refuse to act in this manner. If the person acts, we must assume that the incentives associated with taking the action are greater than the incentives associated with refusing to act. In an experiment, the person may act to avoid hurting the experimenter's feelings, to advance science, and so on. On the other hand, the person is impelled not to act in this manner because an attitude or belief dictates that this behavior should not occur. Thus, the induced compliance situation can be thought of as a decision between acting in the manner suggested or refusing to act in this manner. If there is commitment to the behavior, then the behavior may serve as the focal cognition. Once the person behaves, the reasons for acting in this manner are consonant cognitions, and the reasons for refusing to act (the attitude) are dissonant cognitions. Consonant cognitions support the decision, whereas dissonant cognitions are inconsistent with the decision. The greater the number and importance of the reasons for acting in this manner, the lesser the dissonance. In contrast, the greater the number and importance of the reasons for refusing to act in this manner, the greater the dissonance.

In one of the first induced compliance experiments, Festinger and Carlsmith (1959) paid participants either $1.00 (low justification) or $20.00 (high justification) to tell a "fellow participant" (confederate) that dull and boring tasks were interesting and exciting. After participants told this to the confederate, they were asked how interesting and enjoyable the tasks were. As predicted, participants given little justification for performing the counterattitudinal behavior rated the tasks as more interesting than did participants given much justification. That is, in this experiment, the cognition about the behavior was conceived of as being more resistant to change than the attitude, and thus the attitude, the least resistant-to-change of the cognitions involved, was the one to change. In later research, dissonance was manipulated using perceived choice, assuming that being forced (i.e., having low choice) to behave counterattitudinally is a cognition consonant with that behavior, whereas being given the illusion of choice to behave counterattitudinally (i.e., having high choice) is not. These experiments (e.g., Brehm & Cohen, 1962) found that participants who were subtly induced to write counterattitudinal essays and given an illusion of choice over writing the essay changed their attitudes to be more consistent with their behavior, whereas participants who were given no choice and were simply told that they had to write the essays did not change their attitudes.

Many experiments have been conducted using the induced compliance paradigm, with numerous replications and extensions of the early research (for reviews, see Harmon-Jones & Mills, 1999; Wicklund & Brehm, 1976). In a recently conducted experiment on belief change, Leippe and Eisenstadt (1994) gave White college students low or high choice to write an essay that endorsed a counterattitudinal policy – double the percentage of the available money for scholarships for Blacks and reduce the amount of scholarship money available to Whites. After completion of the essay, participants' attitudes toward the policy and their beliefs about Blacks were assessed. As compared to participants given low choice, participants given high choice to write the essay changed their attitudes to be more supportive of the policy and increased the positivity of their sympathetic beliefs about Blacks.

Exposure to attitude or belief discrepant information

Dissonance is also aroused when persons are exposed to information inconsistent with their beliefs or attitudes. If the dissonance is not reduced by attitude or belief change (e.g., Zimbardo, 1960), the dissonance can lead to misperception, misinterpretation, or misrecall of the information (e.g., Russell & Jones, 1980), rejection or refutation of the information (e.g., Brock & Balloun, 1967; Cacioppo & Petty, 1979), seeking support from those who agree with one's belief or attitude (e.g., Festinger, Riecken, & Schachter, 1956), attempts to persuade others to accept the belief or attitude (e.g., Festinger, Riecken, & Schachter, 1956), intensification of the original belief or attitude (e.g., Batson, 1975; Sherman & Gorkin, 1980), or explaining the disconfirmation by adding new cognitions (Burris, Harmon-Jones, & Tarpley, 1997).

In a study conducted by Batson (1975), females attending a church youth program were asked to declare publicly whether or not they believed in the divinity of Jesus. After completing a measure of Christian orthodoxy, the young women were then presented with belief-disconfirming information (i.e., information that indicated that Jesus was not the son of God). Christian orthodoxy was once again assessed. As expected, those who believed in the divinity of Jesus and accepted the truthfulness of the disconfirming information intensified their belief in Jesus's divinity, whereas those who were not believers or who believed but did not accept the truthfulness of the discon-firming information did not intensify their belief. Batson's (1975) study is an important demonstration of belief intensification in re-sponse to dissonant information.

Experiments explicitly testing the role of emotion in discrepancy reduction

The early experiments on the theory of dissonance were concerned primarily with attitude and belief maintenance, intensification, and change, and not with the emotive processes that led to these cognitive effects. The early researchers simply assumed that the cognitive effects that were being observed resulted from emotive processes, but they rarely directly assessed observable variables related to these mediating constructs to explicitly test this assumption. However, a few early experiments attempted to provide evidence for the motivational and emotional character of dissonance. In the following section, I will briefly describe this research.

There are several questions that can be asked about the role of emotion in producing "dissonance" effects. By dissonance effects, I mean the maintenance, intensification, and changing of attitudes and beliefs that may occur together with and/or through the mispercep-tion, misinterpretation, or misrecall of the information, rejection or refutation of the information, seeking of support from those who agree with one's belief or attitude, and attempts to persuade others to accept the belief or attitude. Two of the more important questions are: (1) Does cognitive discrepancy, as determined by the dissonance ratio, produce negative emotion?; and (2) Does this negative emotion cause these dissonance effects?

Does cognitive discrepancy create negative emotion?

Performance effects
Some early research assessed whether dissonance is accompanied by physiological arousal, because Brehm and Cohen (1962) characterized dissonance as a motivational or drive state that is "tied to specific arousal" (p. 227). It should be noted, however, that the arousal may reflect emotional responses as well. In one line of research, investiga-tors employed a paradigm that attempted to show that dissonance, because it is arousing, would facilitate performance on simple tasks and inhibit performance on complex tasks. These performance effects result because, according to Hull (1943) and Spence (1960), arousal increases the probability of dominant responses. For simple tasks,

correct responses are dominant, whereas for complex tasks, incorrect responses are dominant.

Much of the research designed to test these predictions found that high dissonance manipulations affected task performance in the predicted direction, with dissonance being associated with enhanced performance on simple tasks and poorer performance on complex tasks. However, in these experiments, manipulations of dissonance did not cause cognitive discrepancy reductions (e.g., attitude change), as would be expected (e.g., Cottrell & Wack, 1967; Waterman, 1969; Waterman & Katkin, 1967; see reviews by Kiesler & Pallak, 1976; Wicklund & Brehm, 1976). This suggests that the performance effects may have been due to arousal other than that created by cognitive discrepancy, that the experiments may have failed to yield evidence of cognitive discrepancy reduction because the tasks may have distracted individuals from the cognitive work necessary for this reduction, or that the cognitive discrepancy was reduced in an unmeasured manner (e.g., reduction of perceived importance of the counterattitudinal behavior or the attitude, Simon, Greenberg, & Brehm, 1995).

Physiological arousal
Subsequent research attempted to provide more direct evidence that cognitive discrepancy causes increased arousal, specifically increased sympathetic nervous system activity as measured by peripheral blood flow (Gerard, 1967) and electrodermal activity (Croyle & Cooper, 1983; Elkin & Leippe, 1986; Losch & Cacioppo, 1990). For instance, Harmon-Jones, Brehm, Greenberg, Simon, and Nelson (1996) found that immediately after persons engaged in counterattitudinal behavior, those who had been given the illusion of choice to engage in the behavior evidenced more non-specific skin conductance responses than did those who were forced to engage in the behavior. Moreover, participants given the illusion of choice changed their attitudes to be more consistent with their behavior, whereas participants who were not given choice did not.

Somatic responses
Other research has found that persons respond to cognitive discrepancies with increased somatic responses reflective of negative emotion. For example, Cacioppo and Petty (1979) recorded electromyographic (EMG) activity over several facial muscle regions as persons waited to listen and then listened to a counterattitudinal, proattitudinal, or neutral message. The counterattitudinal message was evaluated less positively, and it evoked fewer favorable thoughts and more counter-arguments than did the proattitudinal message. Moreover, oral (men-

talis) EMG activity was greater when persons anticipated a counter-attitudinal message than when they anticipated a proattitudinal or neutral message, which suggests that more cognitive activity (e.g., counterarguing) may have occurred prior to the presentation of the message "in an effort to rally one's cognitive defenses" (p. 2195). Most important for the present discussion, during the presentation of the message, persons exposed to the counterattitudinal message evidenced less cheek (zygomatic) and more brow (corrugator) muscle region activity than did persons exposed to the proattitudinal message. These facial musculature differences suggest that exposure to the counterattitudinal message evoked less positive and more negative affect than did exposure to the proattitudinal message, as cheek and brow EMG activity have been found to be associated with positive and negative affect, respectively.

Self-reported emotion

Other research has demonstrated that individuals actually experience negative affect in response to cognitive discrepancy (e.g., Elliot & Devine, 1994; Harmon-Jones, in press-b; Kidd & Berkowitz, 1976; Russell & Jones, 1980; Shaffer, 1975). For instance, Zanna and Cooper (1974) found that individuals given high choice to write counter-attitudinal essays reported more tension immediately following the writing of the essays and changed their attitudes more than did individuals given low choice to write the essays.

In another test of the affective consequences of dissonance, Russell and Jones (1980) presented participants with an abstract from a fictitious journal that was consistent or inconsistent with their beliefs in extra-sensory perception (ESP). After reading the abstract, participants completed an affect scale and then completed a recall test. Results showed that increased negative affect occurred when either believers or skeptics were confronted with belief-disconfirming information. However, only believers demonstrated selective learning (discrepancy reduction), recalling less of the abstract than skeptics when ESP was disproven.

Zuwerink and Devine (1996) exposed persons who favored allowing gay persons to serve in the military to an audio-taped counter-attitudinal message. Persons who regarded their attitude on this issue as important were more resistant to attitude change than were persons who regarded their attitude as less important. Moreover, persons who regarded the attitude as important experienced more negative affect (anger, irritation), generated more negative affective and cognitive elaborations, and rated the source of the message more negatively than did persons who regarded the attitude as less important.

In addition, McGregor, Newby-Clark, and Zanna (1999) recently suggested that research and theory on attitudinal ambivalence or naturally occurring inconsistencies between cognitions is consistent with the original theory of dissonance. They presented evidence indicating that the simultaneous accessibility of endorsed positive and negative attitudes toward an issue leads to feelings of ambivalence.

Taken together, this research suggests that cognitive discrepancy causes increases in physiological arousal and experienced negative affect. Other research has examined whether the increased arousal and negative affect actually cause the cognitive effects that occur in dissonance experiments.

Does the increased negative emotion cause the cognitive changes?

Misattribution paradigm

The misattribution paradigm is one way in which the question of whether the increased arousal and negative affect cause the cognitive effects. In the misattribution paradigm, participants are provided a stimulus (e.g., a placebo) that is said to cause specific side effects. Assuming that individuals will search for the cause of an internal state when its source is ambiguous (Schachter & Singer, 1962), researchers have posited that individuals consider internal and external causes, and may occasionally misattribute the actual cause of the increased negative emotion caused by cognitive discrepancy to something else that seems plausible (e.g., the pill they ingested). Misattribution occurs only when the stimulus (e.g., pill) is said to have as a side effect the symptoms the person is actually experiencing. The nature of the internal state can then be inferred indirectly by determining the type of stimuli to which individuals misattribute the state. In the misattribution paradigm, participants are exposed to treatments that will or will not arouse dissonance, and then they are either provided or not provided with a possible external cause for their experienced state.

Zanna and Cooper (1974) first employed the misattribution paradigm. In their experiment, participants were given a "drug" (placebo) to ingest and told that the study concerned the effects of the drug on learning. The drug was said to cause no side effects, tension, or relaxation. The participants then performed an "unrelated" experiment, to allow the drug to take full effect before the learning experiment. In the "unrelated" experiment, participants wrote a counterattitudinal message under high or low choice. The authors reasoned that if discrepancy causes participants to feel tense, and participants change their attitudes to reduce this tension, then participants who believed the pill might cause them to feel tense and who chose to write the counterattitudinal essay would misattribute the internal state induced by dissonance to the pill, and consequently, they would not change their attitudes. Zanna and Cooper's (1974) results supported these ideas. Moreover, they found that high-choice condition participants who were told that the pill would cause them to feel relaxed changed their attitudes more than did other high-choice condition participants. This greater discrepancy reduction may have occurred because participants experienced more negative affect due to the contrast between how they thought they should feel (i.e., relaxed) and how they actually felt (increased negative affect) due to discrepancy.

In the Zanna and Cooper (1974) study, undifferentiated arousal and negative affect were confounded, because participants were told that the pill caused tension, an emotion that is both negative and arousing. Subsequent experiments found that negative affect rather than undifferentiated arousal was responsible for the attitude change in the Zanna and Cooper (1974) study (see Higgins, Rhodewalt, & Zanna, 1979; Zanna, Higgins, & Taves, 1976). Losch and Cacioppo (1990) noted that in the previous experiments, the misattribution sources (e.g., pill) may have been associated with negative experiences, and thus they may have biased participants' interpretations of the dissonance affect in a negative direction. To remedy this problem, Losch and Cacioppo used a misattribution source, prism goggles, found to be novel, affectively malleable, and affectively neutral. Losch and Cacioppo (1990) told participants that the prism goggles would make them tense (negative cue) or pleasantly excited (positive cue). Results indicated that only the negative cue decreased discrepancy reduction (attitude change), suggesting that discrepancy is reduced to decrease the negative affective state rather than undifferentiated arousal.

Independent manipulation of sources of arousal/affect and discrepancy reduction

If the negative affect evoked by cognitive discrepancy causes cognitive discrepancy reduction, then alleviating the negative affect in a manner other than the reduction of cognitive discrepancy might reduce the motivation to reduce the cognitive discrepancy. Similarly, enhancing negative affect might enhance the motivation to reduce the cognitive discrepancy.

In a direct examination of the effects of independent sources of arousal on dissonance processes, Cooper, Zanna, and Taves (1978) had participants write counterattitudinal essays under high or low choice after they ingested a pill. Participants were told that the pill was a placebo, but they were actually given amphetamine (which causes arousal) or phenobarbital (which reduces arousal). Cooper *et al.* (1978) found that participants given amphetamine changed their attitudes in both high- and low-choice conditions, whereas participants given phenobarbital did not change their attitudes. Cooper *et al.* (1978) argued that the results indicated that arousal was a necessary component of the motivation to reduce discrepancy. However, amphetamine may cause individuals to feel more tense than phenobarbital, especially when the drugs taken are thought to be placebos, as Higgins *et al.* (1979) noted. Relatedly, the arousal created by amphetamines may have combined with the discrepancy-produced negative affect to create more negative affect, even in the low-choice condition. Such an explanation is plausible if one assumes that a minimal amount of dissonance is elicited in low-choice conditions. In the phenobarbital condition, the reduction of arousal may have reduced the discrepancy-produced negative affect, which in turn attenuated the discrepancy reduction. Thus, the data could indicate that negative affect that is arousing is necessary for discrepancy reduction to occur. These data suggest that arousal from an independent source can combine with dissonance arousal and increase discrepancy reduction, and that agents that reduce arousal can decrease discrepancy reduction. Research by Brock (1963) and Worchel and Arnold (1974) also manipulated arousal independently of the arousal that resulted from the cognitive discrepancy and found that increased arousal led to increased discrepancy reduction.

Further support for the idea that affect unrelated to dissonance can alter discrepancy reduction comes from an experiment by Rhodewalt and Comer (1979). In their experiment, participants wrote counterattitudinal statements while altering their facial expressions to form a smile, frown, or neutral expression, which has been found to cause positive affect, negative affect, and neutral affect, respectively (Laird, 1974). Control condition participants copied written material from a geology text while holding their face in a neutral position (Laird, 1974). After writing, participants completed an affect scale and then completed an attitude scale. Participants in the smile condition reported the most positive affect; participants in the frown condition reported the least positive affect; control and neutral participants fell in between. Frowning and neutral expression participants changed their attitudes to align them with their behavior, although frowning participants changed their attitudes more than neutral expression participants. In contrast, smiling and control participants did not shift their attitudes. Within-cell analyses of the smile and frown conditions provided further support for the mediating effect of negative affect on discrepancy reduction. By showing that increased positive affect decreases discrepancy reduction and that increased negative affect increases discrepancy reduction, these findings support the hypothesis that discrepancy reduction is motivated by the need to reduce negative affect. [2]

Additional research on whether affect influences discrepancy reduction comes from experiments by Steele, Southwick, and Critchlow (1981) who tested the hypothesis that drinking alcohol would eliminate discrepancy reduction. In their experiment, after participants wrote counterattitudinal essays, they participated in a taste discrimination task. In the taste task, half of the participants drank two mixed vodka drinks and the other half of the participants drank two types of water. Both groups then completed an attitude questionnaire. Results indicated that participants who drank water changed their attitudes, but that participants who drank alcohol did not. Steele *et al.* (1981) suggested that alcohol eliminated the attitude change because of its tension-reducing or disinhibitory effects.

Consistent with the research reviewed in this section, Kidd and Berkowitz (1976) found that a positive mood induced by a humorous audio tape eliminated behaviors that putatively resulted from the motivation to reduce cognitive discrepancy.

The above experiments support the idea that independent increases in negative affect will increase discrepancy reduction as measured by attitude change. However, it is important to note that there are alternative explanations for each of the experiments. The independent manipulations of affect may influence the tolerance of dissonance, the ability to find other discrepancy reduction routes, or the attention to the dissonance or discrepancy. Inclusion of measures of affect and other constructs at critical points during the dissonance process would assist in disentangling the alternative explanations. Future work should be aimed at understanding the exact process by which increased negative affect increases discrepancy reduction and increased positive affect decreases discrepancy reduction.

Correlational analyses of affect and cognitive change
Another way in which the question of whether the affect "causes" the cognitive change could be addressed is through the examination of the correlation of the amount of affect with the amount of cognitive change. Because the data examined are correlational, it is impossible to infer causality, but such data do assist in understanding the relation between affect and cognitive change. In the Zanna and Cooper (1974) experiment, the authors found a positive relation between discrepancy-produced negative affect and discrepancy reduction (attitude

change) in the high-dissonance condition. In the study by Zuwerink and Devine (1996) in which participants were exposed to a message inconsistent with their attitudes, greater experienced negative affect (e.g., anger, irritation) related to more discrepancy reduction. However, others (e.g., Elliot & Devine, 1994; Higgins, Rhodewalt, & Zanna, 1979) failed to find evidence or to report evidence of a positive relation between discrepancy-produced negative affect and attitude change. Thus, these correlational results are ambiguous as to whether self-reported dissonance-related negative affect causes increases in discrepancy reduction.

In a recently conducted induced compliance experiment, Harmon-Jones (in press-b) failed to find evidence of positive correlation between reported negative affect and attitude change. However, a significant curvilinear relationship between reported negative affect and attitude change did emerge, such that persons who reported moderate levels of negative affect in response to behaving counter-attitudinally changed their attitudes more than did persons who reported lower or higher levels of negative affect. Experiments are currently being conducted to examine explanations for this curvilinear effect. For example, it may be that the individuals who reported higher levels of negative affect regarded their attitude as more important and hence the attitude was too resistant to change (Devine, Tauer, Barron, Elliot, & Vance, 1999), or that the individuals who reported higher levels of negative affect were more aware of their negative affect and were less likely to engage in the defensive response of discrepancy reduction (Pyszczynski, Greenberg, Solomon, Sideris, & Stubing, 1993).

Summary and caveat
The reviewed research supports the notion that increased negative affect increases discrepancy reduction. Although most of the research on the role of affect in discrepancy reduction strongly suggests that increased negative affect aroused by cognitive discrepancy increases discrepancy reduction, some exceptions to this causal sequence exist. As reviewed in the section on the correlation between reported affect and discrepancy reduction (most often, attitude change), reported negative affect does not always directly relate to the amount of discrepancy reduction. A number of explanations could be offered for the lack of correlation, such as unreliability of measures of affect and discrepancy reduction. In addition, Pyszczynski *et al.* (1993) found that the expression of dissonance-related affect attenuated the attitude change that typically occurs in the induced compliance situation. Moreover, research suggests that repressors, those who probably have less negative affective experience in general (Weinberger, Schwartz, &

Davidson, 1979), tend to show more evidence of spontaneous discrepancy reduction (Olson & Zanna, 1979). These results suggest that the relation between experienced negative affect and discrepancy reduction may not be direct.

However, it is also wise to consider that dissonance can be reduced in a number of ways, and not all of these ways are assessed within each experiment. Thus, the dissonance may relate directly to the amount of discrepancy reduction but the reduction strategy used by individuals was not assessed in the particular experiment. The idea that dissonance can be reduced via multiple modes was proposed in the original version of the theory (Festinger, 1957), and since then others have discussed the modes persons may use to reduce dissonance (Hardyck & Kardush, 1968; Leippe & Eisenstadt, 1999; Rosenberg & Abelson, 1960; Wicklund & Brehm, 1976). In fact, some scientists have criticized dissonance theory because persons have a variety of ways in which to reduce dissonance (Petri, 1996). This issue, however, is quite interesting, is probably an accurate reflection of the complexity of dissonance reduction, and is in need of further research.

The complexity of multiple modes of discrepancy reduction

The original version of the theory dealt with the complex issue of multiple modes of dissonance reduction by positing that some cognitions are more resistant to change than others and that dissonance reduction would be aimed at the cognition least resistant to change (for supportive research, see Walster, Berscheid, & Barclay, 1967). Another way in which the multiple modes problem can be and has been addressed is by increasing the salience of dissonance reduction strategies (Götz-Marchand, Götz, & Irle, 1974; Wicklund & Brehm, 1976). For instance, Simon, Greenberg, and Brehm (1995) found in an induced compliance experiment that participants reduced dissonance via the route first given to them, regardless of whether it was attitude change or reducing the importance of relevant cognitions.

Most early dissonance theory research seemed to be exclusively concerned with attitude and belief change. Therefore, in the induced compliance research, procedures were undertaken to make the cognition about one's counterattitudinal behavior highly resistant to change by increasing commitment to the behavior. In the belief disconfirmation research, beliefs and attitudes that were personally important and to which persons were deeply committed were often examined. In this research, belief or attitude intensification or change was the only mode of discrepancy reduction assessed.

However, other routes of reducing dissonance may exist, and

persons may prefer these alternative routes. Festinger (1957) posited that individuals could make relevant relations between cognitions not relevant, and that individuals could forget the cognitions involved in a dissonant relation (Festinger, Riecken, & Schachter, 1956). Other theorists proposed additional modes of dissonance reduction (Abelson, 1959; Rosenberg & Abelson, 1960). Following this lead, Hardyck and Kardush (1968) proposed that the different modes of dissonance reduction could be sorted into three broad categories: stopping thinking, changing one cognition of the two that are in a dissonant relation, and restructuring. They also proposed a fourth reaction to dissonance – simply tolerating it – that would be used only when all else failed. For them, stopping thinking could involve passive forgetting or active forgetting (suppression). Passive forgetting was proposed to occur in response to unimportant dissonant relations, whereas active forgetting was proposed to occur in response to important dissonant relations. Changing one of the two cognitions would involve attitude change, denying responsibility for one's behavior, etc. Restructuring could involve increasing the "complexity of *cognitions concerning the two cognitions* in the dissonant relationship" (Hardyck & Kardush, 1968: 685). Restructuring could also involve adding consonant cognitions, making salient consonant cognitions that are already in the psychological situation, or making the relations between cognitions irrelevant. Hardyck and Kardush then proposed that the mode of dissonance reduction selected, when any could be employed, would be a function of (1) effort (2) likelihood of success and (3) the importance of the two cognitions (see Hardyck & Kardush, 1968, for a completion discussion). Hardyck and Kardush (1968) did not present any evidence that had tested this interesting model. In fact, empirical attention to identifying routes of dissonance reduction and to identifying the variables that affect which routes are selected is one of the most neglected areas of research on dissonance theory. Fortunately, some research has attempted to address this lacuna in research.

Intensification of the original belief or attitude

Even though most induced compliance research has produced attitude change in the direction of the counterattitudinal behavior, there are a few experiments in which other ways of reducing discrepancy rather than attitude change occurred. For instance, Sherman and Gorkin (1980) have found bolstering of the pre-existing attitude after their participants behaved contrary to very important beliefs. Cooper and Mackie (1983) also found evidence that could be interpreted as bolstering of the pre-existing attitude after their participants behaved contrary to very important beliefs.

The research just described differs from the majority of induced compliance research in that persons intensified the strength of their beliefs and attitudes rather than changing them to fit with their behavior. Perhaps this belief intensification effect occurs because the research dealt with attitudes and beliefs that were highly resistant to change.

Reducing commitment to the counterattitudinal action

Dissonance can be reduced by altering one of the cognitions involved in the dissonant relationship. After behaving contrary to a belief or attitude, persons can change the belief or attitude to be consistent with the behavior, or persons can deny responsibility for their behavior or perceive it to be less "real" or meaningful. Dissonance theorists and researchers have long recognized the importance of persons believing that they are responsible for their behavior; this has often been operationalized through commitment to the behavior (Beauvois & Joule, 1996, 1999; Brehm & Cohen, 1962; Festinger, 1957, 1964). Much of the reviewed research has provided evidence of attitude or belief change, but persons may instead change the cognition about the counterattitudinal behavior. For example, Brock and Buss (1962) induced participants to administer shocks to an innocent victim. When the victim was a man, participants reduced their estimate of the amount of pain experienced by the victim. In contrast, when the victim was a woman, participants perceived themselves to have been more obligated to participate in the experiment. Perceiving themselves as more obligated may have reduced their sense of responsibility and hence reduced their dissonance.

In another induced compliance experiment that demonstrated attempts to reduce the commitment to counterattitudinal actions, Fleming and Rudman (1993) found that persons would nonverbally distance themselves from their counterattitudinal actions when their actions would harm a person who was present in the experimental room. Moreover, Scheier and Carver (1980) found that manipulations of increased "private" self-awareness (via having participants view themselves in a mirror) caused persons to perceive their counterattitudinal essays as less strong but not to change their attitudes. It is important to note that independent judges rated these participants' essays to be as strong as essays written by participants in a standard induced compliance condition (in which self-awareness was not increased and attitude change occurred).

Altering the importance of relevant cognitions

Simon *et al.* (1995) recently conducted experiments designed to test the idea that persons would reduce dissonance following counterattitudinal behavior by reducing the perceived importance of the cognitions. In one experiment, they found that when the pre-existing attitude was made salient prior to the writing of an essay arguing for mandatory comprehensive final exams, participants given high choice to write the essay reduced dissonance not by changing their attitudes but by reducing the perceived importance of their behavior and attitude toward the issue.

Forgetting or reducing the salience of dissonant cognitions

Evidence also suggests that forgetting about the cognitive discrepancy may reduce dissonance. In an induced compliance experiment (Elkin & Leippe, 1986), electrodermal activity was measured in the minutes following the writing of the counterattitudinal essay and in the minutes following the attitude change opportunity. A number of comparison conditions were included, and the basic effects of the illusion of choice to write the counterattitudinal essays causing increased electrodermal activity and attitude change emerged. Following the attitude change opportunity, electrodermal activity remained elevated for those participants who were given an attitude change opportunity, whereas it was reduced for those participants who were not given an attitude questionnaire but were given a magazine to read for the same time it took to complete the questionnaire. Elkin and Leippe (1986) suggested that participants in this latter condition may have simply forgotten the discrepancy and were less aroused as a result.

Other research has found that when participants' attention is taken away from the dissonance-arousing issue and focused instead on irrelevant communications or technical tasks, discrepancy reduction in the form of attitude change does not occur (e.g., Allen, 1965; Pallak, Brock, & Kiesler, 1967).

Cognitive restructuring

Burris *et al.* (1997) recently examined dissonance reduction via cognitive restructuring. One type of cognitive restructuring may involve transcendence, or reconciling dissonant cognitions under a superordinate principle (Abelson, 1959). Burris, Harmon-Jones, and Tarpley (1997) sought to test an untested idea advanced by Abelson (1959).

Abelson (1959) wrote, "The theosophical dilemma of God's presumed permissiveness toward evil is sometimes resolved by appeal to transcendent concepts" (p. 346). In the experiment by Burris *et al.* (1997), religious individuals read a news story that highlighted the discrepancy between belief in a loving God and knowledge of the gratuitous suffering individuals experience. Participants were then allowed to endorse superordinate principles to explain the discrepancy (transcendence; e.g., "How often does God work in mysterious ways?") or not allowed to make these endorsements (i.e., they completed the transcendence measure prior to arousal of the discrepancy). Then, participants completed a measure of self-reported negative affect, which assessed agitation and discomfort. In support of predictions, within the transcendence condition endorsement of higher levels of transcendence related to lower levels of discomfort and agitation, whereas in the no-transcendence-opportunity condition this relation was not observed. Thus, reducing cognitive discrepancy via transcendence decreased the negative affect aroused by the discrepancy.

Conclusion

The reviewed research strongly suggests that cognitive discrepancy produces negative affect, and that this negative affect motivates attempts to reduce the cognitive discrepancy. The exact manner in which the cognitive discrepancy will be reduced will be influenced by resistance to change of cognitions and the salience of cognitive discrepancy reduction routes. Thus, whether the negative affect produced by cognitive discrepancy influences attitudes and beliefs will be determined in part by whether or not the attitude or belief is more resistant to change than the discrepant information or behavior.

According to the theory of cognitive dissonance, negative affect is aroused when cognition is inconsistent with an existing belief or attitude, and this negative affect may motivate the change or maintenance of the belief or attitude. Indeed, the majority of research on dissonance theory has been concerned with attitude and belief maintenance and change. However, dissonance processes may also contribute the formation of new beliefs and attitudes. That is, dissonance can be reduced by adding consonant cognitions, which might involve the formation of new beliefs. When persons make difficult decisions, when they are confronted with belief-disconfirming evidence, or when they act contrary to their previously held beliefs or attitudes, they may form new beliefs to assist in reducing dissonance. For example, after a difficult decision between career options, a person might believe that their career choice not only provides excellent wages, but that it helps other persons. In addition, persons may form new beliefs to justify their actions or feelings. The creation of rumors of impending disasters to justify feelings of anxiety is an example. Although the formation of beliefs is a theoretically plausible means of reducing dissonance, little research has investigated it. Part of the difficulty in conducting the necessary research is that in demonstrating the formation of a new belief, one would need to demonstrate that no previous belief existed. It is likely that a belief existed and then became more salient or important because of its utility in reducing dissonance, or that an existing belief was modified as a result of dissonance pressures.

The theory of cognitive dissonance has been widely influential and generative within the study of attitudes and beliefs. The exact manner in which the negative affect influences attitudes and beliefs via dissonance processes and the important concept of resistance to change of cognitions has received less attention. These important issues are in need in further inquiry. With theoretical and empirical advances in the study of affect and cognition, the future of research on the role of cognitive dissonance processes looks promising.

Notes

[1] I would like to thank Cindy Harmon-Jones for providing helpful comments on drafts of this chapter. Correspondence concerning this chapter should be addressed to Eddie Harmon-Jones, Department of Psychology, University of Wisconsin – Madison, 1202 West Johnson Street, Madison, Wisconsin, USA, 53706–1696. Electronic mail may be sent to eharmonj@facstaff.wisc.edu.

[2] However, as suggested by Rhodewalt and Comer (1979), because the facial expressions were posed during the writing of the essays, commitment to the position taken in the essay rather than emotion may have caused the attitude effects. That is, relative to persons who posed neutral expressions, persons who frowned may have taken their essays more seriously and been more committed to them while persons who smiled may have taken their essays less seriously and been less committed to them. These differences in commitment to the essay may have, in turn, caused the differences in attitude change.

References

Abelson, R. P. (1959). Modes of resolution of belief dilemmas. *Journal of Conflict Resolution, 3*, 343–352.

Allen, V. L. (1965). Effect of extraneous cognitive activity on dissonance reduction. *Psychological Reports, 16*, 1145–1151.

Aronson, E. (1968). Dissonance theory: Progress and problems. In R. P. Abelson, E. Aronson, W. J. McGuire, T. M. Newcomb, M. J. Rosenberg, & P. H. Tannenbaum (Eds.), *Theories of cognitive consistency: A sourcebook* (pp. 5–27). Chicago: Rand McNally.

Aronson, E. (1995). *The social animal*, 7th ed. New York: W. H. Freeman.

Aronson, E. (1999). Dissonance, hypocrisy, and the self-concept. In E. Harmon-Jones & J. Mills (Eds.), *Cognitive dissonance: Progress on a pivotal theory in social psychology* (pp. 103–126). Washington, DC: American Psychological Association.

Aronson, J., Cohen, G., & Nail, P. R. (1999). Self-affirmation theory: An update and appraisal. In E. Harmon-Jones, & J. Mills (Eds.), *Cognitive dissonance: Progress on a pivotal theory in social psychology* (pp. 127–148). Washington, DC: American Psychological Association.

Batson, C. D. (1975). Rational processing or rationalization?: The effect of disconfirming information on a stated religious belief. *Journal of Personality and Social Psychology, 32*, 176–184.

Beauvois, J. L., & Joule, R. V. (1996). *A radical dissonance theory.* London: Taylor and Francis.

Beauvois, J. L., & Joule, R. V. (1999). A radical point of view on dissonance theory. In E. Harmon-Jones & J. Mills (Eds.), *Cognitive dissonance: Progress on a pivotal theory in social psychology* (pp. 43–70). Washington, DC: American Psychological Association.

Beckmann, J., & Irle, M. (1985). Dissonance and action control. In J. Kuhl & J. Beckmann (Eds.), *Action control: From cognition to behavior* (pp. 129–150). Berlin: Springer-Verlag.

Brehm, J. W. (1992). An unidentified theoretical object. *Psychological Inquiry, 3,* 314–315.

Brehm, J. W., & Cohen, A. R. (1962). *Explorations in cognitive dissonance.* New York: Wiley.

Brock, T. C. (1963). Effects of prior dishonesty on post-decision dissonance. *Journal of Abnormal and Social Psychology, 66,* 325–331.

Brock, T. C., & Balloun, J. C. (1967). Behavioral receptivity to dissonant information. *Journal of Personality and Social Psychology, 6,* 413–428.

Brock, T. C., & Buss, A. H. (1962). Dissonance, aggression, and the evaluation of pain. *Journal of Abnormal and Social Psychology, 65,* 197–202.

Burris, C. T., Harmon-Jones, E., Tarpley, W. R. (1997). "By faith alone": Religious agitation and cognitive dissonance. *Basic and Applied Social Psychology, 19,* 17–31.

Cacioppo, J. T., & Petty, R. E. (1979). Attitudes and cognitive response: An electrophysiological approach. *Journal of Personality and Social Psychology, 37,* 2181–2199.

Cooper, J. (1999). Unwanted consequences and the self: In search of the motivation for dissonance reduction. In E. Harmon-Jones & J. Mills (Eds.), *Cognitive dissonance: Progress on a pivotal theory in social psychology* (pp. 149–173). Washington, DC: American Psychological Association.

Cooper, J., & Fazio, R. H. (1984). A new look at dissonance theory. In L. Berkowitz (Ed.), *Advances in experimental social psychology* (Vol. 17, pp. 229–264). Orlando, FL: Academic Press.

Cooper, J., & Mackie, D. M. (1983). Cognitive dissonance in an intergroup context. *Journal of Personality and Social Psychology, 44,* 536–544.

Cooper, J., Zanna, M. P., & Taves, P. A. (1978). Arousal as a necessary condition for attitude change following induced compliance. *Journal of Personality and Social Psychology, 36,* 1101–1106.

Cottrell, N. B., & Wack, D. L. (1967). Energizing effects of cognitive dissonance upon dominant and subordinate responses. *Journal of Personality and Social Psychology, 6,* 132–138.

Croyle, R. T., & Cooper, J. (1983). Dissonance arousal: Physiological evidence. *Journal of Personality and Social Psychology, 45,* 782–791.

Devine. P. G., Tauer, J. M., Barron, K. E., Elliot, A. J., & Vance, K. M. (1999). Moving beyond attitude change in the study of dissonance-related processes. In E. Harmon-Jones & J. Mills (Eds.), *Cognitive dissonance: Progress on a pivotal theory in social psychology* (pp. 297–323). Washington, DC: American Psychological Association.

Elkin, R. A., & Leippe, M. R. (1986). Physiological arousal, dissonance, and attitude change: Evidence for a dissonance-arousal link and a "don't remind me" effect. *Journal of Personality and Social Psychology, 51*, 55–65.

Elliot, A. J., & Devine, P. G. (1994). On the motivational nature of cognitive dissonance: Dissonance as psychological discomfort. *Journal of Personality and Social Psychology, 67*, 382–394.

Festinger, L. (1957). *A theory of cognitive dissonance*. Stanford, CA: Stanford University Press.

Festinger, L. (1964). *Conflict, decision, and dissonance*. Stanford, CA: Stanford University Press.

Festinger, L., & Carlsmith, J. M. (1959). Cognitive consequences of forced compliance. *Journal of Abnormal and Social Psychology, 58*, 203–210.

Festinger, L., Riecken, H. W., & Schachter, S. (1956). *When prophecy fails*. Minneapolis: University of Minnesota Press.

Fleming, J. H., & Rudman, L. A. (1993). Between a rock and a hard place: Self-concept regulating and communicative properties of distancing behaviors. *Journal of Personality and Social Psychology, 64*, 44–59.

Frijda, N. H. (1986). *The emotions*. Cambridge: Cambridge University Press.

Frijda, N. H. (1993). Moods, emotion episodes, and emotions. In M. Lewis & J. M. Haviland (Eds.), *Handbook of emotions* (pp. 381–403). New York: Guilford Press.

Gerard, H. B. (1967). Choice difficulty, dissonance and the decision sequence. *Journal of Personality, 35*, 91–108.

Götz-Marchand, B., Götz, J., & Irle, M. (1974). Preference of dissonance reduction modes as a function of their order, familiarity, and reversibility. *European Journal of Social Psychology, 4*, 201–228.

Greenwald, A. G., & Ronis, D. L. (1978). Twenty years of cognitive dissonance: Case study of the evolution of a theory. *Psychological Review, 85*, 53–57.

Hardyck, J. A., & Kardush, M. (1968). A modest modish model for dissonance reduction. In R. P. Abelson, E. Aronson, W. T. McGuire, T. M. Newcomb, M. J. Rosenberg, & P. H. Tannenbaum (Eds.), *Theories of cognitive consistency: A sourcebook* (pp. 684–692). Chicago: Rand-McNally.

Harmon-Jones, E. (1999). Toward an understanding of the motivation underlying dissonance effects: Is the production of aversive consequences necessary? In E. Harmon-Jones & J. Mills, *Cognitive dissonance: Progress on a pivotal theory in social psychology* (pp. 71–99). Washington, DC: American Psychological Association.

Harmon-Jones, E. (in press-a). An update on dissonance theory, with a focus on the self. In A. Tesser, R. Felson, & J. Suls (Eds.), *Psychological perspectives on self and identity*. Washington, DC: American Psychological Association.

Harmon-Jones, E. (in press-b). Dissonance and affect: Evidence that dissonance-related negative affect occurs in the absence of aversive consequences. *Personality and Social Psychology Bulletin*.

Harmon-Jones, E., Brehm, J. W., Greenberg, J., Simon, L., & Nelson, D. E. (1996). Evidence that the production of aversive consequences is not necessary to create cognitive dissonance. *Journal of Personality and Social Psychology, 70*, 5–16.

Harmon-Jones, E., & Mills, J. (1999). *Cognitive dissonance: Progress on a pivotal theory in social psychology.* Washington, DC: American Psychological Association.

Higgins, E. T., Rhodewalt, F., & Zanna, M. P. (1979). Dissonance motivation: Its nature, persistence, and reinstatement. *Journal of Experimental Social Psychology, 15*, 16–34.

Hull, C. L. (1943). *Principles of behavior.* New York: Appleton-Century-Crofts.

Jones, E. E. (1985). Major developments in social psychology during the past five decades. In G. Lindzey & E. Aronson (Eds.), *Handbook of social psychology: Vol. 1. Theory and methods*, 3rd ed., pp. 47–107. New York: Random House.

Jones, E. E., & Gerard, H. B. (1967). *Foundations of social psychology.* New York: Wiley.

Kidd, R. F., & Berkowitz, L. (1976). Effect of dissonance arousal on helpfulness. *Journal of Personality and Social Psychology, 33*, 613–622.

Kiesler, C. A., & Pallak, M. S. (1976). Arousal properties of dissonance manipulations. *Psychological Bulletin, 83*, 1014–1025.

Laird, J. D. (1974). Self-attribution of emotion: The effects of expressive behavior on the quality of emotional experience. *Journal of Personality and Social Psychology, 29*, 475–486.

Lawrence, D. H., & Festinger, L. (1962). *Deterrents and reinforcement.* Stanford, CA: Stanford University Press.

Leippe, M. R., & Eisenstadt, D. (1994). The generalization of dissonance reduction: Decreasing prejudice through induced compliance. *Journal of Personality and Social Psychology, 67*, 395–413.

Leippe, M. R., & Eisenstadt, D. (1999). A self-accountability model of dissonance reduction: Multiple modes on a continuum of elaboration. In E. Harmon-Jones & J. Mills (Eds.), *Cognitive dissonance: Progress on a pivotal theory in social psychology* (pp. 201–232). Washington, DC: American Psychological Association.

Losch, M. E., & Cacioppo, J. T. (1990). Cognitive dissonance may enhance sympathetic tonus, but attitudes are changed to reduce negative affect rather than arousal. *Journal of Experimental Social Psychology, 26*, 289–304.

McGregor, I., Newby-Clark, I. R., & Zanna, M. P. (1999). "Remembering" dissonance: Simultaneous accessibility of inconsistent cognitive elements moderates epistemic discomfort. In E. Harmon-Jones & J. Mills (Eds.), *Cognitive dissonance: Progress on a pivotal theory in social psychology* (pp. 325–353).Washington, DC: American Psychological Association.

Mills, J. (1999). Improving the 1957 version of dissonance theory. In E. Harmon-Jones & J. Mills (Eds.), *Cognitive dissonance: Progress on a pivotal theory in social psychology* (pp. 25–42).Washington, DC: American Psychological Association.

Olson, J. M., & Zanna, M. P. (1979). A new look at selective exposure. *Journal of Experimental Social Psychology, 15*, 1–15.

Pallak, M. S., Brock, T. C., & Kiesler, C. A. (1967). Dissonance arousal and task performance in an incidental verbal learning paradigm. *Journal of Personality and Social Psychology, 7*, 11–21.

Petri, H. L. (1996). *Motivation: Theory, research, and applications*, 4th ed. Pacific Grove: Brooks/Cole.

Pyszczynski, T., Greenberg, J., Solomon, S., Sideris, J., & Stubing, M. J. (1993). Emotional expression and the reduction of motivated cognitive bias: Evidence from cognitive dissonance and distancing from victims' paradigms. *Journal of Personality and Social Psychology, 64,* 177–186.

Rhodewalt, F., & Comer, R. (1979). Induced-compliance attitude change: Once more with feeling. *Journal of Experimental Social Psychology, 15,* 35–47.

Rosenberg, M. J., & Abelson, R. P. (1960). An analysis of cognitive balancing. In M. J. Rosenberg, C. I. Hovland, W. J. McGuire, Abelson, R. P., & Brehm, J. W. (Eds.), *Attitude organization and change* (pp. 112–163). New Haven: Yale University Press.

Russell, D., & Jones, W. H. (1980). When superstition fails: Reactions to disconfirmation of paranormal beliefs. *Personality and Social Psychology Bulletin, 6,* 83–88.

Sakai, H. (1999). A multiplicative power function model of cognitive dissonance: Toward an integrated theory of cognition, emotion, and behavior after Leon Festinger. In E. Harmon-Jones & J. Mills (Eds.), *Cognitive dissonance: Progress on a pivotal theory in social psychology* (pp. 267–294). Washington, DC: American Psychological Association.

Schachter, S., & Singer, J. E. (1962). Cognitive, social, and physiological determinants of emotional states. *Psychological Review, 69,* 379–399.

Scheier, M. F., & Carver, C. S. (1980). Private and public self-attention, resistance to change, and dissonance reduction. *Journal of Personality and Social Psychology, 39,* 390–405.

Shaffer, D. R. (1975). Some effects of consonant and dissonant attitudinal advocacy on initial attitude salience and attitude change. *Journal of Personality and Social Psychology, 32,* 160–168.

Sherman, S., & Gorkin, L. (1980). Attitude bolstering when behavior is inconsistent with central attitudes. *Journal of Experimental Social Psychology, 16,* 388–403.

Simon, L., Greenberg, J., & Brehm, J. W. (1995). Trivialization: The forgotten mode of dissonance reduction. *Journal of Personality and Social Psychology, 68,* 247–260.

Spence, K. W. (1960). *Behavior theory and learning.* Englewood Cliffs, NJ: Prentice-Hall.

Steele, C. M. (1988). The psychology of self-affirmation: Sustaining the integrity of the self. In L. Berkowitz (Ed.), *Advances in experimental social psychology* (Vol. 21, pp. 261–302). San Diego, CA: Academic Press.

Steele, C. M., Southwick, L. L., & Critchlow, B. (1981). Dissonance and alcohol: Drinking your troubles away. *Journal of Personality and Social Psychology, 41,* 831–846.

Walster, E., Berscheid, E., & Barclay, A. M. (1967). A determinant of preference among modes of dissonance reduction. *Journal of Personality and Social Psychology, 7,* 211–216.

Waterman, C. K. (1969). The facilitating and interfering effects of cognitive dissonance on simple and complex paired associates learning tasks. *Journal of Experimental Social Psychology, 5,* 31–42.

Waterman, C. K., & Katkin, E. S. (1967). The energizing (dynamogenic) effect of cognitive dissonance. *Journal of Personality and Social Psychology, 6,* 126–131.

Weinberger, D. A., Schwartz, G. E., & Davidson, R. J. (1979). Low-anxious, high-anxious, and repressive coping styles: Psychometric patterns and behavioral and physiological responses to stress. *Journal of Abnormal Psychology, 88,* 369–380.

Wicklund, R. A., & Brehm, J. W. (1976). *Perspectives on cognitive dissonance.* Hillsdale, NJ: Erlbaum.

Worchel, S., & Arnold, S. E. (1974). The effect of combined arousal states on attitude change. *Journal of Experimental Social Psychology, 10,* 549–560.

Zanna, M. P., & Cooper, J. (1974). Dissonance and the pill: An attribution approach to studying the arousal properties of dissonance. *Journal of Personality and Social Psychology, 29,* 703–709.

Zanna, M. P., & Cooper, J. (1976). Dissonance and the attribution process. In J. H. Harvey, W. J. Ickes, and R. F. Kidd (Eds.), *New directions in attribution research.* Vol. 1. Hillsdale, NJ: Erlbaum.

Zanna, M. P., Higgins, E. T., & Taves, P. A. (1976). Is dissonance phenomenologically aversive? *Journal of Experimental Social Psychology, 12,* 530–538.

Zimbardo, P. G. (1960). Involvement and communication discrepancy as determinants of opinion conformity. *Journal of Abnormal and Social Psychology, 60,* 86–94.

Zuwerink, J. R., & Devine, P. G. (1996). Attitude importance and resistance to persuasion: It's not just the thought that counts. *Journal of Personality and Social Psychology, 70,* 931–944.

9

Relationship beliefs and emotion: Reciprocal effects[1]

Margaret S. Clark and Ian Brissette

Beliefs and emotions are tied together in many ways. In recent years the connections between beliefs and emotions receiving the most attention are those existing within a single person. That is, many researchers have asked just how and why a person's beliefs influence his or her own affective experiences; others have asked just how and why a person's affective states influence his or her own beliefs. Such work is well represented in the present volume. This chapter, however, is written from a different perspective – an interpersonal rather than an intrapersonal perspective – something that, as Ekman and Davidson (1994) have noted, has been given "short shrift" among psychologists interested in emotion.[2] We address two broad questions: First, how do people's beliefs about their relationships with others influence their expressions of emotions to those others? Second, how do experiences and expressions of emotion influence beliefs about relationships?

In answering these questions we argue for the idea that the structure of social relationships has important implications for understanding the experience, expression and interpretation of emotions. In so doing, we follow in the tradition of others who have noted the importance of understanding social structure for understanding emotion. This tradition includes researchers who have emphasized how status and power influence expressions of emotion (Kemper, 1978, 1993), those who emphasize how gender roles influence the expression of emotion (Brody, 1985; Brody & Hall, 1993; Timmers, Fischer, & Manstead, 1998), and Hochschild who has argued that the nature of one's job may require "emotion work" (Hochschild, 1975, 1979, 1990). However, we differ from these others in the aspects of social relationships on which we focus. Unlike others in this tradition, we *emphasize how feeling a special responsibility for the needs of one's partner and how believing that one's partner feels such a responsibility for one's own* needs influence emotional life. To put this in our own theoretical terms, we argue that whether one believes one has a communal relationship with the other (Clark & Mills, 1979, 1993; Mills & Clark, 1982), how strong that communal relationship is believed to be, how certain one is of the communal relationship (Clark & Mills, 1993; Mills & Clark, 1982), and whether that communal relationship is believed to be obligate or discretionate (Brissette & Clark, 1998) all have implications for the expression and interpretation of emotions.

Our arguments are based upon some simple assumptions. First we assume that one important function of experiencing and expressing emotion is to *communicate need states* – both to oneself, but most importantly for this chapter, to others who care about one's welfare and about whose welfare one cares. Although many emotion re- searchers have noted the communication function of emotion, most have emphasized how our own emotions serve to alert us to our own needs (Frijda, 1993; Simon, 1967). We along with a few others (e.g., Levenson, 1994) emphasize two *inter*personal communication func- tions as well. One is that expressing many emotions (e.g., fear, sadness, happiness, contentment) serves to communicate our needs (or lack thereof) to others thus allowing those others to address those needs and us to mobilize external resources (Watson & Clark, 1994; Scott, 1958, 1980). The other is that experiencing and expressing a narrower set of emotions (e.g., guilt, empathic distress, empathic happiness) serve to convey to our relationship partners and to ourselves that we care about *their* needs. Second we assume that social relationships can be distinguished from one another on the basis of the extent to which members feel responsible for one another's needs (Clark & Mills, 1979, 1993; Mills & Clark, 1982). These two assump- tions in conjunction imply that understanding relationship context is crucial to understanding the roles emotions play in people's lives.

Beliefs about relationships influence the expression and sometimes the experience of emotion

We begin our arguments by discussing how beliefs about relationships influence expression of emotion. Relationship beliefs that we argue are important include beliefs about whether a relationship is communal or not, how strong a communal relationship it is, whether the com- munal relationship is obligate or discretionate as well as the certainty with which such beliefs are held.

Communal relationships and communal relationship strength

Clark and Mills have drawn distinctions between social relationships based upon the implicit rules governing the distribution of benefits in relationships (Clark & Mills, 1979, 1993; Mills & Clark, 1982). In communal relationships, they argue, members are concerned about the other's welfare. To the best of their ability, they keep track of the other's needs (Clark, Mills, & Powell, 1986; Clark, Mills, & Corcoran, 1989), and strive to give benefits to fulfill the other person's needs or to demonstrate a general concern for the other person (Clark, Ouellette, Powell, 1987). At the same time, members of communal relationships are not expected to neglect their own needs (Clark, Dubash, & Mills, 1998). Friendships, romantic relationships, and family relationships often exemplify communal relationships. In communal relationships, when a benefit is given to a person, that person does not incur a specific debt which must be repaid with a comparable benefit (Clark & Mills, 1979; Clark & Waddell, 1985).

Clark and Mills have contrasted communal relationships with other relationships in which members feel no special sense of responsibility for the other's welfare. Their most frequently used examples of such relationships are exchange relationships. In exchange relationships people keep track of benefits given and received (Clark, 1984; Clark *et al.*, 1989) and benefits are given on the basis of comparable benefits received in the past or with the expectation of being repaid with comparable benefits in the future (Clark & Mills, 1979; Clark & Waddell, 1985). Exchange relationships are often exemplified by relationships between people who do business with one another (e.g., a store owner and a customer), and by acquaintances who exchange circumscribed benefits but do not take on responsibility for one another beyond that (e.g., parents who work out a car pool to transport their respective children to and from athletic practices). However, exchange relationships are not the only example of noncommunal relationships. Exploitative relationships, in which members are primarily concerned with their own needs and are willing to act in unjust ways to extract benefits for themselves also are examples of noncommunal relationships.

We believe that the distinction between communal relationships and other relationships is important to understanding emotions because *emotions very often convey information about the need states of the person expressing the emotion* and *about our reactions to another person's needs*. For instance, a sad person is feeling a loss and may be in need of comfort or help in recovering from that loss whereas a happy or content person is not feeling needy. Negative feelings generated through empathy convey that one feels badly because another is in need, whereas happy feelings generated through empathy indicate one is pleased that another's welfare has received a boost. A guilty person feels badly about having neglected another person's needs or about having harmed another. Because it is in communal relationships, according to our analysis, that people feel a special responsibility for the other's needs and expect the other to care about their welfare, it follows that expressing emotions should be far more important to communication within the context of communal relationships than to communication within other types of relationships.

Although Clark and Mills began their work with a simple qualitative distinction between communal relationships and noncommunal relationships, they have pointed out a quantitative dimension to communal relationships as well (Mills & Clark, 1982). Specifically, Clark and Mills assert that communal relationships vary in strength or, in other words, the *degree* to which members feel responsible for the other person's needs. In weak communal relationships members feel a small amount of responsibility for the other person's needs and give low cost benefits on a communal basis; as communal relationships become stronger members feel greater amounts of responsibility for the other's needs and give higher cost benefits. Most people have weak communal relationships even with strangers. They will tell the stranger the time or give directions without expecting comparable benefits in return but they will not return the stranger's library books or give the stranger a ride to the airport on the same basis.[3] They have stronger communal relationships with friends – they would tell a friend the time, give directions, return the friend's books to the library and give the friend a ride to the airport. However, they would not pay the friend's college tuition. They have even stronger communal relationships with their children. They would do almost anything for their children on a communal basis including paying the children's college tuition. This dimension of communal strength is depicted in Figure 9.1.

The implication of communal relationship strength for emotional expression is simple. Because emotions very often signal one's own needs or one's concern for one's partner's needs, expressing one's own emotions and emotional experience and expression in response to one's partner's needs ought to be seen as more appropriate and ought to occur more in stronger communal relationships.[4]

Do we express emotions more often when we believe the relationship to be a communal relationship, especially a strong one?

If one assumes that existing friendships and romantic relationships often exemplify communal relationships – an assumption for which there is considerable support (Clark, 1984; Clark et al., 1989; Clark & Grote, 1998; Grote & Clark, in press), there is, indeed, evidence that communal relationships – especially strong ones – involve more

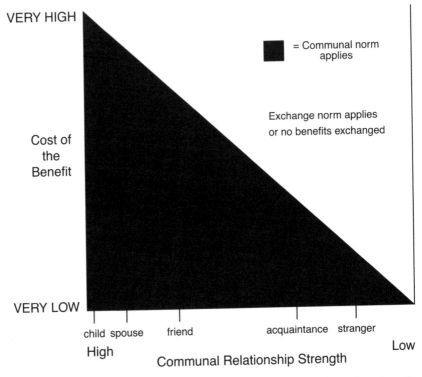

VERY HIGH

■ = Communal norm
applies

Exchange norm applies
or no benefits exchanged

Cost of
the
Benefit

VERY LOW

child spouse   friend   acquaintance stranger

High   Low

Communal Relationship Strength

Figure 9.1 When the communal norm will be applied as a function of communal relationship strength and cost of benefit. (The placement of stranger, acquaintance, friend, spouse and child on the communal relationship strength axis is for illustrative purposes. The placement and ordering of relationships in terms of communal strength will vary from person to person.)

emotional expression. For example, in a study by Clark and Taraban (1991, Study 2) participants were randomly assigned to have a discussion with their friend or with a stranger. The experimenter gave them a list of fifteen potential topics, five involving talking about emotions (i.e., "times you have felt especially serene," "your fears," "things that make you sad," "things that make you angry," and "what makes you happy"); the rest not (e.g., "your future plans," "your opinions of Carnegie Mellon," "your favorite restaurants"). Participants ranked the topics in terms of their preferences. The results were clear. All emotional topics received higher rankings in the Friends than in the Strangers condition with the difference in ranks reaching traditional levels of significance for four of the five topics.

Recently Barrett, Robin, Pietromonaco, and Eyssell (1998) also reported data linking the existence and strength of communal relationships with emotional expression. They had college students keep daily diaries of happiness, sadness, nervousness, surprise, anger, embarrassment, and shame experienced and expressed within the context of any interaction lasting for ten minutes or longer. Participants did this for seven days. They also indicated the closeness of their ongoing relationships with the other people. (Barrett *et al.* did not define closeness for their participants, but we believe most people interpret close to mean communal in nature.) On the average, the intensity of participants' emotional experiences and the *degree to which they expressed those emotions* was positively and significantly associated with the rated closeness of their relationship with the other person. (See also Shimanoff, 1988, for findings making the same point.)

Finally, in a questionnaire study we recently conducted, we again obtained evidence that more emotion is expressed in communal – especially strong communal – relationships than in other relationships. First, we defined the communal strength of a relationship to participants as the extent to which a person responds to the other's needs without requiring or expecting a comparable benefit in return. We added that, in these relationships, people do not keep track of who has provided what to whom, but that they do keep track of who needs what. Then the participants rated the communal strength of a number of their relationships including those with a stranger, their mother, a casual friend, a sister or brother, their boss at work, their professor, a neighbor, a close friend, a fellow member of a sports team, a classmate, their cousin, a member of their church or temple, their priest, minister, or rabbi, a fellow employee at work, their father, a member of their fraternity or sorority, and their roommate. On a separate sheet they also rated the extent to which they would express hurt, sadness, anger, disgust, guilt, fear, happiness, and contentment within each of these relationships (both when caused by that partner and when caused by someone or something else). Ratings of how communal each relationship was were made on nine-point Likert scales. Ratings of the extent to which one was likely to express each of the specific emotions within those relationships were made on seven-point Likert scales.

Were people, indeed, most willing to express each of these emotions in the relationships they considered to be the most communal in nature? Yes. We found large and consistent positive correlations between how communal particular relationships were perceived to be and the extent to which people reported being willing to express both positive and negative emotions in those relationships. When the emotions were caused by the other those correlations were .23 for anger, .27 for disgust, .40 for fear, .39 for guilt, .39 for hurt, .43 for sadness, .43 for contentment, and .48 for happiness. When the emotions were caused by someone or something else the correlations were .45 for anger, .48 for disgust, .57 for fear, .45 for guilt, .54 for hurt, .51 for sadness, .43 for contentment, and .49 for happiness. All correlations were statistically significant.

We believe the correlations for anger and disgust caused by the other were smaller than the other correlations because in mutual communal relationships not only is one's partner supposed to be concerned about one's welfare, one is supposed to be concerned about one's partner's welfare as well. As a result, one sometimes may suppress expression of disgust and anger so as not to hurt one's partner's feelings.

Overall, on average, people said they would *suppress* feelings of hurt, guilt, sadness anger, fear and disgust when with people such as strangers, coworkers, neighbors, and professors – relationships which they also reported being low in communal strength. However, they reported that they *would express* those feelings to mothers, fathers, close friends, siblings and roommates – relationships which were reported to be higher in communal strength. On average, our participants also told us they would be more likely to express emotions such as happiness and contentment to such people as mothers fathers, close friends and siblings than to such people as strangers, bosses, coworkers and neighbors.

In sum, the more communal a relationship is, the more likely we are to express the emotions – both positive and negative– that we feel and that will inform the other about our current need state. Moreover, by expressing more emotion in communal relationships, people may also come to experience more emotion in these relationships. After all, many have argued that the very act of expressing emotion provides feedback that may intensify that emotion (Laird, 1974; Laird & Bresler, 1992; Riskind & Gotay, 1982; Riskind, 1984). Turning now to a related point, we address whether we are also more likely to experience and express emotion in response to our partners' need states in communal than in other relationships.

Do we experience and express more emotions in response to the other person's need states when we believe we have communal obligations to the other?

Most communal relationships between peers are mutual – not only do we assume that the other cares about our needs, and that he or she should and will respond to those needs on a communal basis; we also care about the other's needs and feel we should respond to those needs on a communal basis. Moreover, there are certain asymmetric communal relationships (to be discussed in more detail below) in which one actually feels *greater* responsibility for the welfare of the other than one expects that other to feel for oneself (e.g., one's relationship with one's own newborn child). Feelings of responsibility for another's welfare have clear implications for expressing certain emotions (i.e., those experienced in response to the other's needs, such as guilt, empathic sadness, and empathic happiness) and they also have implications for *experiencing* these emotions in the first place.

Consider the experience of these emotions first. Guilt usually implies that one feels badly about having not met another person's needs or about having harmed the other's welfare in some way. As a result of people having greater responsibilities for the other's needs in stronger communal relationships, there should be more opportunities for feeling that one has unjustly neglected those needs and more opportunities for guilt to occur in stronger relative to weaker communal relationships. Moreover, given the same neglectful actions, guilt should be greater in stronger than in weaker communal relationships. For example, most people would feel more guilty if they forgot their mother's birthday than if they forgot a friend's birthday, and more guilty if they forgot a good friend's birthday than if they forgot a casual friend's birthday. Or consider empathic sadness. This implies that one cares about the loss another has experienced and, holding the magnitude of the other's loss constant, such sadness should be greater the stronger the communal relationship with the other. Finally, consider experiencing empathic happiness when another's welfare has received a boost. It too should be greater the stronger the communal relationship with the other.

Is there evidence for people experiencing and expressing more of these "other oriented" emotions within communal relationships? Yes. First consider some recent work on guilt by Baumeister, Stillwell, and Heatherton (1994, 1995). These authors asked students to write two stories describing incidents in which they had angered someone. They were to pick two incidents that were important and memorable and thoroughly describe them. One was to be of an incident after which the participant "felt bad or suffered from a feeling of having done something wrong"; the other an incident after which the participant "did not feel bad or suffer from a feeling of having done something wrong." The stories were coded for whether the victim was someone with whom the subject had a communal relationship or not. As predicted, the incidents participants chose as examples of ones in which they felt bad or suffered from a feeling of having done something wrong (that is, guilt, as operationally defined by the authors) were more likely to have taken place in the context of a communal

relationship than were the incidents chosen to represent times participants did not feel bad or suffer from a feeling of having done something wrong.[5] In other words guilt appears to have been experienced
more often in the context of communal relationships.

What about empathic compassion or happiness? Are these emotions also experienced more often in communal relationships? Again,
the answer is yes. Consider evidence for empathic compassion first
(i.e., feeling sympathetic, compassionate, softhearted and tender – to
use Batson's conception of this emotion). Batson and his colleagues
have often used a manipulation of similarity to experimentally create
the experience of this emotion and they have done so with considerable success. People who feel similar to another person in need have
been shown to experience more empathic compassion for that
person than do those not manipulated to feel similar to another (e.g.,
Batson, Duncan, Ackerman, Buckley, & Birch, 1981; Batson, Turk,
Shaw, & Klein, 1995; Krebs, 1975). Importantly for the present
argument, the reason that a similarity manipulation appears to result
in these enhanced feelings of empathic compassion is that it increases the degree to which experimental participants care about the
welfare of the other person. In other words, manipulating similarity
seems to increase the strength of the communal relationship between
the two people in question. The evidence for this comes from Batson
et al. (1995, Studies 1 & 2). In two studies, these researchers manipulated how similar college females felt to another college female by
providing feedback that the other had answered a "personal profile
and interest inventory" either in very much the same way as the
participant or in quite a different way. Later participants in the
highly similar conditions reported feeling more similar to the other
and also valuing the other's welfare more. Apparently people who
perceive themselves to be similar to another also perceive themselves
to have a stronger communal relationship with the other and, in
turn, experience more empathic compassion when that other is in
need.

Finally consider empathic happiness. Research evidence suggests
that it too is experienced more frequently within the context of
communal relationships. Specifically, Williamson and Clark (1989,
Study 3; 1992) reported two studies in which they measured positive
and negative moods at the beginning of their studies, and then
manipulated desire for a communal versus desire for an exchange
relationship with another "participant." Later participants were either
induced to help that other participant or not. Then the experimenters
measured mood again. In both studies helping the other was associated with improvements in mood, *but only when a communal relation-*

ship was desired. Moreover, in the 1992 study this improvement in mood occurred whether the help was freely given or required. The fact that the needy other was benefited, not the fact that the helper could think of him- or herself as a wonderful person for having provided the help freely, seems key to the improvement in mood when help was provided. This overall pattern is consistent with the idea that empathic happiness when another is benefited is something that occurs selectively, within communal relationships.[6]

Taken together this evidence suggests that any emotion that indicates to oneself that one cares about the welfare of another person should occur more frequently and more intensely the more communal one's relationship with that other person. Further, existing literature on the experience of guilt, empathic compassion, and empathic happiness experienced when one's relationship partner has been benefited supports this contention.

Our theoretical position also suggests, of course, that not only should one *experience* more guilt, empathic compassion, and empathic happiness within the context of communal relationships; one also should *express* these emotions more often in the context of communal relationships. In mutual communal relationships, after all, not only should it be important that one expresses one's own emotions to the other, thereby alerting one's partner to one's own needs; it should also be important that one express the guilt, empathic compassion, and empathic happiness that one experiences on the partner's behalf to convey to that partner that one cares about him or her. There is little empirical evidence to support this idea. However, we note that Baumeister *et al.* (1995) found that guilt was not only experienced but also expressed more often within communal than within other relationships. Of course, these results could be accounted for by simply arguing that one must experience an emotion before it can be expressed. However, even if the experience of emotions such as guilt, empathic compassion, and empathic happiness was constant, we hypothesize that these emotions would still be expressed more often in communal relationships.

Also, in our own study, described above in connection with expressing emotions conveying one's own needs, we included one of the three emotions indicating concern for the other's welfare – that is, guilt. We asked participants to tell us, when they experienced guilt, the extent to which they would express it to others. They told us they would be far less likely to express guilty feelings to others with whom they had weak communal relationships (e.g., strangers, coworkers, neighbors, professors, and classmates) than they would be to express guilty feelings to those with whom they reported having stronger communal relationships (e.g., roommates, siblings, close friends, mothers, and fathers).

Believing a communal relationship is symmetrical versus asymmetrical and expressing emotion

To this point we have discussed communal relationships as if both members of such a relationship feel equally responsible for one another's needs and thus equally able (or unable) to express emotions in their relationship. Indeed, many communal relationships (such as communal relationships between friends, romantic partners and family members occupying similar roles) are symmetrical. However, communal relationships can be asymmetrical and the degree of symmetry in a communal relationship has implications for expressing emotions. An asymmetrical communal relationship occurs when one person feels more communal responsibility for the other than vice versa. The parent of a young child, for example, typically feels a much greater responsibility for the welfare of the child than the child does for the parent.

The implications of asymmetry of communal responsibility for understanding emotional expression are straightforward. The person who feels more communal responsibility for the other is more restricted in expressing emotions that carry information about his or her own needs but more likely to express feelings of tenderness and sympathy for the other. For instance, it is far more appropriate for a child to express sadness and to cry in front of his or her parents than for the parent to express sadness and to cry in front of his or her child. Indeed, the relationship would probably be considered a troubled one if the child was unwilling to express his or her fears, anger, and frustrations to the parent *or* if the parent regularly expressed all of his or her fears, anger, and frustrations to the child. Moreover, especially early in the relationship, the parent is expected to express tenderness, care, and empathy to the child while the reverse is not expected. Of course, as a child grows, the communal nature of the relationship is likely to become more symmetrical and, with that change, expressions of emotion should also become more symmetrical.

In our questionnaire study of emotion expression described earlier in this chapter, we did find evidence of people being especially reluctant to express their emotions to their very young children and becoming increasingly willing to do so as those children age. Specifically, we asked our participants the extent to which they would be willing to express their emotions to a preschool child, an adolescent child, and an adult child. People reported they would be quite reluctant to express anger, sadness, fear, disgust, guilt and hurt to very young children but they become increasingly willing to express those emotions as those children grow older.

The norm that parents should not express emotions indicative of their own needs to young children is not absolute. It only should apply insofar as the child is perceived as being unable to meet the parent's needs and/or when it is perceived that it would be unhealthy for the child to have to meet the parent's needs given the child's level of maturity. In other words, the key conceptual variable here is the degree of responsibility for the other person's welfare. There certainly will be some occasions when a child *is* seen as having the ability to act in ways that meet the parent's needs or fulfill the child's duty to a family. For instance, a parent might quite appropriately express irritability at a young child who is interfering with the parent's needs by making noise while the parent is trying to speak on the phone, as long as the child is perceived as having the ability and responsibility to be quiet at that time. So too is it likely to be perceived as appropriate to express irritability if the child leaves his or her belongings scattered on the floor when the parent believes the child has the ability not to do so. Indeed, fostering these levels of responsibility in a child fulfills part of the parent's responsibility to socialize the child. The general point is not that parents' emotions can *never* be expressed to the child but rather that, in general, because the parent has greater responsibility for the child's welfare than vice versa, the child will have more leeway to express his or her emotions to the parent than does the parent to the child.

Being certain about the nature of a communal relationship and expressing emotion

We have pointed out that communal relationships can be qualitatively distinguished from other relationships in that they are characterized by members benefiting one another in response to needs without creating a specific debt. We have noted that there also is a quantitative dimension to people's communal relationships in that they feel a greater responsibility for some people's needs than they do for others. Going beyond those dimensions, Mills and Clark (1982) have also noted that communal relationships can vary in terms of how *certain* we are that a particular relationship is communal. Certainty reflects the degree of confidence that the other person will treat one's relationship in a communal fashion and/or that the other truly desires a communal relationship.

Sometimes, due to one's history with another person and/or to cultural dictates, one is very certain that the relationship is a strong communal one. Other times, one may very much desire a communal relationship, perhaps even a strong one, and may suspect or hope that the other does as well, while feeling uncertain about that other's intention. This might occur, for instance, when one is not romantically involved with another person and meets an attractive personable other. One would like to form a strong communal relationship with this other and has begun to indicate that interest to the other, but is still uncertain of the other's interest in a similarly strong communal relationship. We suspect that certainty will vary, to some extent, as a function of the length of communal relationships – newly developing friendships and romantic relationships are often characterized by more uncertainty than more established ones. We further suspect that there are important and stable individual differences in people's certainty about whether their relationships with others are highly communal or not. For instance, we would suspect that those who have insecure attachment styles might be chronically lower in certainty about their communal relationships than are those with secure attachment styles.

What are the implications of uncertainty about communal relationships? It seems likely that the greater the uncertainty about a communal relationship, the more reluctance there will be to express negative emotions to the other lest such emotions put too much pressure on the other to respond to one's needs. On the other hand, given that people have strong motives to present themselves in a favorable light when trying to form new friendships or romantic relationships (Bell & Daly, 1984; Burger & Bell, 1988), people may quite intentionally, even strategically, present more positive than negative emotions to the other, so as not to seem too needy and to present themselves in a positive, likable light (Clark, Pataki, & Carver, 1996).

Aune, Buller, and Aune (1996) have recently reported findings from two laboratory observational/questionnaire studies involving dating and married couples that are consistent with our ideas about the effects of communal relationship certainty on the expression and perceived appropriateness of emotional expression. In both studies, the perceived appropriateness of expressing both positive and negative emotions increased with relationship development. In terms of actual management of emotion in their conversations, partners in more developed relationships managed positive emotions less than negative emotions, and less than early daters managed either negative or positive emotions.

Believing a communal relationship to be obligate or discretionate and expressing emotion

Our definition of communal relationships is that they are characterized by people feeling a responsibility for the welfare of the other person and responding to that person's needs accordingly. It is, presumably, believing that the other cares for one's welfare that leads one to feel free to express one's emotions.

The factors that lead a person to have a communal relationship with another and that maintain that communal relationship may also have important implications for understanding people's willingness to express certain emotions. As Brissette and Clark (1998) point out, motivations to form communal relationships can vary. Sometimes our biology and/or culture seem to strongly dictate that we adopt a communal norm for interacting with a particular other. For instance, new parents typically feel obligated to adopt a communal norm for purposes of interacting with their infants, many family members feel obligated to adopt a communal norm for purposes of caring for the elderly members of their family, members of a church may feel obligated to adopt a communal norm for interactions with needy people within the church, and so forth. There will be social or even legal sanctions if we fail to treat such people in a communal fashion (Finch & Mason, 1993). We call these sorts of relationships "obligate" communal relationships. In contrast, people sometimes form communal relationships with others even though their biology or culture does not dictate that they should have communal relationships with these particular others. Friendships and romantic relationships often exemplify such voluntary communal relationships. We call these sorts of relationships "discretionate" communal relationships.

It is our belief that whether a communal relationship is "obligate" or "discretionate" has implications for the expression of some types of emotion in that communal relationship. Specifically, we suspect that it has implications for the expression of negative emotions directed toward the other person. These expressions of negative emotions imply that the other person has failed to meet one's needs and ought to be more responsive to those needs (or that the person is feeling stressed or needy for reasons extrinsic to the relationship, and would like the partner to be more responsive toward his or her needs). When a communal relationship is "obligate" in nature expression of such emotions may be more common than when it is "discretionate" in nature. The rationale is straightforward. Being the target of such emotions can be aversive, and, in a discretionate communal relationship, the other has the option of leaving the relationship altogether and not having to meet the needs. In an obligate communal relation-ship, however, the other does not have that option. Thus, we suspect that if a parent upsets his or her child by misplacing something that belongs to that child, the child will express more anger than he or she would have expressed to a friend who had done exactly the same thing and had elicited exactly the same feelings of anger. The parent will not end the relationship with the child; the friend is more likely do so.

In obligate relationships, expressing negative emotions toward another person with the intention of making that person feel bad or guilty may actually help a person to get what they need. For example, in response to feelings of loneliness an elderly woman may express feelings of anger to her son in order to get him to visit. In contrast, in discretionate relationships negative emotions aimed at making the other person feel bad or guilty might have a different impact. For example, expressing anger about the fact that a friend has not visited recently may actually decrease the likelihood of a future visit.

Summing up our points thus far

To this point we have argued that, to fully understand the experience and expression of emotion, it is crucial to take the extent to which a relationship is communal into account. Just as emotion alerts us to our own needs and the necessity of attending to those needs (Frijda, 1986, 1993; Simon, 1967), so too can emotional expression alert our relation-ship partners about our needs and the necessity of their responding to those needs (see also Buck, 1984, 1989). However, whereas we are all presumably concerned about our own needs (one could say we all have communal responsibilities to ourselves), not everyone else is concerned about our needs and we do not feel equal responsibilities for all other people's needs. This suggests that we will be selective in expressing emotions conveying information about our needs to others, choosing to express them primarily to those whom we believe to feel a communal responsibility for us – especially when the communal relationship is believed to be strong and we feel certain about it. It also suggests that we will experience more emotions in response to others' needs when we feel a communal responsibility toward those others – especially when the communal relationship is believed to be strong and we feel certain about it. Existing research, we have argued, supports our claims. Beliefs about relationships do influence the experience and expression of emotion.

Expressions of emotion influence beliefs about relationship partners and relationships

Effects of emotional expression on judgments about the person who expresses it

Two studies from our laboratory suggest that expressing emotions is judged to be more appropriate and is reacted to with more favorable evaluations of the other within the context of communal relationships than within the context of other relationships. One was reported by Clark and Taraban (1991, Study 1); the other by Clark *et al.* (1987). In the Clark and Taraban (1991, Study 1) study participants, who expected to play word games with another person, were seated in front of a monitor. On the monitor, each participant could see his or her supposed partner seated at a desk in another room. The experimenter told the participant that, despite the way it had been advertised, the study actually dealt with impression formation. The first person to arrive (i.e., the one shown on the monitor) always became the stimulus person and that person continued to believe the study was about word games. However, the second person to arrive (i.e., the participant) was to form an impression of the stimulus person, first on the basis of a background information sheet filled out by the first person and then again after the two participants had briefly interacted.

At this point the participant received a background information sheet supposedly filled out by the other person. It contained a manipulation of desire for a communal as opposed to an exchange or no particular relationship with this person. In the communal relationship condition, the partner was described as new to the university and quite interested in meeting new people. In the exchange or no relationship condition, the other was described as married and busy. This other person obviously was unavailable for new friendships or romantic relationships. (See Clark, 1986, for evidence of the effectiveness of this manipulation in creating desire for a friendship or romantic relationship – or, in other words, a relationship that is typically communal in nature.) Importantly for present purposes, the background sheet also contained a manipulation of the confederate's expressed emotion. The person either reported feeling no particular emotion (the control condition), happiness, sadness, or irritability.

After seeing this information, each participant rated the other on a number of dimensions (e.g., agreeableness, pleasantness, likeability). The ratings were then summed to form an overall measure of likeability. The results were clear. When no emotion was expressed, beliefs about how agreeable, pleasant and likeable the other was did not depend upon relationship type. However, when happiness, sadness or irritability was expressed, more positive beliefs were held about that other in the communal than in the exchange condition. In other words emotional expressions took on different meanings in different relationship contexts. When exchange relationships were desired expressions of irritability and sadness led to significantly more negative beliefs about the other. In contrast, when communal relationships were desired, expressions of irritability did not significantly decrease liking for the other and expressing sadness actually was associated with a tendency toward greater liking.

Fitting with these findings is the fact that when other researchers have asked people to evaluate a person *whom they have never met before*, negative emotions (e.g. feeling angry, gloomy, frustrated) cause the person to be evaluated negatively – i.e., as unsociable, unpopular, and nonconventional (Sommers, 1984, Study 3). In contrast, when spouses (who undoubtedly have more communal relationships with one another) have been asked to evaluate messages from their mates, messages that include unpleasant emotions, disclosures of vulnerabilities, and hostilities toward persons other than the spouse, these often prompt the recipient to respond with *more positive* messages and a *more positive* attitude toward request compliance, and their relationship with the spouse (Shimanoff, 1987).

Why does the same expression of emotion lead to different beliefs in different relationship contexts? We think the answer is simple. In communal relationships members are supposed to respond to one another's needs. Thus, those who express emotions (which carry information about needs) are seen as understanding the relationship context and behaving appropriately. In turn, expressions of negative emotions are accepted and liking does not drop. Indeed, expressing emotions that reveal vulnerabilities can even be taken as a sign that the other trusts one and wants to form or maintain a communal relationship. It is that sort of inference, we believe, that led to the slight increase in liking as a result of displaying sadness in a communal relationship in the Clark and Taraban study and to spouses having a positive attitude toward their partner's disclosure of unpleasant emotions caused by others. In contrast, emotions expressed in the context of an exchange relationship carry a different meaning. The person expressing the emotion is seen as failing to understand the relationship context and as behaving inappropriately. In turn, liking drops. Interestingly Hoover-Dempsey, Plas, and Strudler-Wallston (1986) also argue that expressions of sadness may result in negative reactions within the sorts of relationships we would expect to be low in communal strength, that is, relationships at work. Specifically, they argue that when women weep in work settings it results in embarrass-ment, confusion and even anger, whereas this does not occur in what they call "intimate" or "personal" relationships.

In the second study suggesting that emotions are more appropri-ately expressed and lead to more positive beliefs about the other within communal as opposed to non-communal relationships (Clark *et al.*, 1987), participants were led to believe that they and another person were involved in a study of mood and creativity. Measures of mood were collected and participants were told they would paint a picture; the other person would create a balloon sculpture. The participant was led to desire a communal or an exchange relationship with the other (in the same manner as in the Clark and Taraban, 1991 study) and also discovered that the other was in a neutral or sad mood state. Finally the participant was given a chance to help the other by blowing up balloons but was not required to do so. The dependent variable was the time the participant spent (if any) helping the other blow up balloons. The results appear in Figure 9.2.

As expected, participants helped more when they had been manipu-lated to desire a communal relationship. Most interesting for the present chapter, though, is the fact that the impact of the other's sadness on helping depended upon the nature of the desired relation-ship. When a communal relationship was desired, the other's sadness significantly increased the time participants spent helping. When no communal relationship was desired, the other's sadness had no impact on the time participants spent helping.

Why did expressing sadness increase helping in communal but not in exchange relationships? Again our view is that expressing emotions such as sadness lead to different beliefs about others depending upon relationship context. When sadness is expressed in communal rela-tionships, the sad person is likely to be seen as needing help and, because the relationship calls for helping when help is needed, as behaving appropriately. Thus, beliefs about the other remain positive and help is given. When sadness is expressed in exchange relation-ships the story is very different. The person will still be seen as needing help – perhaps even as being especially in need of help given that sadness is being expressed in an inappropriate context. However, the person will also be seen as behaving inappropriately, will be judged harshly as a result, and help is unlikely to be given. Indeed, we suspect that when a person expresses too much sadness in a non-communal relationship setting, he or she may be actively avoided. (Due to "floor effects" on the helping measure in the exchange conditions of the Clark *et al.* (1987) study, however, it was impossible for such avoidance, should it exist, to be detected.)

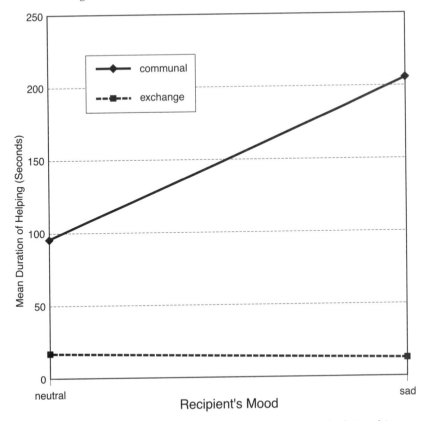

Figure 9.2 Mean duration of helping as a function of relationship manipulation and recipient mood

Judging the nature of the relationship that exists between oneself and another or between two other people

One straightforward implication of the position we have taken in this chapter is that emotional expression, particularly expressions of emotions that convey need (e.g., fear, hurt, sadness), distress over having failed to meet another person's needs (e.g. guilt), or empathy/sympathy with another person ought to be important signals to outside observers, as well as, through self-perception processes (Bem (1972), to the participants in a relationship themselves, that a communal relationship does or may exist between two other people. The intensity and frequency of emotional expression can also be taken as an indicator of the strength of that communal relationship. Thus, if someone whom a person considers to be a casual friend breaks down in tears in front of that person, the effect may be to signal to the person and, perhaps to the other, that the person crying considers the relationship to be a closer friendship (i.e., a stronger communal relationship) than was previously thought to be the case. The absence of emotional expression may also be an important signal that a communal relationship does not exist and or that it is not desired. Thus, if a friend expresses no emotion to us when experiencing something (e.g., a job loss, a death in the family) assumed to elicit emotion in just about anyone, we may conclude that the friendship is not a very strong one.

Relevant to this general point are some recent findings reported by Batson, Turk, Shaw, and Klein (1995). They deal specifically with the inferences we can draw about relationships with others as a function of how much empathy we feel for them when they are in need. Specifically, in two studies the authors directly manipulated the extent to which participants felt empathy when exposed to a confederate in need and measured the inferences they drew about their relationship with the other.

In the first of these studies this was accomplished by assigning female participants to one of the following conditions: (a) a control condition in which they neither heard about another participant's troubles nor were induced to feel empathy for the other; (b) a high empathy condition in which they were to imagine how another participant (who had just been dropped by a boyfriend and was depressed) felt, and "how it has affected his or her life and how he or she feels as a result"; or (c) a low empathy condition in which participants were exposed to the same information about the other person's troubles but were instructed to take an objective perspective toward that person, and to "Try not to get caught up in how he or she feels: just remain objective and detached." As expected, participants did report feeling more empathy for the other in the high than in the low empathy condition. Most importantly for the present point, participants also inferred having a stronger communal relationship with the other after having experienced the enhanced empathy. Specifically, participants were asked to respond to the following: "Think of someone whose welfare you value highly (e.g., a best friend or favorite family member). Now think of someone whose welfare you do not value highly (e.g., someone you know nothing about at all). Compared to these two extremes, how much do you value the welfare of (the other participant)? (1 = not highly (like a person you know nothing about), 9 = very highly (like a best friend)." (p. 306). The results revealed no statistically significant difference between ratings on this measure for participants in the control and low empathy conditions (means = 4.40 and 5.65, respectively) but ratings on this measure were significantly higher in the high than in the low empathy condition (6.95 as opposed to 5.65).

Analogous findings were obtained in a second study in which the perception that participants were feeling empathy with another person in need were manipulated by providing participants in the high empathy condition with false physiological feedback indicating that they had experienced arousal upon hearing another's plight or not. Again, those participants believing that they had experienced empathy upon hearing another's plight were especially likely to infer that they had a communal relationship with the other.

Viewing Batson *et al.*'s (1995) findings from our perspective, we believe that participants in these studies inferred the existence of communal relationships based on their own experience of emotions. Our more general point is that experiencing guilt when failing to meet another's needs, expressing empathy or guilt under the same circumstances, or expressing one's own fears, sadness, happiness, or contentment to another, should all lead to greater inferences that a communal relationship exists between oneself and another person.

Judging just how emotional or needy another person is

Knowledge of a relationship type may be an important determinant of the meaning attached to emotional expression (or lack thereof). For instance, *can we safely infer that a person who is not expressing emotion is not feeling any emotion?* Certainly not. It is, after all, well known that people do not always express the emotions they are feeling (Zammuner & Frijda, 1994). But when should we be most likely to suspect that emotions are being felt that are not being expressed? The above analysis suggests that, in general, the less communal a relationship is, the more suspicious we should be that felt emotions are not being expressed. For example, if a parent's own child fails to express distress after a disappointment, that parent ought to feel more confident that no distress is being experienced than if a stranger's child fails to express distress to him or her under the same circumstances.

There is, however, an important caveat to this rule which has to do with inferences that can or cannot be drawn from the lack of expressing negative emotions directed at the other person in a relationship. Strong communal relationships probably are far more important relationships to people than are weaker communal relationships. Thus, to the extent that expressing an emotion can damage a communal relationship (especially one which we would characterize as a discretionate communal relationship as, for instance, expressing anger at a friend may do), such emotions may be suppressed. As a result, lack of expression of such emotions within important, discretionate communal relationships may also be uninformative.

What about when an emotion *is* expressed? Does a given expression of emotion indicate the presence of the same amount of emotion and/ or the same amount of neediness no matter what the relationship context? Our analysis suggests that this is unlikely. We have argued that expressing emotion becomes less normative the less communal a relationship is. Moreover, behavior that breaks a norm (or goes beyond what everyone else does) should cause perceivers to feel more confident that the behavior indicates something unique or special about the behaving person (Jones & Davis, 1965). It follows that the more a given emotion is expressed outside the context of a communal relationship, the more seriously it may be taken. (This is simply an application of what is known in social psychology as an "augmentation effect.")

Some empirical evidence supporting this contention is provided by Clark and Taraban (1991). We have already referred to their evidence supporting the idea that expressing emotion – happiness, sadness, or irritability – will be met with greater liking when a communal rather than when an exchange relationship is expected. They also had people rate the extent to which they perceived the target person to be needy and dependent. When no emotion was expressed there was no significant difference in the extent to which the other was seen as needy and dependent. However, when happiness, sadness, or irritability was expressed, the exchange target was perceived to be more needy and dependent than the communal person. Moreover, it is interesting to note that while expressing sadness increased perceived neediness and dependency in both the communal and exchange conditions, the increase tended to be larger in the exchange condition. Furthermore, although there was a tendency for expressions of happiness and irritability to be associated with decreases in perceived dependency in the communal conditions, they tended to be associated with increases in perceived dependency in the exchange conditions. Clark and Taraban (1991: 330) speculated that, "Perhaps when a person expresses emotions in an inappropriate context (i.e., when he or she does not have or is not seeking to have a communal relationship) that person seems *especially* emotional and needy."

Judging the sincerity of an emotional expression

People sometimes strategically present emotions to elicit certain behaviors from others (Andersen & Guerreo, 1998; Clark, Pataki, & Carver, 1996; Vangelisti, Daly, & Rudnick, 1991). They may present happiness to make someone like them (Clark *et al.*, 1996), sadness to elicit help, anger to intimidate another person (Clark *et al.*, 1996), or guilt to cause another to think they care for them. Doing so may involve presenting more intense emotions than they actually feel (Ekman, 1978; Saarni, 1985), emotions that they are not feeling (Bugental & Shennum, 1984), or even substituting expressions of an emotion they are not feeling for expressions of emotion that they are feeling (Ekman, 1978; Saarni, 1993). For instance, parents certainly comment that their children, even when quite young, do just this by displaying more tears following minor accidents when they have a potentially sympathetic audience than when they do not (Saarni,1993). Parrott (1993), talking about adults, has noted that, "acting like one is in a bad mood can cause one to obtain desirable attention from others, as well as sympathy, aid, and exemption from normal duties" (p. 294). He also made the related point that displaying a negative mood may serve as a test to see if the other person cares enough to respond, and Hill, Weary, and Williams (1986) have noted that displaying depressive symptoms may be utilized to "obtain sympathy and permit the avoidance of performance demands" (p. 214).

There clearly are many potential reasons for strategically presenting emotion and, thus, there are many reasons for doubting the sincerity of an emotional expression. However, *to the extent that emotions convey one's needs*, there is particular reason to suspect insincerity within the context of a communal relationship. After all, these are the only relationships in which the target of such expressions ought to feel particularly compelled to do something about those needs. Thus, it should be primarily within the context of communal relationships that people attempt to exploit each other (thereby violating the norm that is supposed to be followed) by illicitly exaggerating their needs (Mills & Clark, 1986). Such exaggeration may be particularly likely to take the form of expressing emotions that convey neediness (e.g., sadness, fear, repulsion) because emotions are often considered to be spontaneous and thus may be less likely to be openly questioned than explicit verbal statements of needs. Thus the sincerity of such emotions should be especially likely to be *doubted* or *questioned* when they occur within the confines of a communal relationship.

Of course, in mutual communal relationships people not only expect their partners to be responsive to their needs; they also feel responsibility for meeting the other's needs and this, too, may have implications for strategic self-presentation of emotion. For instance, strategic expressions of guilt, because they imply concern about having failed to meet the other's needs, also may be more common in communal than in other relationships. Reacting to another's expression of emotion with one's own expression of emotion may also be used strategically in an effort to get out of having to respond to another's emotions. For instance, one partner may express a fear or anxiety over dealing with a particular problem, thereby placing pressure on the other person to do the task. The other may respond by saying he or she feels the same way, in an effort to avoid doing the task. In all of these cases, members of communal relationships may feel compelled to be especially wary of emotional expressions, lest they be taken in by such strategic self-presentation.

Concluding comments

In this chapter, in contrast to most chapters in this book and to most emotion research in psychology, we have taken an *interpersonal approach* to understanding emotional expressions, emotional experience (especially when another's needs have elicited our emotions), the inferences people may draw from those expressions, and their behavioral reactions to those emotional expressions. Our primary points have been simple: *First, beliefs about our relationships with others will influence the expression and experience of emotion.* To the extent to which we believe our relationship partners have communal obligations to us, we will express more emotions because emotions communicate information about our needs and help the other to respond to those needs. In turn, expressing those emotions may result in our experiencing more of those emotions in our communal relationships as well. Moreover, to the extent to which we believe we have communal obligations to our relationship partners, we will experience and express more emotions such as guilt, empathic sadness, and empathic happiness that convey both to ourselves and to our relationship partner that we are concerned with that person's needs. *Second, the experience and expression of emotions will have influenced beliefs about our relationship partners and our relationships.* This will occur because we implicitly know that about the links between expressing and experiencing emotion discussed above. Thus, when we observe our own and others' emotional expressions it conveys information about people and relationships. Emotion expressed within communal relationships is appropriate and will lead to positive beliefs about the other, the relationship and to behaviors (e.g., helping) that will promote the relationship. Emotion expressed outside communal relationships will lead to different beliefs – negative judgments about the other and the relationship and to behaviors (e.g., avoidance of the other if a communal relationship is not desired) that may harm the relationship.

There is certainly much which follows from our claims that is left to be investigated. For instance, one might search for empirical evidence to support our claims about drawing inferences about the nature of relationships on the basis of emotional expression. One also might ask how the ideas here relate to other literatures within the emotion field. The literature on gender differences, for instance, is one we suspect our analysis might help to illuminate. In particular, although there is little evidence that women *experience* more emotion than men, there is considerable evidence that they *express* more emotion than men (Brody & Hall, 1993; Hall, 1984) and that they also are better decoders of others' emotional expressions (Hall, 1978, 1984). People have also been observed to be more likely to express emotion to women than to men (e.g., Fuchs & Thelen, 1988) and women are widely considered to be more relationship-oriented than men. Given all these things, perhaps the differences in expression of emotion that have been linked to gender can be explained in terms of the extent to which women, compared to men, feel they have or should have communal relationships with others. Our analysis might also help to explain findings in the relationship area which suggest that a secure attachment style is linked to a greater willingness to express emotion (e.g., Feeney, 1995; Kirkpatrick & Hazan, 1994). A secure attachment style undoubtedly provides the basis for a well-functioning communal relationship. These findings also may represent a specific manifestation of the more general principle that communal relationships are characterized by high levels of emotional expression. In any case, we hope we have convinced the reader that the communal strength of a relationship is a crucial factor to take into account if we are to understand emotional experience and expression fully.

Notes

[1] We gratefully acknowledge NSF grant SBR9630898 which supported Margaret Clark's participation in this project and graduate training grant T32MH19953 which supported Ian Brissette's participation in this project. We thank Elizabeth Ferrick for help in searching relevant literatures and for comments on earlier versions of this manuscript.

[2] See, however, Frijda, 1986; Parkinson, 1997; Timmers, Fischer, & Manstead, 1998. Also note that this perspective has been far less neglected among sociologists than among psychologists (e.g., Hochschild, 1975, 1979, 1990; Thoits, 1989).

[3] Exceptions to providing only very low cost help to a stranger on a communal basis may occur in emergency situations in which one greatly benefits the stranger at relatively low cost to oneself – especially when no one with a stronger communal relationship with the victim is present.

[4] Exceptions to keeping emotional expression low in low strength communal relationships may occur when the other's needs are very great or when one's own needs are very great and those needs are not being met.

[5] Two other studies also have appeared in which similar results are reported (Baumeister *et al.*, 1995, Study 2; Vangelisti, Daly, & Rudnick, 1991).

[6] The Williamson and Clark (1989, 1992) results can also be explained in terms of participants feeling good about promoting the development of their communal relationships rather than in terms of empathic happiness. Still, the results are certainly compatible with our overall argument that feeling emotions in response to another's welfare is something that occurs primarily when we feel a sense of communal responsibility for that other.

References

Andersen, P. A., & Guerrero, L. K. (1998). Principles of communication and emotion in social interaction. In P. A. Andersen & L. K. Guerrero (Eds.), *Handbook of communication and emotion: Research, theory, applications, and contexts* (pp. 49–96). San Diego, CA: Academic Press.

Aune, K. S., Buller, D. B., & Aune, R. K. (1996). Display rule development in romantic relationships: Emotion management and perceived appropriateness of emotions across relationship stages. *Human Communication Research, 23,* 115–145.

Barrett, L. F., Robin, L., Pietromonaco, P. R., & Eyssell, K. M. (1998). Are women the "more emotional" sex? Evidence from emotional experiences in social context. *Cognition and Emotion, 12,* 55–578.

Batson, D. C., Duncan, B. D., Ackerman, P., Buckley, T., & Birch, K. (1981). Is empathic emotion a source of altruistic motivation? *Journal of Personality and Social Psychology, 40,* 290–302.

Batson, C. D., Turk, C. L., Shaw, L. L., & Klein, T. R. (1995). Information function of empathic emotion: Learning that we value the other's welfare. *Journal of Personality and Social Psychology, 68,* 300–313.

Baumeister, R. F., Stillwell, A. M., & Heatherton, T. F. (1994). Guilt: An interpersonal approach. *Psychological Bulletin, 115,* 243–267.

Baumeister, R. F., Stillwell, A. M., & Heatherton, T. F. (1995). Personal narratives about guilt: Role in action control and interpersonal relationships. *Basic and Applied Social Psychology, 17,* 173–198.

Bell, R. A., & Daly, J. A. (1984). The affinity-seeking function of communication. *Communication Monographs, 51,* 91–115.

Bem, D. J. (1972). Self-perception theory. In L. Berkowitz (Ed.), *Advances in experimental social psychology* (Vol. 6, pp. 1–62). New York: Academic Press.

Brissette, I., & Clark, M. S. (1998). Obligate and discretionate communal relationships. Unpublished paper, Carnegie Mellon University.

Brody, L. R. (1985). Gender differences in emotional development: A review of theories and research. *Journal of Personality, 53,* 102–149.

Brody, L. R., & Hall, J. A. (1993) Gender and emotion. In M. Lewis & J. M. Haviland (Eds.), *Handbook of emotions* (pp. 447–460). New York: Guilford.

Buck, R. (1984). *The communication of emotion.* New York: Guilford.

Buck, R. (1989). Emotional communication in personal relationships: A developmental-interactionist view. In C. Hendrick (Ed.), *Close relationships: Review of Personality and Social Psychology* (Vol. 10, pp. 144–163). Newbury Park, CA: Sage.

Bugental, D. B., & Shennum, W. A. (1984). "Difficult" children as elicitors and targets of adult communication patterns: An attributional-behavioral transactional analysis. *Monographs of the Society for Research in Child Development, 49,* 79–123.

Burger, C. R., & Bell, R. A. (1988). Plans and the initiation of social relationships. *Human Communication Research, 15,* 217–235.

Clark, L., & Watson, D. (1994). Distinguishing functional from dysfunctional affective responses. In P. Ekman & R. J. Davidson (Eds.) *The nature of emotion: Fundamental questions* (pp. 131–136). New York: Oxford University Press.

Clark, M. S. (1984). Record keeping in two types of relationships. *Journal of Personality and Social Psychology, 47,* 549–557.

Margaret S. Clark and Ian Brissette

Clark, M. S. (1986). Evidence for the effectiveness of manipulations of communal and exchange relationships. *Personality and Social Psychology Bulletin, 12,* 414–425.

Clark, M. S., & Grote, N. K. (1998). Why aren't indices of relationship costs always negatively related to indices of relationship quality? *Personality and Social Psychology Review, 2,* 2–17.

Clark, M. S., Dubash, P., & Mills, J. (1998). Interest in another's consideration of one's needs in communal and exchange relationships. *Journal of Experimental Social Psychology, 34,* 246–264.

Clark, M. S., & Mills, J. (1979). Interpersonal attraction in exchange and communal relationships. *Journal of Personality and Social Psychology, 36,* 1–12.

Clark, M. S., & Mills, J. (1993). The difference between communal and exchange relationships: What it is and is not. *Personality and Social Psychology Bulletin, 19,* 684–691.

Clark, M. S., Mills, J., & Corcoran, D. (1989). Keeping track of needs and inputs of friends and strangers. *Personality and Social Psychology Bulletin, 15,* 533–542.

Clark, M. S., Mills, J., & Powell, M. C. (1986). Keeping track of needs in communal and exchange relationships. *Journal of Personality and Social Psychology, 51,* 333–338.

Clark, M. S., Ouellette, R., Powell, M. C., & Milberg, S. (1987). Recipient's mood, relationship type, and helping. *Journal of Personality and Social Psychology, 53,* 94–103.

Clark, M. S., Pataki, S. P., & Carver, V. H. (1996). Some thoughts and findings on self-presentation of emotions in relationships. In G. J. O. Fletcher and J. Fitness (Eds.), *Knowledge structures in close relationships: A social psychological approach* (pp. 247–274). Mahwah, NJ: Erlbaum.

Clark, M. S., & Taraban, C. B. (1991). Reactions to and willingness to express emotion in two types of relationships. *Journal of Experimental Social Psychology, 27,* 324–336.

Clark, M. S., & Waddell, B. (1985). Perception of exploitation in communal and exchange relationships. *Journal of Social and Personal Relationships, 2,* 403–413.

Ekman, P. (1978). Facial expression. In W. Siegman & S. Feldstein (Eds.), *Nonverbal behavior and communication* (pp. 90–116). Hillsdale, NJ: Erlbaum.

Ekman, P., & Davidson, R. J. (1994). Afterword: What is the function of emotions? In P. Ekman & R. J. Davidson (Eds.), *The nature of emotion: Fundamental questions* (pp. 137–139). New York: Oxford University Press.

Feeney, J. A. (1995). Adult attachment and emotional control. *Personal Relationships, 2,* 143–160.

Finch, J., & Mason, J. (1993). *Negotiating family responsibilities.* London: Tavistock/Routledge.

Frijda, N. H. (1986). *The emotions.* Cambridge: Cambridge University Press.

Frijda, N. H. (1993). Moods, emotion episodes, and emotions. In M. Lewis and J. M. Haviland (Eds.) *Handbook of emotions* (pp. 381–404). New York: Guilford.

Fuchs, D., & Thelen, M. (1988). Children's expected interpersonal consequences of communicating their affective state and reported likelihood of expression. *Child Development, 59,* 1314–1322.

Grote, N. K., & Clark, M. S. (in press). Distributive justice norms and family work: What is perceived as ideal, what is applied, and what predicts fairness. *Social Justice Research.*

Hall, J. A. (1978). Gender effects in decoding nonverbal cues. *Psychological Bulletin, 85,* 845–857.

Hall, J. A. (1984). *Nonverbal sex differences: Communication accuracy and expressive style.* Baltimore, MD: Johns Hopkins University Press.

Hill, M. G., Weary, G., & Williams, J. (1986). Depression: A self-presentation formulation. In R. Baumeister (Ed.), *Public self and private self* (pp. 213–240). New York: Springer-Verlag.

Hochschild, A. R. (1979). Emotion work, feeling rules and social structure. *American Journal of Sociology, 85,* 551–575.

Hochschild, A. R. (1975). The sociology of feeling and emotion: Selected possibilities. In M. Millman & R. M. Kanter (Eds.), *Another voice: Feminist perspectives on social life and social science* (pp. 280–307). New York: Anchor.

Hochschild, A. R. (1990). Ideology and emotion management: A perspective and path for future research (pp. 117–144). In T. D. Kemper (Ed.) *Research agendas in the sociology of emotion.* Albany, NY: SUNY Press.

Hoover-Dempsey, K. V., Plas, J. M., & Strudler-Wallston, B. (1986). Tears and weeping among professional women: In search of new understanding. *Psychology of Women Quarterly, 10,* 19–34.

Jones, E. E., & Davis, K. E. (1965). From acts to dispositions: The attribution process in social psychology. In L. Berkowitz (Ed.), *Advances in experimental social psychology* (Vol. 2, pp. 219–266). New York: Academic Press.

Kemper, T. D. (1993). Sociological models in the explanation of emotions. In M. Lewis and J. M. Haviland (Eds.), *Handbook of emotions* (pp. 41–51). New York: Guilford.

Kemper, T. D. (1978). *A social interactional theory of emotions.* New York: Wiley.

Kirkpatrick, L. A., & Hazan, C. (1994). Attachment styles and close relationships: A four-year prospective study. *Personal Relationships, 1,* 123–142.

Krebs, D. (1975). Empathy and altruism. *Journal of Personality and Social Psychology, 32,* 1134–1146.

Laird, J. D. (1974). Self-attribution of emotion: The effects of expressive behavior on the quality of emotional experience. *Journal of Personality and Social Psychology, 33,* 475–486.

Laird, J. D., & Bresler, C. (1992). The process of emotional experience: A self-perception theory. In M. S. Clark (Ed.), *Emotion* (pp. 213–234). Newbury Park, CA: Sage.

Levenson, R. W. (1994). Human emotion: A functional view. In P. Ekman & R. J. Davidson (Eds.) *The nature of emotion: Fundamental questions* (pp. 123–126). New York: Oxford University Press.

Mills, J., & Clark, M. S. (1982). Exchange and communal relationships. In L. Wheeler (Ed.), *Review of personality and social psychology* (Vol. 3, pp. 121–144). Beverly Hills, CA: Sage.

Mills, J., & Clark, M. S. (1986). Communications that should lead to perceived exploitation in communal and exchange relationships. *Journal of Social and Clinical Psychology, 4,* 225–234.

Parkinson, B. (1997). Untangling the appraisal-emotion connection. *Personality and Social Psychology Review, 1,* 62–79.

Parrott, W. G. (1993). Beyond hedonism: Motives for inhibiting good moods and for maintaining bad moods. In D. M. Wegner & J. W. Pennebaker

240 *Margaret S. Clark and Ian Brissette*

(Eds.), *Handbook of mental control* (pp. 278–305). Englewood Cliffs, NJ: Prentice-Hall.

Riskind, J. H. (1984). They stoop to conquer: Guiding and self-regulatory functions of physical posture after success and failure. *Journal of Personality and Social Psychology, 47*, 479–492.

Riskind, J. H., & Gotay, C. C. (1982). Physical posture: Could it have regulatory or feedback effects on motivation and emotion? *Motivation and Emotion, 6*, 273–298.

Saarni, C. (1989). Children's understanding of strategic control of emotional expression in social transactions. In C. Saarni & P. L. Harris (Eds.), *Children's understanding of emotion* (pp. 181–208). Cambridge: Cambridge University Press.

Saarni, C. (1993). Socialization of emotion. In M. Lewis & J. M. Haviland (Eds.), *Handbook of emotions* (pp. 187–209). New York: Plenum.

Scott, J. P. (1958). *Animal behavior.* Chicago: University of Chicago Press.

Scott, J. P. (1980). The function of emotions in behavioral systems: A systems theory analysis. In *Emotion: Theory, research, and experience, Vol. 1: Theories of emotion* (pp. 35–56). New York: Academic Press.

Shimanoff, S. B. (1988). Degree of emotional expressiveness as a function of face-needs, gender, and interpersonal relationship. *Communication Reports, 1*, 43–59.

Shimanoff, S. B. (1987). Types of emotional disclosures and request compliance between spouses. *Communication Monographs, 54*, 85–100.

Simon, H. A. (1967). Motivational and emotional controls of cognition. *Psychological Review, 74*, 29–39.

Sommers, S. (1984). Reported emotions and conventions of emotionality among college students. *Journal of Personality and Social Psychology, 46*, 207–215.

Thoits, P. A. (1989). The sociology of emotions. *Annual Review of Sociology, 15*, 317–342.

Timmers, M., Fischer, A. H., & Manstead, A. S. R. (1998). Gender differences in motives for regulating emotions. *Personality and Social Psychology Bulletin, 24*, 974–985.

Vangelisti, A. L., Daly, J. A., & Rudnick, J. R. (1991). Making people feel guilty in conversations: Techniques and correlates. *Human Communication Research, 18*, 3–39.

Williamson, G. M., & Clark, M. S. (1989). Providing help and desired relationship type as determinants of changes in moods and self-evaluations. *Journal of Personality and Social Psychology, 56*, 722–734.

Williamson, G. M., & Clark, M. S. (1992). Impact of desired relationship type on affective reactions to choosing and being required to help. *Personality and Social Psychology Bulletin, 18*, 10–18.

Zammuner, V. L., & Frijda, N. H. (1994). Felt and communicated emotions: Sadness and jealousy. *Cognition and Emotion, 8*, 37–53.

Index of authors

Index of subjects

Studies in Emotion and Social Interaction

First Series
Editors: Paul Ekman and Klaus R. Scherer